First World War
and Army of Occupation
War Diary
France, Belgium and Germany

66 DIVISION
198 Infantry Brigade
Royal Dublin Fusiliers
6th Battalion
1 July 1918 - 29 April 1919

WO95/3140/2

The Naval & Military Press Ltd
www.nmarchive.com
Published in association with The National Archives

Published by

The Naval & Military Press Ltd

Unit 10 Ridgewood Industrial Park,

Uckfield, East Sussex,

TN22 5QE England

Tel: +44 (0) 1825 749494

www.naval-military-press.com

www.nmarchive.com

This diary has been reprinted in facsimile from the original. Any imperfections are inevitably reproduced and the quality may fall short of modern type and cartographic standards.

© **Crown Copyright**
Images reproduced by permission of The National Archives, London, England, 2015.

Contents

Document type	Place/Title	Date From	Date To
Heading	WO95/3140/2		
Heading	66th Division 198th Infy Bde 6th Bn Roy Dublin Fus Jly 1918-Apr 1919		
Heading	Vol 1		
War Diary	Kantara	01/07/1918	02/07/1918
War Diary	Alexandria	03/07/1918	04/07/1918
War Diary	At Sea	05/07/1918	08/07/1918
War Diary	Taranto	09/07/1918	13/07/1918
War Diary	Train Route	14/07/1918	15/07/1918
War Diary	Serqueux	16/07/1918	31/07/1918
Miscellaneous	Train Arrangements		
Miscellaneous	March Table		
Miscellaneous	O.C. 2/24th London Regt.	01/07/1918	01/07/1918
Miscellaneous	O.C. 2/24th Bn London Regiment	01/07/1918	01/07/1918
Miscellaneous	O.C., 2/24th Londons	01/07/1918	01/07/1918
Miscellaneous	Disembarkation Orders By Lieut Colonel J.P.G. Crosbie D.S.O. Commanding Troops H.T. "Malwa"	07/07/1918	07/07/1918
Miscellaneous	Disembarkation Orders By Lieut Colonel W.H. Whyte D S O Commanding 6 (S) Bn Royal Dublin Fusiliers	07/07/1918	07/07/1918
Miscellaneous	Programme of Train No.T.F.		
Heading	War Diary 6th (S) Bn Royal Dublin Fusiliers From 1st To 31st August 1918 Volume 38		
War Diary	Serqueux	01/08/1918	31/08/1918
Heading	War Diary 6th (S) Bn Royal Dublin Fusiliers Period-1/9/18 To 30/9/18 Volume 39		
War Diary	Serquex	01/09/1918	12/09/1918
War Diary	Abancourt	13/09/1918	13/09/1918
War Diary	Gueschart	14/09/1918	19/09/1918
War Diary	Bonniers	21/09/1918	21/09/1918
War Diary	Leincourt	22/09/1918	29/09/1918
War Diary	Bayonvillers	30/09/1918	30/09/1918
Map	Map 'D'		
War Diary	Bayonvillers	01/10/1918	01/10/1918
War Diary	Cappy	02/10/1918	02/10/1918
War Diary	Guillemont	03/10/1918	04/10/1918
War Diary	Moilands	05/10/1918	05/10/1918
War Diary	Ste Emille	06/10/1918	07/10/1918
War Diary	Le Catlet	07/10/1918	12/10/1918
War Diary	Maurois	12/10/1918	13/10/1918
War Diary	Maretz	14/10/1918	15/10/1918
War Diary	Remont	16/10/1918	16/10/1918
War Diary	Le Cateau	17/10/1918	18/10/1918
War Diary	Q.2.	19/10/1918	20/10/1918
War Diary	Maurois	21/10/1918	21/10/1918
War Diary	Premont	22/10/1918	31/10/1918
Miscellaneous	6th Bn Royal Dublin Fusiliers Operations-7th-11th October 1918		
Miscellaneous	6th Lancs Fus	21/10/1918	21/10/1918
Miscellaneous	Guns Captured by the 6th (S) Bn Royal Dublin Fusiliers	10/10/1918	10/10/1918
Diagram etc	Ville an Cateau		

Type	Description	From	To
Map	Map 'A'		
Map	Map 'B'		
Map	Map 'C'		
War Diary	Premont	01/11/1918	09/11/1918
War Diary	Le Jonquiere Farm	10/11/1918	24/11/1918
War Diary	Hastiere	30/11/1918	30/11/1918
Heading	War Diary 6th Royal Dublin Fusiliers From 1 12 1 18 To 31 12 18 Volume 42		
Miscellaneous			
Miscellaneous	198th Inf. Bde, No. 1977/2/A	12/12/1918	12/12/1918
Miscellaneous	6th Bn Lancs Fusrs	11/12/1918	11/12/1918
Miscellaneous	March Table "B" to Accompany 198th Infantry Brigade Order No, 145	12/10/1918	12/10/1918
Miscellaneous	March Table "A" To Accompany 198th Infantry Brigade Order No, 145		
Miscellaneous			
Operation(al) Order(s)	198th Infantry Brigade Order No. 145	11/12/1918	11/12/1918
War Diary	Hastiere	01/12/1918	15/12/1918
War Diary	Houyet	16/12/1918	16/12/1918
War Diary	Jemelle	18/12/1918	31/12/1918
Heading	War Diary 60th Royal Dublin Fusiliers From 1 2 19 To 28 2 19 Volume 44		
War Diary	Jemelle	01/02/1919	26/02/1919
Heading	War Diary 60th (S) Bn The Royal Dublin Fusiliers Period 1/3/19 To 31/3/19 Volume 45		
Heading	O.C. Div Cadre Herewith Copy of War Diary For March 1919		
War Diary	Jemelle	01/03/1919	01/03/1919
War Diary	Belgium	02/03/1919	04/03/1919
War Diary	Achene	05/03/1919	05/03/1919
War Diary	Belgium	08/03/1919	31/03/1919
Operation(al) Order(s)	198th Infantry Brigade Order No. 147	03/03/1918	03/03/1918
Miscellaneous	Table "A"		
Heading	War Diary 60th Royal Dublin Fusiliers Period 1/4/19 To 30/4/19 Volume 46		
War Diary	Achene Belgium	04/04/1919	29/04/1919
Heading	6 R D F Vol 3		
Heading	D A G G H Q 3rd Echelon		
Miscellaneous	O C 6 R Dublin Fus		
Miscellaneous	Addendum To 198 Infantry Brigade Order No.107	29/09/1918	29/09/1918
Miscellaneous	March Table		
Operation(al) Order(s)	198th Infantry Brigade Order No. 102	10/09/1918	10/09/1918
Miscellaneous	Administrative Instructions Issued In Reference To 198th Infantry Brigade Order No. 102	11/09/1918	11/09/1918
Miscellaneous	5th Inniskilling Fus	10/09/1918	10/09/1918
Miscellaneous	Billeting List		
Miscellaneous	5th Royal Inniskilling Fusiliers	15/09/1918	15/09/1918
Miscellaneous	66th Division 7068/Q	10/09/1918	10/09/1918
Miscellaneous	198th Inf. Bde No./807/10/A	10/09/1918	10/09/1918
Miscellaneous	197th Inf. Bde. 66th Divn 7068/ Q	09/09/1918	09/09/1918
Miscellaneous	B.M.L. 28/3/2	09/09/1918	09/09/1918
Operation(al) Order(s)	197th Infantry Brigade Operation Order No. 98	09/09/1918	09/09/1918
Miscellaneous	35 Bn R Innisk's Fus	11/09/1918	11/09/1918
Miscellaneous	Table		
Miscellaneous	Administrative Instructions Issued In Reference To 198th Infantry Brigade Order No.103	15/09/1918	15/09/1918

Category	Description	Date 1	Date 2
Operation(al) Order(s)	198th Infantry Brigade Order No. 104	19/09/1918	19/09/1918
Miscellaneous	Administrative Instructions Issued In Reference To 198th Infantry Brigade Order No. 104	19/09/1918	19/09/1918
Miscellaneous	Reference 198th Inf. Bde. Order No. 104	19/09/1918	19/09/1918
Miscellaneous	Table "A" To Accompany 198th Infantry Brigade Order No.104		
Miscellaneous	A Form Messages And Signals		
Operation(al) Order(s)	198th Infantry Brigade Order No. 105	20/09/1918	20/09/1918
Miscellaneous	Table "A" To Accompany 198th Infantry Brigade Order No. 105		
Miscellaneous	Administrative Instructions Issued 198th Infantry Brigade Order No.106	27/09/1918	27/09/1918
Miscellaneous	5th Bn. R. Innis Fus	20/09/1918	20/09/1918
Miscellaneous	Amendment To Administrative Instructions Issued In Reference To 198th Infantry Brigade Order No. 106	27/09/1918	27/09/1918
Operation(al) Order(s)	198th Infantry Brigade Order No. 107	28/09/1918	28/09/1918
Miscellaneous	Entrainment Programme "A"		
Heading	6 R Div Fus Oct 18		
Operation(al) Order(s)	198th Infantry Brigade Order No. 108	30/09/1918	30/09/1918
Miscellaneous	Appendix 1		
Miscellaneous	Appendix 1	30/09/1918	30/09/1918
Miscellaneous	6th Royal Dublin Fusiliers Tactical Scheme No. 1		
Miscellaneous	Reference Addendum No. 1 To 198th Infantry Brigade Order No. 110	01/10/1918	01/10/1918
Miscellaneous	6th Lancs Fus	01/10/1918	01/10/1918
Miscellaneous	Appendix 2		
Miscellaneous	Situation Report IV		
Miscellaneous	Situation Report I		
Miscellaneous	Situation Report III		
Miscellaneous	Situation Report II		
Miscellaneous	Situation Report V		
Operation(al) Order(s)	198th Infantry Brigade Order No.110	01/10/1918	01/10/1918
Operation(al) Order(s)	198th Infantry Brigade Order No.109	01/10/1918	01/10/1918
Miscellaneous	March Table to accompany ? No. 1		
Miscellaneous	Addendum No.1 To 198th Infantry Brigade Order No.110	01/10/1918	01/10/1918
Miscellaneous	66th Division	30/08/1919	30/08/1919
Operation(al) Order(s)	198th Infantry Brigade Order No.113	05/10/1918	05/10/1918
Miscellaneous	March Table To Accompany 198th Infantry Brigade Order No. 113		
Miscellaneous	66th Division Instruction No.1	05/10/1918	05/10/1918
Operation(al) Order(s)	198th Infantry Brigade Order No.114	06/10/1918	06/10/1918
Miscellaneous	Warning Order	07/09/1918	07/09/1918
Miscellaneous	6th Bn. Lancs Fus	07/10/1918	07/10/1918
Miscellaneous	Instructions No. 2 Issued Under 198th Infantry Brigade Order No. 115 Machine Guns	07/10/1918	07/10/1918
Miscellaneous	Issued Down to Platoon Commanders	06/10/1918	06/10/1918
Miscellaneous	6th Lancs Fus	07/10/1918	07/10/1918
Miscellaneous	A Form Messages And Signals		
Miscellaneous	Appen 5		
Miscellaneous	A Form Messages And Signals		
Operation(al) Order(s)	198th Infantry Brigade Order No.115	07/10/1918	07/10/1918
Miscellaneous	6th Bn. Lancs. Fusrs	07/10/1918	07/10/1918
Miscellaneous	198th Infantry Brigade Preliminary Order No.1	07/10/1918	07/10/1918
Miscellaneous	198th Infantry Brigade Report On Operations	12/10/1918	12/10/1918
Miscellaneous	Part II		

Miscellaneous	Part III		
Miscellaneous	Message Map		
Map	Map		
Miscellaneous	198th Infantry Brigade		
Miscellaneous	9th Lancs. Fus	08/10/1918	08/10/1918
Heading	6 Divl. Fus		
Operation(al) Order(s)	198th Infantry Brigade Order No.116	08/10/1918	08/10/1918
Miscellaneous			
Miscellaneous	198 Inf Bde No. B.M 201	08/10/1918	08/10/1918
Miscellaneous	Messages And Signals		
Heading	1K 6 Wounded		
Miscellaneous	Messages And Signals		
Miscellaneous	198 Infantry Instruction No.1	10/10/1918	10/10/1918
Miscellaneous	A Form Messages And Signals		
Miscellaneous	Appendix 7		
Miscellaneous	Messages And Signals		
Miscellaneous	O.C. 'B' Coy	15/09/1918	15/09/1918
Miscellaneous			
Miscellaneous	A Form Messages And Signals		
Heading	6th Div Fus		
Miscellaneous	A Form Messages And Signals		
Miscellaneous	198th Inf Bde. No. B.M 234	11/10/1918	11/10/1918
Miscellaneous	198th Inf Bde No.B.M. 231	11/10/1918	11/10/1918
Miscellaneous	A Form Messages And Signals		
Miscellaneous	198th Inf Bde No.B.M.231	11/10/1918	11/10/1918
Miscellaneous	198th Inf Bde No. B.M. 234/1	11/10/1918	11/10/1918
Miscellaneous	Appendix 8	11/10/1918	11/10/1918
Operation(al) Order(s)	198th Infantry Brigade Order No.117	11/10/1918	11/10/1918
Miscellaneous	198th Inf Bde No.B.M. 239	11/10/1918	11/10/1918
Miscellaneous	A Form Messages And Signals		
Miscellaneous	198th Inf Bde No. B.M. 229	11/10/1918	11/10/1918
Miscellaneous	A Form Messages And Signals		
Operation(al) Order(s)	198th Infantry Brigade Order No.117	13/10/1918	13/10/1918
Operation(al) Order(s)	198th Infantry Brigade Order No.121	10/10/1918	10/10/1918
Miscellaneous	A Form Messages And Signals		
Miscellaneous	Preliminary Instructions In Connection With 198th Infantry Brigade Order No.120	16/10/1918	16/10/1918
Miscellaneous	Relief Table		
Miscellaneous	A Form Messages And Signals		
Miscellaneous	March Table To Accompany 198th Infantry Brigade Order No.119	16/10/1918	16/10/1918
Operation(al) Order(s)	198th Infantry Brigade Order No.119	16/10/1918	16/10/1918
Miscellaneous	198th Infantry Brigade Order No.119	16/10/1918	16/10/1918
Miscellaneous	A Form Messages And Signals		
Miscellaneous	Reference 198th Infantry Brigade Order No.120	10/10/1918	10/10/1918
Miscellaneous	Addendum No.1 To 198th Infantry Brigade Order No.120	16/10/1918	16/10/1918
Miscellaneous	Administration Instruction Issued In Reference To 198 Infantry Brigade Order No.120	16/10/1918	16/10/1918
Miscellaneous	A B C D No	16/10/1918	16/10/1918
Miscellaneous	Order Of Battle	14/10/1918	14/10/1918
Operation(al) Order(s)	198th Infantry Brigade Order No.120	16/10/1918	16/10/1918
Miscellaneous	A Form Messages And Signals		
Miscellaneous	Addendum No.2 To 198th Infantry Brigade Order No.120	16/10/1918	16/10/1918
Miscellaneous	A Form Messages And Signals		

Miscellaneous	Appendix 13	17/10/1918	17/10/1918
Miscellaneous	To OC P Coy	17/10/1918	17/10/1918
Miscellaneous	To C.O. 6th R.D.F.		
Miscellaneous	To C.O. 6th R.D.F.	17/10/1918	17/10/1918
Miscellaneous	To O.C.6th R D Fus		
Miscellaneous	To O.C 6th R. D. F		
Miscellaneous	A Form Messages And Signals		
Miscellaneous	Messages And Signals		
Miscellaneous	Account of Operations		
Miscellaneous	Part IV		
Miscellaneous	Part V The Advance To The Red Line		
Miscellaneous	Part VI		
Miscellaneous	A Form Messages And Signals		
Miscellaneous	C Form Messages And Signals		
Heading	6th R.D.F		
Miscellaneous	C Form Messages And Signals		
Heading	6th R Dub. Fus		
Miscellaneous	Appendix 12	16/10/1918	16/10/1918
Miscellaneous	Reference P.8 Para VI	16/10/1918	16/10/1918
Miscellaneous	A Form Messages And Signals		
Miscellaneous	Messages And Signals		
Miscellaneous	A Form Messages And Signals		
Miscellaneous	6 Dub. Fus	17/10/1918	17/10/1918
Miscellaneous	A Form Messages And Signals		
Miscellaneous	198th Inf Bde No. B.M.259	18/10/1918	18/10/1918
Miscellaneous	C Form Messages And Signals		
Miscellaneous	A Form Messages And Signals		
Miscellaneous	Appendix 14		
Miscellaneous	Messages And Signals		
Miscellaneous	A Form Messages And Signals		
Miscellaneous	C Form Messages And Signals		
Operation(al) Order(s)	198th Infantry Brigade Order No.123	20/10/1918	20/10/1918
Miscellaneous	Reference 198th Infantry Brigade Order No.123		
Miscellaneous	A Form Messages And Signals		
Map	Map		
Heading	6 R Dub, Fus Nov 18		
Miscellaneous	Copies of Orders And Messages (Sept Oct & Nov 1918 Supplied by Lieut.-Colonel W.B. Little DSO. MC (Late Comdg 6/R. Dublin Fusiliers)		
Miscellaneous	Operation Order No	16/10/1918	16/10/1918
Miscellaneous	C.O.X.33		
Miscellaneous	6th Bn Royal Dublin Fusiliers	17/10/1918	17/10/1918
Miscellaneous	O.C. "B" Coy		
Miscellaneous	198th Inf. Bde	09/11/1918	09/11/1918
Miscellaneous	Warning Order	09/11/1918	09/11/1918
Miscellaneous	Notes Issued With O.O.No.19	04/11/1918	04/11/1918
Miscellaneous		08/11/1918	08/11/1918
Miscellaneous	C.O.X. 63	08/11/1918	08/11/1918
Miscellaneous	C.O.X.67		
Miscellaneous	C.O.5		
Operation(al) Order(s)	198th Infantry Brigade Order No.125	01/11/1918	01/11/1918
Miscellaneous	6 R Dub Fus Movement Order No. 16		
Miscellaneous	6th Bn. Lancs. Fusrs	01/11/1918	01/11/1918
Miscellaneous	Administration Of The Town Of Le Cateau	31/10/1918	31/10/1918
Miscellaneous	Forwarded for Information	01/11/1918	01/11/1918
Operation(al) Order(s)	198th Infantry Brigade Order No.126	02/11/1918	02/11/1918

Type	Description	Date	Date
Miscellaneous	March Table To Accompany 198th Infantry Brigade Order No.128	02/11/1918	02/11/1918
Miscellaneous	Reference 198th Infantry Brigade Order No.128		
Miscellaneous	Reference 198th Infantry Brigade Order No.128	02/11/1918	02/11/1918
Miscellaneous	198th Infantry Brigade Instruction No.5	04/11/1918	04/11/1918
Miscellaneous	Warning Order	03/11/1918	03/11/1918
Miscellaneous	Reference 198th Infantry Brigade Order No.120	03/08/1918	03/08/1918
Operation(al) Order(s)	198th Infantry Brigade Order No.129	04/10/1918	04/10/1918
Operation(al) Order(s)	198th Infantry Brigade Order No.130	04/10/1918	04/10/1918
Miscellaneous	6th Lancs Fus	04/11/1918	04/11/1918
Operation(al) Order(s)	198th Infantry Brigade Order No.131	05/11/1918	05/11/1918
Operation(al) Order(s)	198th Infantry Brigade Order No.132	05/11/1918	05/11/1918
Miscellaneous	A Form Messages And Signals		
Miscellaneous	Messages And Signals		
Miscellaneous	A Form Messages And Signals		
Miscellaneous	198th Inf Bde No. B.M 114	07/11/1918	07/11/1918
Operation(al) Order(s)	198th Infantry Brigade Order No.135	07/11/1918	07/11/1918
Operation(al) Order(s)	6 Royal Dublin Fusiliers Order No.20	08/11/1918	08/11/1918
Miscellaneous	Messages And Signals		
Miscellaneous	A Form Messages And Signals		
Operation(al) Order(s)	198th Infantry Brigade Order No.136	08/11/1918	08/11/1918
Miscellaneous	Addendum To 198th Infantry Brigade Order No.136	08/11/1918	08/11/1918
Miscellaneous	C.O.X.70	08/11/1918	08/11/1918
Miscellaneous	198th Inf Bde No. G32/14	09/11/1918	09/11/1918
Miscellaneous	Account of Operations Part VII 2nd November 1918-11th November 1918		
Miscellaneous	Part VII		
Miscellaneous	Total Captures 1st Nov-11th Nov.		
Operation(al) Order(s)	198th Infantry Brigade Order No.138	11/11/1918	11/11/1918
Miscellaneous	198th Inf Bde No. G 32/16	12/11/1918	12/11/1918
Miscellaneous	Reference	11/11/1918	11/11/1918
Miscellaneous	Order of Battle Fourth Army Advanced Guard And Locations On 12th November 1918	12/11/1918	12/11/1918
Operation(al) Order(s)	198th Infantry Brigade Order No.139	15/11/1918	15/11/1918
Miscellaneous	March Table To Accompany 198th Inf. Bde Order No.139	15/11/1918	15/11/1918
Miscellaneous	198th Inf Bde No.G	16/11/1918	16/11/1918
Miscellaneous	A Form Messages And Signals		
Miscellaneous	Advanced Guard Commander's Order No.1		
Miscellaneous	Administrative Arrangements In Reference To The March To The Rhine	14/11/1918	14/11/1918
Miscellaneous	66th Division 1948/1/Q	14/11/1918	14/11/1918
Miscellaneous	Administrative Instructions No.2	18/11/1916	18/11/1916
Operation(al) Order(s)	198th Infantry Brigade Preliminary Order No.140	16/11/1918	16/11/1918
Miscellaneous	March to the Rhine	17/11/1918	17/11/1918
Miscellaneous	198th Inf. Bde No. G 38/6	18/11/1918	18/11/1918
Miscellaneous	Administrative Instructions	17/11/1918	17/11/1918
Miscellaneous	Administrative Instructions No.1 In Connection With 66th Div	16/11/1918	16/11/1918
Miscellaneous	66th Divn 7948/8/Q	16/11/1918	16/11/1918
Miscellaneous	To All Recipients Of 66th Div. No. 7948/8/Q	17/11/1918	17/11/1918
Operation(al) Order(s)	198th Infantry Brigade Order No.141	14/11/1918	14/11/1918
Miscellaneous	March Table To Accompany 198th Inf. Bde Order No.141	17/11/1918	17/11/1918
Miscellaneous	198th Infantry Brigade	22/11/1918	22/11/1918

Miscellaneous	6th (S) Bn Royal Dublin Fusiliers Movement Order No.29	22/11/1918	22/11/1918
Miscellaneous	6th (S) Bn Royal Dublin Fusiliers Movement Order No.29	23/11/1918	23/11/1918
Operation(al) Order(s)	198th Infantry Brigade Order No.143	22/11/1918	22/11/1918
Miscellaneous	March Table To Accompany 198th Infantry Brigade Order No.143		
Miscellaneous	6th Lancs. Fus	23/11/1918	23/11/1918
Operation(al) Order(s)	198th Infantry Brigade Order No.144	23/11/1918	23/11/1918
Miscellaneous	March Table To Accompany 198th Infantry Brigade Order No.144		

WO 95/3140/2

66TH DIVISION
198TH INFY BDE

6TH BN ROY. DUBLIN FUS.
JLY 1918 - APR 1919.

FROM EGYPT
to DIVISION & BDE

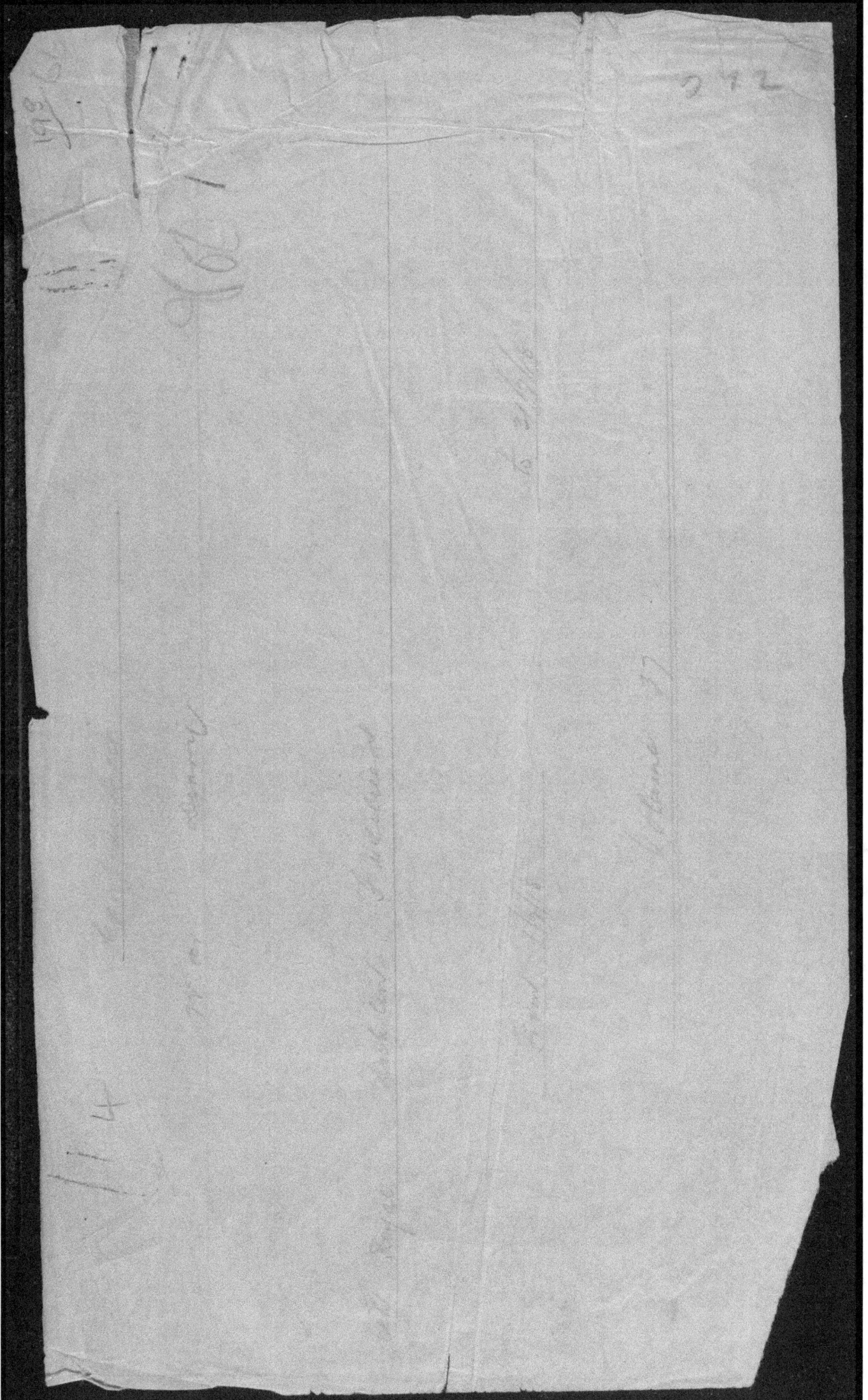

Army Form C. 2118.

WAR DIARY
or
INTELLIGENCE SUMMARY.
(Erase heading not required.)

Instructions regarding War Diaries and Intelligence Summaries are contained in F.S. Regs., Part II. and the Staff Manual respectively. Title pages will be prepared in manuscript.

Place	Date	Hour	Summary of Events and Information	Remarks and references to Appendices
KANTARA	1/7/43		8th Lt Wing TD. 31 officers 834 OR Indian Recruits for No 6 Labour at Cheps stores	(1)
	2		Marched from No 5 Tr at 14.30 and entrained at MAHFUZA W stated at 1800. 200 Details RAMC & 279 f/JO Indian Repl embarked for this unit	
Alexandria	3		We received at GABBARI sheds at 0445 and embarked in S.S. HAZWA APPENDIX (2) Proceeded alongside by 0700. After loaded left harbour some ship at 12.00 for Croatia at 0700. After loaded life equipment of troops & crew	
	4		emergency stations of SS HAZWA various serials exercised out of routine	
	5		At 12.00 sighted by 7 Ital aeroplanes but wind cloudy & short STOL but clear as SW #5 W waited convoy instructions	
	6		Dense Haze (up to noon) but found at 09.00	
	7		Arrived at TARANTO at 10.30 anchored intense forced + water rated APP. (3) Troops moved on shore at 13.00 the transporters at 17.30 and unroaded	
	8		6 C.M.P's Bat. Pers. resting for the night.	
	6/7		Lorried transport train 532 cpl. H. Browne left at 18.00 Leaving town debarked the train T.E. 27 W. Laurebury 286z at 1870 at train T.E. 27 W. Laurebury 286z and 13 vehicles attached	APP. (4)
			Route Posses landed in our Sec Collinois 23/7 to train Aosto M.T. News Fort MEOLA	
			Ritartford - SAN PERDAPENA - twice my train SAVONA - dinner for men at	
			VENTIMIGLIA (crowded station) 2/8	
			Menton - NICE - Cruette - Tours - St Etienne -	
	9		reached U- MIRIMAS	

Army Form C. 2118.

WAR DIARY
or
INTELLIGENCE SUMMARY.
(Erase heading not required.)

Instructions regarding War Diaries and Intelligence Summaries are contained in F. S. Regs., Part II. and the Staff Manual respectively. Title pages will be prepared in manuscript.

Place	Date	Hour	Summary of Events and Information	Remarks and references to Appendices
PARAY	14/76		ROLL CALL MUSTER Transfers and March for Mal	
	15		Arr. ordered all FORCES to EAUX at 12.30 retiring from Marshes to Camp	
SEROCEUX			near SEROCEUX loaded and defenses from Meleure full out-could be made	
	16		H destroyed A.G.B. Hospital bombed for twelve Army Transports the	
	17		young strength 30 officers SCY. Avenue evacuated to go forward for administration	
	18		Red blood for these while 87th shells to aid 50 Bens for admission	
	19		Strong at Terme on the slope 827 the bn Can send LOTS off handler to the	
	20		Zigzag through 30 off 827	Capt John Willa
	21		30 " 827 " 3	Bn total 6 147 Bn all Ranks Bng Gnrl Mr Wallace
	22		31 " 827 1	Park arrived 1100p Bns all Ranks Lost 1 to my p.m. Lost
	23		31 " 827 "	Lost 1 Col the Lotes Lost
	24		31 " 827 1	A Battle CFC CF (Reception) I.M.C. 1 off 141 ordered
	25		31 " 827 1	1A the front of Hosp self killed to the Butter lost
	26		" 38 " 818	Quartermaster I below the form total Richard Hospital
	27		" 38 " 822	Bn duty lost on
	28		" 37 " 825	hospital duty of experiences
	29		" 38 " 844	Bn Rank
	30		" 38 " 845	R.S.y or ministers dept Withdrew but he awarded
	31		" 38 " 830	Lty Rates

H. Wightman Lieut. Col. O.C. Batt. Gal.

Train Arrangements.

Reference SD/1780/IV of today, the following Train arrangements have been made :-

		Offr.	O.R.	Ldg. Sta.	Ready to Load	Depart.	Arrive Gabbari Quays.
1st Train to convey (night of July 2nd/3rd)	6th R. Dublin Fus.	30	813	Kantara W. No.1 Mil.Sdg.	July 2. 1700	1840	July 3rd 0545
	2nd/20th London Regt.	9	266	" "	" "	"	" " "
	R.A.M.C. Details.		100	" "	" "	"	" " "
2nd Train to convey	2/24th London Regt.	29	793	Kantara W. No.2 Mil.Sdg.	July 2. 1915	2115	July 3rd 0540
	74th Div. Details.	4	244	" "	" "	"	" " "
	R.A.M.C. Details.		100	" "	" "	"	" " "
3rd Train to convey	52nd Div. Details.	5	171	Kantara W. No.1 Mil.Sdg.	July 2. 2000	2210	July 3rd 0645
	6th Connaught Rangers.	1	65	" "	" "	"	" " "
	5th Munsters Fus.	2	87	" "	" "	"	" " "
	Other Details for France less 2/14th London and 6th Leinsters	8	448	" "	" "	"	" " "
	R.A.M.C. Details.		100	" "	" "	"	" " "
	Tank Corps.		2	" "	" "	"	" " "
4th Train to convey (night of July 3rd/4th)	2/14th London Regt.	123		Kantara W. No.1 Mil.Sdg.	July 3. 1700	1840	July 4th 0545
	6th Leinsters.	8	110	" "	" "	"	" " "
	R.A. Details (from No.2 I.B.D)		808	" "	" "	"	" " "
	R.A.M.C. Details.		100	" "	" "	"	" " "
5th Train to convey	R.A. Details.		1000	Kantara W. No.2 Mil.Sdg.	July 3. 2000	2210	July 4th 0645
	Conducting Officers.	7		" "	" "	"	" " "
	R.A.M.C. Details.	1	100	" "	" "	"	" " "

MARCH TABLE.

for Crossing South Bridge July 2nd.

Unit.	Commence Cross.	Complete Cross.
6th R.Dublin Fus.	1630	1645
Detachment 2/20 Londons.	1645	1650
R.A.M.C. Details	1655	1700
2/24th London Regt.	1900	1915
74th Div.Details.	1915	1925
R.A.M.C. Details.	1925	1930
Details for 3rd Train.		
From No.1 Base Depot	1930	1940
From No.2 Base Depot	1940	1955
R.A.M.C. Details.	1955	2000

for Crossing South Bridge July 3rd.

Unit.	Commence Cross.	Complete Cross.
Details for 4th Train.		
From No.2 Base Depot	1630	1645
R.A.M.C. Details	1650	1655
Details for 5th Train.		
From General Base Depot	1930	1945
From No.2 Base Depot	1945	1950
R.A.M.C. Details	1955	2000

E.S.O. will make necessary arrangements with Suez Canal Co.

Police orders will be issued by A.P.M.

To:- O.C. 2/24th London Regt.
    O.C. 2/20th " "
    O.C. 6th Bn. R. Dublin Fus.
    O.C. No.1 Infantry Base Depot.
    O.C. No.2 " " "
    O.C. General Base Depot.
    O.C. R.A.M.C. Base Depot.

SECRET.

No. SD/1780/17

1. As Artillery Details do not proceed on the same day as Battalions, Conducting Officers will not be found by 6th Dublin Fus. and 2/24th London Regt. as detailed in para.5 of SD/1780/17 of today. Conducting Officers for Train 5 will be found as under to proceed to ALEXANDRIA and return on Completion of Duty.
    1 Officer from No.2 I.B.D. in charge details on Train 5.
    6 Officers from No.1 I.B.D. who will report to O.C. G.B.D. at 1000 July 3rd, and take charge of details from that Depot.

2. R.A.M.C. Details will be marched to Kantara West Station, under arrangements to be made by O.C. R.A.M.C. Base Depot. On arrival at Station they will be handed over to O.C. Train who will detail an Officer to take charge of party proceeding on his Train.

3. March Table and Train Timings are attached.

4. Water Bottles will be filled before leaving Camp.

5. Lorries have been ordered to report as follows:-
    To O.C. 2/24th Londons at 0600 July 2nd   3 Lorries.
    " " 2/20th " " " "   1 Lorry.
    " " 6th Dublin Fus. " " " "   3 Lorries.
Baggage for 2/24th Londons will be stacked at N. end No.2 Platform Military Siding and baggage of 2/20th Londons and 6th R. Dublin Fus at N. end No.1 Platform by 1500 July 2nd.
    Baggage of details proceeding from Base Depots will be conveyed under arrangements to be made by Depots concerned, but all heavy kit must be stacked on Platform from which Train leaves by 1500 on day of departure. Any baggage for 3rd Train will be stacked 50 yards from N. end of No.1 Platform. Guards will be provided by Units or Depots concerned.

6. Loading parties under an Officer will be detailed by Units or Depots concerned before leaving Camp on arrival at Station all other Details will entrain at once.

7. Train states will be handed to R.T.O. by Officers Commanding Units and/or portions of Units proceeding by each Train.

8. Troops will not detrain on arrival until ordered to do so by the Embarkation Staff Officer.
    Embarkation will take place immediately after detrainment. No leave will be granted to personnel embarking.

9. Tents, Latrines, etc. in Dueidar Road Camps will be left standing.

H. Tomkinson
Major,
D.A.Q.M.G.
CANAL ZONE.

KANTARA.
1st July, 1918.

Copies to:- R.T.O., Kantara West.
    E.S.O.
    S.T.O.
    A.P.M.

M.
To:-
O.C., 2/24th Bn. London Regiment.
O.C., 2/20th Bn. London Regiment.
O.C., 6th Bn. R. Dublin Fusiliers.
O.C., No.1 Infantry Base Depot.
O.C., No.2 Infantry Base Depot.
O.C., General Base Depot.

SECRET.

SD/1780/17.

(2)

1. This office No.CMQ 11982/5 dated June 27th is cancelled.

2. The following will embark at Alexandria on the 3rd July:-

(I) On Ship "A"

	Off.	O.R.
Now at Kantara.		
2/24th London Regiment.	29 ø	798
6th R. Dublin Fusiliers.	30 ø	813
2/20th London Regiment.	9	266
ø-includes Medical Officer.		
52nd Division Details	5	171
74th " "	4	244
Tank Corps.	-	2

(II) On Ship "B". To embark at Alexandria on 3rd and 4th July.

	Off.	O.R.
Now at Kantara.		
R.A. Details for U.K., ex "Kashgar"	-	1806
R.A.M.C. for U.K.	1	
For France:-		
2/4th Somerset L.I.	-	33
2/4th Hants Regt.	4	46
7th Bn. Dublin Fusrs.	2	62
5th Bn. R. Inniskg. Fusrs.	-	38
5th Bn. R. Irish Fusrs.	1	-
6th Bn. R. Inniskg. Fusrs.	-	51
2/14th Bn. London Regt.	-	123
2/15th Bn. " "	-	64
2/16th Bn. " "	-	46
2/17th Bn. " "	-	56
2/20th Bn. " "	-	20
2nd Bn. L. N. Lancs. Regt.	1	32
6th Bn. Leinster Regt.	8	110

3. The following will also proceed to ALEXANDRIA (Camp "A") for embarkation on the 5th July. Further orders will be issued:-

	Off.	O.R.
5th Bn. Connaught Rangers	1	65
6th " R. Munster Fusrs.	2	87

4. It is understood that the numbers to proceed from KANTARA may be increased. All details becoming available for embarkation will proceed, but 6th Dublin Fusiliers, 2/24th Londons, 2/20th Londons must not embark above strength of Infantry Off. 29 including those who have already proceeded. Numbers actually entraining will be reported to this office by 1000 July 2nd.

5. R.A. details from KANTARA will be commanded - until arrival on board ship - by Officers of other units proceeding for embarkation from that place, who will be detailed by G.O.C., Kantara Area.
These and other details will be taken over on board by Officers of the R.A.F and organized into Companies.
O.C., No.2 Infantry Base Depot will detail Officers to take charge of Artillery Details proceeding from that Depot. O's C. 6th R. Dublin and 2/24th Londons will each detail 4 Officers (one not below Rank of Captain) from those proceeding to report to O.C., General Base Depot at 1000 July 2nd to take charge of 850 Artillery Details now in that Depot.

Continued.

- 2 -

6. Medical Officers proceeding (whether on duty or leave) will be distributed proportionately amongst all ships. One Medical Officer will be detained by G.O.C., Alexandria District, for embarkation on another vessel on the 5th July.

7. Rations will be issued on board from and including the dinner meal on the date of embarkation.

8. Four copies of Embarkation Returns and three copies of Nominal Rolls of those embarking will be required by the Embarkation Staff Officer. These documents will clearly show, in the case of details in transit, the destination (U.K. or France) and the name of the vessel by which the personnel were conveyed to this command.

9. Train arrangements for the moves entailed by the above order will be notified.

10. Iron rations will be taken.

H. Tomkinson
Major,
D.A.Q.M.G.
KANTARA AREA.

KANTARA.
1st July, 1918.

Copies to :- R.T.O., Kantara West.
E.S.O.
A.D.S.T.
S.T.O.
O.C., Main Supply Depot.
C. O. O.
S. M. O.
A. D. W.
A. P. M.
O.C., 114th Sanitary Section.
O.C., 121st Sanitary Section.

M.

To:-
O.C., 2/24th Londons.
O.C., Detch. 2/20th Londons.
O.C., 6th R. Dublin Fusiliers.
O.C., No.1 Infantry Base Depot.
O.C., No.2 Infantry Base Depot.
O.C., General Base Depot.

Please note that orders issued under OMQ 11982/5 of June 27th have been cancelled. Embarkation will take place at Alexandria on July 3rd. Particulars will be sent as soon as possible.

KANTARA.
1st July, 1918.

H. Jenkinson
Major,
D.A.Q.M.G.
KANTARA AREA.

S E C R E T.
HEADQUARTERS
No./1780/17.
Date
* KANTARA AREA *

DISEMBARKATION ORDERS
by
Lieut.Colonel J.P.G.Crosbie, D.S.O.,
Commanding Troops H.T. "Malwa".

(3)

1. LIFEBELTS:- Lifebelts will be worn until the Ship anchors - word will be passed round - Officers will put theirs in respective cabins.

   Sections "A","B","C","D" & "J" will stow their lifebelts in Kit Room No.3 flat ("B" Section).

   Sections "E","F","G","H" & "I" will stow their lifebelts in Port No.5, Mail Room ("G" Section).

   No lifebelts to be lying about Troop Decks prior to O.C. Troop's final inspection.

2. TROOP DECKS. Officers of Units will see that Troop Decks are left scrupulously clean prior to O.C.Troop's final inspection.

3. SWEEPING PARTY. The Officer Commanding the last Unit to disembark (probably 2/24th Battn.London Regt) will be required to find one Platoon as a working party for thoroughly sweeping the Troops decks and upper decks prior to O.C.Troop's final inspection.

4. BAGGAGE - WORKING PARTIES. Each Unit will be ready to provide working parties of the following strength, required in No.2 hold and on the lighters.

   1 Officer supervising.
   1 N.C.O. & 10 men in the hold.
   1 N.C.O. & 15 men in the lighter.

   The Officer and lighter parties will proceed ashore with the respective Unit's baggage to unload and provide necessary guards and working parties.

5. TROOP DECK CLEANING GEAR. All Troop Deck cleaning gear will be returned to store No.3 flat ("B" Section) by 0930 hours 8th inst. Brooms will be issued to the sweeping party.

6. The following times are considered possible.

   Arrival. 10/1100 hrs. 8th inst. Baggage parties redd. 1900. 8th.

   Disembarkation. 0500 hours, 9th.

   Captain.
   Ship's Adjutant,
   "H.T."Malwa".

7-7-18.

Copies issued to.
    O.C.Troops.
    " 6th Royal Dublin Fusiliers.
    " 2/24th Battn.London Regt.
    " 2/20th " " "
    " 52nd Divisional Details.
    " 74th " "
    " Detachment, R.A.M.C.
    Ship's Quartermaster.

DISEMBARKATION ORDERS
BY
LIEUT-COLONEL W.H. WHYTE D.S.O.
COMMANDING 6(S) BN. ROYAL DUBLIN FUSILIERS.

---

1. **LIFEBELTS.** Lifebelts will be worn untill the ship anchors- word will be passed round- Officers will put theirs in respective cabins.
Sections "A" "B" "C" & "J" will stow their lifebelts in kit room No.3 Flat ("B" Section)
No lifebelts will be lying about troop decks prior to O.C. Troops final inspection.

2. **TROOP DECKS.** Officers Commanding Sections will see that troop decks are scrupulously clean proir to O.C. Troops final inspection.

3. **BAGGAGE-WORKING PARTIES.**
O.C. "B" Coy will detail the following baggage party :-
   1 Officer supervising
   1 N.C.O. & 10 men in the hold.
   2 Sgts & 50 O.Rks. Lighter party.
The Officer & Lighter party will proceed ashore with the baggage to unload and provide necessary guards.
In the event of the Battalion being last to disembark O.C. "B" Coy will detail one platoon to thoroughly sweep Troop Decks and Upper Deck prior to O.C. Troops final inspection.

4. **TROOP DECK CLEANING GEAR.**
All troop deck cleaning gear will be returned to store No. 3. Flat ("B" Section) by 0930 hours 8th inst. Brooms will be issued to the sweeping party.

5. **TIME OF ARRIVAL ETC.**
The following times are considered probable:-
   Arrival- 1000/1100hrs 8th inst.
   Baggage parties
      ready- 1900 hrs 8th inst.
   Disembarkation- 0500 hrs 9th inst.

AT SEA
7th July 1918.

J. Esmonde
Capt & Adjutant.
6TH (S) Bn. Royal Dublin Fusiliers.

SECRET. PROGRAMME OF TRAIN NO. TD. LEAVING CIMINO   HOURS ON / /18.

ENTITLED FOR FRANCE.   6th R. Lab: ~~~~ (4)
                                                    Officers. O.Ranks.
No.   " ....Regt.   30   900

   1.   Entrain at 15.04 hours on 9/7/ 1918.
        Baggage to start loading three hours before time fixed for departure

   2.   Troops to parade at Siding, on road, two hours before time fixed for
departure.

   3.   Officer Commanding Train to arrange with A.S.C., through CAMP QUARTER
MASTER, for the rationing of the Train.

   4.   O.C., Train with Entrainment Statement, to report to the Officer of
the D.A.A.G. (M) at 11am hours on   1918.

   5.   O.C., Train to confer with the R.T.O. CIMINO, at the Station Office,
at   10   hours on 9/7/ 1918.

   6.   O.C., Train is responsible that, Personnel having entrained, are not
left behind. He will take such ~~necessary~~ steps for picquetting the Train as
he may consider necessary.

ALL RANKS TO ENTRAIN WITH WATER BOTTLES FULL.

CAMP HEADQUARTERS.   W. R. Wilson
No.9. Rest Camp,   Captain.
  / /1918.   CAMP ADJUTANT.

$$\frac{55}{29}$$ $$\frac{849}{808-12-25}$$
$$31$$

A 18 $$\frac{849}{37}$$
$$\overline{81}$$

1. NCO Each Vehicle
2 Guards 1 Each End
Officer i/c Each
Train Guard Emergency
Train Baggage Officer

1818

Army Form C. 2118.

WAR DIARY
or
INTELLIGENCE SUMMARY.
(Erase heading not required.)

Instructions regarding War Diaries and Intelligence Summaries are contained in F. S. Regs., Part II. and the Staff Manual respectively. Title pages will be prepared in manuscript.

Place	Date	Hour	Summary of Events and Information	Remarks and references to Appendices

A5834 Wt. W4973/M687 750,000 8/16 D. D. & L. Ltd. Forms/C.2118/13

CONFIDENTIAL

WAR DIARY

6th (s) Bn ROYAL DUBLIN FUSILIERS.

From 1st To 31st August 1918.

VOLUME 38

Army Form C. 2118.

WAR DIARY
or
INTELLIGENCE SUMMARY.
(Erase heading not required.)

Instructions regarding War Diaries and Intelligence Summaries are contained in F. S. Regs., Part II. and the Staff Manual respectively. Title pages will be prepared in manuscript.

Place	Date	Hour	Summary of Events and Information	Remarks and references to Appendices
SEROUEH	1/2/18		Inspection through 20 officers No 9 I.B.D. Coy training	
"	2 "		Coy Inspected training	R
"	3 "		Coy Inspected training. A.A. Scouts intelligence taken by G.O.C 197 I.B to see themselves	R
"	4 "		Training Ranges 2/Lt 2/Lt Burns Joining P.I.I.B. Force & 16 O.Rs Scouts	R
"	5 "		Going as on 3rd 1 Bn Catriment Arras	R
"	6 "		G.O.C 66th Div Inspects the Batt marching past 09.30	R
"	7 "		Settled Reveille at 1000 for Route March. Commence training scheme	R
"	8 "		1st A/Tg Coy commenced scheme issued indent dated 10.2.18 I.O	R
"	8 "		Coy Returned training. No Parades at 15.00 for lecture on Bayonet by Capt by Lt Col R13 Capt Hamm. OBE	R
"	9 "		Coy went Musketry Range. Remainder of Btn Route marching	R
"	10 "		Coy Returned training. Lecture by Bn.Cmdr 11.00 to all Officers arrival	R
"	11 "		Orders received by Bn that new draft arrived by H.M. T.W.W.F on arriving	R
"	12 "		Coy Returned training	R
"	13 "		All Coys Route Marching Reveille. Remainder training	R
"	14 "		Rehearsal on to stop Appendix A. Reveille turns M.O of 1/Lt 1/6 time taper site	R
"	15 "		Training in Coys Command. of the Bn from 1/Lt 1/7/2 to Lt Coy	R
"	16 "		Coy Training Scheme. 28 arrived 236 OR. 1 of Byrne Injured by shell 1 N.C.O	R
"	17 "		Same Reveille at 09.00 Draft 2/Lt 8 Officers 321 ORs inspected by Maj O Nott O N/C	R
"	18 "		Training Reveille at 09.00 Major W Inness Reported to Bn W/C	R
"	19 "		Coy to Rifle Ranges Capt Lockhart Y Gordon Allowed home leave.	R

D. D. & L., London, E.C.
(A8001) Wt. W1771/M2031 750,000 5/17 Sch. 52 Forms/C2118/14

Army Form C. 2118.

WAR DIARY
or
INTELLIGENCE SUMMARY.
(Erase heading not required.)

Instructions regarding War Diaries and Intelligence Summaries are contained in F. S. Regs., Part II. and the Staff Manual respectively. Title pages will be prepared in manuscript.

Place	Date	Hour	Summary of Events and Information	Remarks and references to Appendices

CONFIDENTIAL

WAR DIARY.

6TH (S) BN. ROYAL DUBLIN FUSILIERS.

Period - 1/9/18 to 30/9/18.

VOLUME 39.

Army Form C. 2118.

WAR DIARY
or
INTELLIGENCE SUMMARY.
(Erase heading not required.)

Instructions regarding War Diaries and Intelligence Summaries are contained in F.S. Regs., Part II. and the Staff Manual respectively. Title pages will be prepared in manuscript.

Place	Date	Hour	Summary of Events and Information	Remarks and references to Appendices
SERQUEX	1/9/18		Fighting strength 30 Officers 761 O.R. Lt Col W.H. Little D.S.O.A.C. returned from leave and assumed command of the Bn.	
"	2		Bn Carry out Morning & Evening operating orders	
"	3		Coy and Section Training	B
"	4		Reorganization of Platoons 4yo	
"	5		Extension Musketry Training	B
"	6		Company & Platoon Training	
"	7	6.45	Bn on 4.45 inspection Ceremonial Parade	
"	8		Drum service and Coy ½ on 09.00. Orders received for Bn to relieve 198 Coy	
"	9		Bn at H.Qrs. of 198 Coy Conference an the 198 Coy Scheme near the handing over the bn by ABBEVILLE Station at little 250 attended Conference at SR QUEUX at 09.00 arrived at ABBEVILLE about 11.10	
"	10		Bn moved by March route from SR QUEUX Companies transferred from tfamol 238 B 15.40 Reaching 2nd Version A51-1 103 men Bn 16/com to FORMERI and Echerine BOMEX L	
"	12		Bn moved by March route 65.8 B CHATEAU. Offing (3) Supper 658 B	
ABANCOURT	13		Bn arrived at AUXI le CHATEAU at 07.30 Billeting Complete by 05.00 Bn moved by march route to Belette. – H.Q & Coys GUESCHART. B Coy at IVERGNY. D Coy VACQUERETTES Billeting Complete by 18.00pm	
GUESCHART	14		Orders received to form when Jore for Cavalry manoeuvres & a Divisional reference for the G.S. Cav GUESCHART. CHURCH at 09.30	
"	15		Divine Service at H.Qrs.	
"	16		Company Training	
"	17		Cavalry manoeuvres Bn in Reserve along the GENNE-IVERGENY VACQUERETTE Rd Cavalry- Infantry Conference at Rue River Commander Known about 08.00 GUESCHART - Infantry Conference at Rue River Commander Known about 08.00 and Covers were given the new Commanders Rendezvous at Covers v Tables. B Coy moved from IVERGNEY to H.Q at 21.00	
"	18		Coy moved from VACQUERETTE to H.Q at 11.00. Lt W.H. OSBORNE joined from England. Coy & D attached to 11cm	
"	19		From GUESCHART to BONNIERS by March route	

Army Form C. 2118.

Page V

WAR DIARY
or
INTELLIGENCE SUMMARY.

(Erase heading not required.)

Instructions regarding War Diaries and Intelligence Summaries are contained in F.S. Regs., Part II. and the Staff Manual respectively. Title pages will be prepared in manuscript.

Place	Date	Hour	Summary of Events and Information	Remarks and references to Appendices
BONNIERS	21		Bn moved by road route at 0730 arrived LEINCOURT at 1200 Enemy into Billets	
LEINCOURT	22		Divine Service at 10-11am for A,B & C Coy remainder by Platoon training	
"	23		" " " "	
"	24		" " " "	
"	25		" Orders received to move	
"	26		Bayonet route march	
"	27		" " " "	
"	28		" Bn kicking moved by road to CORBIE	
"	29/9		Bn moved from LEINCOURT at 0715am arrived at PT HOVEIN at 1000 Entrained at 1600 arrived at CORBIE at 0730 detrained marched to AVEIGNY going into Billets about 02 on 29/9/18	
			Bn moved by road route to BAYONVILLERS arriving about 1630 Enemy aircraft	
BAYONVILLERS	30/9		into billets	
			Fighting strength 31 officers 876 O.Rs Bn reorganising at a decisive View nothing kept in offensive and were S.O.C 198 was bidets to all officers early date. N Chefice at upton further offensive operates	

General East
Asst. Adjt.

MAP 'D'.

LEGEND.

6ᵗʰ Lancs. Fus.
5ᵗʰ R. Innis. Fus.
6ᵗʰ R. Dublin Fus.

Army Form C. 2118.

6th R. Dub. Fus.

WAR DIARY or INTELLIGENCE SUMMARY

(Erase heading not required.)

Instructions regarding War Diaries and Intelligence Summaries are contained in F. S. Regs., Part II. and the Staff Manual respectively. Title Pages will be prepared in manuscript.

Place	Date	Hour	Summary of Events and Information	Remarks and references to Appendices.
BAYONVILLERS	1.10.18		Bn move by march route at 1040 arriving at CAPPY 1430 Lt Horney Joined Bn	Appen (1)
CAPPY	2.	"	" " " " at 1000 to GUILLEMONT Tactical scheme en route	" (2)
GUILLEMONT	3.	"	Bn Training Tactical scheme for all Officer and Platoon Commdrs Bn hurried off to MOILANDS at 1830 arriving about 0005 (march route)	
MOILANDS	4.	"		Appen (3)
STE EMILIE	5.	"	Bn less B. Team move by march route STE EMILIE going into Bivouac.	
"	6.	"	Bn preparing for Battle.	
"	7.	"	Bn move under Adjutant by march route to LE CATLET taking up position support trenches HINDENBERG LINE.	Appen (4)
LE CATLET	8.	"	Bn move cut to assembly Tape for attack 2200 (see appendic 5.) see appendic (6) & L.F.99.	
	9.	"	see appendic (7) & L.F.99	
	10.		" 2 " (8) & L.F.99.	
	11.		" " (9) & L.F.99.	
	12.		Bn resting and reorganising 2nd R.Dub.Fus quartered alongside the Bn.	Appen (10)
MAUROIS	13.		Bn move to MARETZ at 0955.	
MARETZ	14.		Bn Training and reorganising As on 14th 2/Lt ARMSTRONG, BELL & O'HEA joined from U.K. Warning order XIII Corps Commdr visited Bn in Billets at 1345.	Appen (11)
	15.		Bn move to RUFMONT en route for operations in LE CATEAU see appendic 12. & L.F. 99.	
REMONT	16.		Bn mopping up LE CATEAU see appendic (13) and L.F.99.	
LE CATEAU	17.		Bn relieved by 6th Lanc Fus. Relief complete 1300. Coys moved independent to Reserve Trenches in Q.2. see appendic 14 Slight hostile shelling (Casualties 4.)	
"	18.		Bn still in Reserve at Q.2. Slight Hostile Shelling, Lt Thornton, Rooker and Byrne Joined.	
Q.2.	19.		Bn moved from Reserve Trenches at 0200 to RUFMONT see appendic (15) Bn moved from RUFMONT to MAUROIS at 1630, Going into Billets. Capt Sproule and 2/Lt J.J.Purcell and P.P.Purcell join	
	20.		Bn move from MAUROIS to PREMONT.	
MAUROIS	21.		Reorganising and Lewis Gun Training.	
PREMONT	22.		As on 22nd Fighting Strength Off. 20 Orks. 240	
"	23.			

Army Form C. 2118.

WAR DIARY
or
INTELLIGENCE SUMMARY

(Erase heading not required.)

Instructions regarding War Diaries and Intelligence Summaries are contained in F.S. Regs., Part II. and the Staff Manual respectively. Title Pages will be prepared in manuscript.

Place	Date	Hour	Summary of Events and Information	Remarks and references to Appendices
PREMONT	24.10.18		Training as on 23rd Lt & Q.M. Unwin General List joined for duty as Q.M. 2/Lts McMillan & Wing Joined for duty. Bn under 2hrs notice to move.	
"	25.	"	Bn route march to old Battle Sector Buried some of our dead and salved Equipment etc.	
"	26.	"	Bn route march.	
"	27.	"	Divine service and Rest.	
"	28.	"	Bde Route March (11 miles Battalions) .Capt SHADFORTH to Bde (Staff under study)	
"	29.	"	Major J. LUKE to 2nd Roy. Dub. Fus as temporary 2nd Command.	
"	30.	"	Bn Training. Fighting Strength 31 Officers 472 ORs.	
"	31.	"	Bn took part in Divisional Scheme Vicinity WALLINCOURT, ELLINCOURT, BERTRY-CLARY returning to PREMONNT at 1800 hours.	

Captain & Adjutant.
6th (s) Bn The Royal Dublin Fusiliers

9th Bn Royal Dublin Fusiliers. No, D.F.99
OPERATIONS -- 7th-11th October 1918.

7/10/18

0730. C.O. went forward from ST EMELIE with Coy Commdrs to reconnoitre Battle Sector

1045. Bn moved by march route from ST EMELIE to LE CATELET under the Adjutant arriving 1430.

2200. Bn moved to Tape Line via Canal Bridge – A.18 Central-Fork Road B.1,d 21 night very dark and slight hostile shelling.

8/10/18

0445 C, Coy reached the assembly Tape and commenced taking up positions.

0450 Intensive Gas Shell and M.G. Barrage opened by enemy. B, Coy were only a short distance from the Tape and laid down in groups, A, & D Coys were in the Valley and scattered out. Considerable confusion was caused and about 100 Casualties, inc. 4 Officers resulted.

0530. Barrage still intense Parties who were scattered were collected together and sent forward to the Tape.

0400. Barrage slackened somewhat but M.Guns kept up heavy fire.

0445 Coy now in position on the Tape with 5th R,Innis Fus on right Considerable Gap between Battalions.

0510 Zero,- Our Guns put down a splendid Barrage and Coys went forward to the attack A. & C. leading with D.&B in support.
Bn frontage 650 yds- Each Coy was a Two Platoon front. As right Coys were very weak Capt Shadforth Commdg A, Coy was ordered to send one of his Platoons from left support to the Right.
This was done in the first stage of the Barrage.

0530 DENAMED FARM was captured under the barrage without difficulty and yielded 40 Prisoners to No,5 Platoon.
Advance to PETIT VERGER FARM continued, troops keeping well under barrage. At this stage heavy M,Gun Fire was brought to bear from T.25 C & D T21.B and T.15 D, No, C Platoon from support deployed to the left and destroyed the nearest Guns which were in another Battalion area.By so doing they enabled the leading line which had halted to catch up the barrage before reaching PETIT VERGER FARM. This Farm and the Rifle Pits in the vicinity were captured with little difficulty and about 50 Prisoners collected Time 0600.
The attack was continued but was held up on the line T 23 A 6 7 - T23b.Y.Y mainly primarily by 5 M.Gs firing from 200 x WEST of MARLIGHES FRM and snipers. An endeavour was made to get a Stokes Mortar into action but it was found impossible as the team had become Casualties. Our artillery at this time was firing smoke shells and 18pdrs short. As good smoke screen was afforded however and taking advantage of it B, Coy under Capt Shadforth leap frogged and pushed on for MARLIGHES FARM. One Platoon 4/60th Rifles at this point got in touch with our left flank. The sunken road T23b B.5 - T.17c cc was assulted and yielded about 40 Prisoners. The Farm was then captured but was untenable owing to M.G. Fire from the front left flank and left rear. Field Guns were also firing over open sights but these three guns were silenced by a Lewis gun section which enfiladed their flank. The front line now fell back gradually to the sunken road and the right Coy got in touch with the 7th R.I. Fus on the flank by shutter.
Capt SHADFORTH now took over command of all coys, they having been considerably reduced in strength and reorganised. The SUNKEN ROAD became very unhealthy as enemy Machine gunners had worked out on the left flank and were enfilading it. The shooting however was bad and in the meantime the troops on the left had advanced and had commenced clearing VILLERS OUTREAUX. Just at this time a Whippet Tank came up but got stuck in the SUNKEN ROAD and was Machine gunned until the crew all became Casualties. An Officer Lt MANSION 4/60th Rifles was also wounded in trying to rescue them. By now resistance in the left flank had slackened and the advance again commenced.

1500 Little or no opposition was met with and Coys proceeded to establish posts near LARPE FARM where touch with the 5th Manchester Regt was gained,T.12C and T.11 central,
Casualties Total OFFICERS-7 O.RKS-262

Contd.

```
Captured - Prisoners   170
    "      Field Guns   14
    "      Anti-Tanks
           Rifles        3
    "      M.Gs         41
    "      L.T.Ms        2
```

9/10/18

0330. Orders received from Brigade for advance to continue, Bn was told off in support with orders to Mop up ELINCOURT from the WEST with the 5th R.I. Fus on the right flank.

0430 Coys assembled in SUNKEN ROAD T.12a and b.

0520 Advance commenced and as touch with the right flank could not be obtained 2 Coys were sent in to mop up the whole of ELINCOURT. Later touch with 1 Coy R.I. Fus was made. Only 11 Prisoners were taken in ELINCOURT. The enemy had apparently made a hurried departure as food was found on the tables in some houses.

1000 Reorganised, having come into Reserve and marched in Column of route with Advanced Guard out for IRIS COPSE G.55 Central.

1250 Reached IRIS COPSE.

10/10/18

0001 Orders received to continue the advance to LE CATEAU.
        Advance Guard 6th Lanc Fus.
        Main   "   5th R. Innis Fus.
                       6th Roy Dub. Fus.

0530 Bn marched via L'EPINETTE and MARETZ alongReaux Road to RUESMONT.

0630 Passed through RUESMONT under artillery fire and received orders to be in Brigade Reserve following up the 5th R.I.Fus who were in support with the 6th Lanc Fus leading Right Flank boundary-ROMAN ROAD exclusive.

0730 Advance continued in artillery formation, considerable hostile shelling. Leading 2 Coys--A.C.D. crossed LE CATEAU-CAMBRAI road and dug in.
      Bn H.Qrs established in T.70a.9.
                Casualties - Officers 2,
                             O.Rks.   45.

11/10/18

0800 Orders received for Bn to relieve 6th Lanc Fus in outpost position.

1400 Reconnaissance of outpost line completed.

1830 Orders to relieve 6th Lanc Fus cancelled. Had orders to withdraw into Divisional Reserve received.

2100 Moved back to Billets in MARCIS (3 Casualties on way)

Total Casualties to Date
```
              K.   W.   M.    Total
Officers      1    12.          13
O.Rks        41   258   2      301.
```

12/10/18

1000 Bn moved by march route from MARETZ to RUESMONT.

1200 Attended G.O.C. Conference at RUESMONT and received instructions for the Bn to Mop up LE CATEAU in combination with Coys operating on the morning of the 13th inst.

1330 C.O. and Coy Cmdrs went forward to reconnoitre point of Assembly for 2 Coys and H.Q. and to arrange details for the relief of the 2nd Bn S.A.I with remaining 2 Coys in outpost line EAST of LE CATEAU.
Arrangements for mopping up LE CATEAU were as follows:- B & C Coys were detailed to cross bridges between RIFTS SPLES between X.29a 30 29 and X.29d 39.39 in rear of the assaulting troops (SOUTH AFRICAN BRIGADE) entered the Town from the NORTH EAST and clear the Town in bounds, which were definitely arranged. A & D Coys were to cross the river if circumstances permitted with patrols and gain touch with the C Coys working from the NORTH EAST. If this crossing couldn't be effected a sally the forward posts were to keep the enemy on the EAST BANK engaged while they were taken in rear by the other Coys. B & C Coys under the command of Capt BRADFORTH and MAJOR LUKE respectively had orders to

(3) Contd.

cross the bridges at Zero plus 3 hours.

1800   Bn H.Qrs moved to house at K.33d 5.8 and Coys to respective positions.

1900   Capt. W. B. ENGLISH O.C. D Coy reported that on the night of the 15th inst the 2nd Bn S.A.I. had effected a crossing of the SHELD about K.34d 4.5 and had established a post on the Eastern Bank with 1 Officer and 160 O.Rks but that nothing had been heard from it since the early hours of the 16th inst. O.C. gave orders to O.C. D. Coy to try and cross the River and investigate matters. This he endeavoured to do but failed owing to M.G Fire at close range from Eastern Bank. A Post was then established on the W.Bank O.C. A. Coy reported that the post which the S.As had previously held on the West Bank of the River about K.36a 9.2 had been driven in earlier in the evening. Orders were given for one platoon to reestablish this post at all costs The night was very light and the patrols proceeding down the street Heavy M.G. Fire was brought to bear on it by the enemy. A Lewis Gun was quickly got into action and after some skirmishing our men got into the houses on both sides of the street near the demolished bridge, with two casualties.

17/10/18
0700.   B & C COYS left position of assembly and proceeded via K.33b 5.8-K33c 7.8 GATEAU-Road in K 30d to bridges. A very thick fog prevailed and at the time a Heavy Gas and H.E. Barrage was being put down by the enemy. Box Respirators had to be worn and this made the question of keeping direction and touch a very difficult problem. B Coy lost No.5 Platoon and C Coy its H.Qrs Platoon the former owing to the connecting files having become casualties.

0815   Both Coys got touch with the S.A Bde about CHATEAU DESBONS and at this point came under heavy M.G.Rifle and T.M. Fire. Several casualties resulted. Information was received that the S.As were held up on the East Side of the River.

0915   Coys crossed the bridges near DAHOMEY FACTORY. No5 Platoon was ordered direct to Railway Crossing at K.33c 7.5 to make good this point and intercept enemy retreating from LE CATEAU. No.8 Platoon was ordered to establish a strong point about K.33c 4.5 to further assist in cutting off the enemy. Nos.7 Platoon and C Coy commenced in mopping up the Town. Later it was ascertained that Nos 6 and 8 Platoons had become involved in the fighting with the SOUTH AFRICANS as they were held up on the right. One Lewis Gun Section had been ordered to consolidate in K.33 a 5.3. On this information reaching R.C B. Coy (less one Platoon holding river crossing K34d 4.5) was ordered to reinforce B.Coy. In the meantime No.5 Platoon which had lost direction, had been located near an M.Gun and was sent under the Adjutant to rejoin its Coy. Capt SHADFORTH had not learned that one of his platoons had been involved in the fighting with the S.As and proceeded to get in touch with them at 1130. He went direct to K.33c 6.5 with 5 men and was promptly cut off by the enemy who commenced to M.Gun and Bomb the party. They got into a house just N.E of 34 reference Town Plan and managed to keep the enemy at bay until 1500 when by piling furniture against the wall they got out through a shell hole in the wall at the back of the house and pushed back to K.33c 7.5. In the meantime O.C.Major SINCLY B. COY who had escaped in the first instance located Major LUKE informing him of what had happened. A party was sent to rescue Capt SHADFORTH and his 4 men but failed to get near the house owing to M.G Fire. In the Railway Major LUKE then took command of all the mopping up parties and set to work systematically.

At 1600 the mopping up from the North East was not proceeding sufficiently fast it was decided to effect a crossing of the SHELD from the West Bank and work up the street from bridge K33b.0.1 to church to join forces with those working from the N.E 1 Platoon of A Coy was ordered to effect this crossing. This they did by avoiding the bridge at K34 Central and fording the stream lower down. A Machine post consisting of 9 men was quickly captured. This being successful a second platoon of A was ordered to follow up the first and work from bridge to K.34d K1-K34i 6.8 and K 34d 6.8. The remaining two Platoons less one Lewis gun section left to guard bridge at K,34b 0.1 were dispatched soon afterwards to clear in a North Easterly direction (this was made possible by orders being received from Bde that all the Bn would be used for mopping up purposes and that two Coys 5th R.I.Fus were to be sent to support) A Coy met with considerable opposition from all quarters by M.G and snipers. The enemy were a very brave and stout lot of fellows and regret to say treacherous. About 1900 one platoon had just taken two snipers when a runner reported that another platoon was held up and the platoon Officer and others killed.

No.(4) Contd.

Lt HARKIN and 2nd I.O Section immediately put two prisoners in front of them and proceeded direct along the street and called on them to surrender. Ten came out with their hand up apparently for this purpose but instead of surrendering opened fire with a M.Gun killing some of our men and taking cover needless to say the prisoners in possession were promptly dispatched to another world.

Our party then quickly fell back to cover and errected a barricade in front of 2 Lewis Guns which were turned on to the house and good street fighting began. Half an hour later C.S.Major Cooke reported to his Coy Comndr Capt HAYES that there was another strong party of about 20 in a house with a M.Gun in street and that he had captured another 4. Lt WHYTE who speaks German fluently instructed one of them to go down the street and tell his Comrades that if they would surrender they would get a safe conduct through our lines and that if he himself who was covered with rifles did not return his other 3 comrades would be shot. This prisoner did as he was instructed but the reply he got was No Surrender. Curiously enough this man was allowed by the party referred to to return safely to our men. On hearing of this obstinacy a platoon of the 9th R.Innis Fus who had come up was sent round south of the Town for the purpose of enveloping these parties.
This was successfully done.

1500 A Coy got touch with B & C Coys coming from the NORTH EAST, These Coys had also had several M.Guns and snipers to deal with.

1400 Capt SHADFORTH on urgent message from D.A. Scottish collected 60 men of B. C and D. Coys and reorganised into 3 Platoons to defend bridges over River.

1210 On learning that 2 Platoons of B Coy had become involved with the S.As and fearing that other platoons would be called upon to halt an order was sent to Major LUKE and Capt SHADFORTH that all 6th R.I.Fus from this time would be employed in mopping up and defending LE CATEAU. Capt SHADFORTH did not receive this message being at the time imprisoned.

1227 Reported to Bde that mopping up from the West going well and the Church had been reached.

1200 Hearing that Railway Crossing K.35 c 2.3 had not been made good 1 Platoon 9th R.I.Fus was dispatched to this point.

1500 Report received from this platoon Comndr that he was held up in K36d N.2

1730 Southern portion of Town was cleared of the enemy and posts definitely established at Q4 b.7.2. Q.8 a 2.3 and R. 31a 7.7.
6 platoon 9th R. Innis Fus and 2 Vickers Guns were sent to support Capt SHADFORTH in NORTH of Town but only 3 men reached him as remainder has become casualties by shell fire.

1700 Sent 2 Vickers Guns with Sgt MORLEY A. Coy to about point 5.1 Town Plan to command eastern exists of Town.

1830 Post established at K.35a 7.5. This area of the Town was under constant Fire from Railway Embankment.

1900 Streets being actively patrolled in case of Snipers coming out.

1930 Posts established at K.35a 4.8 and K 35a 5.6.

2030 2 Vickers Guns dispatched to these posts.
18/10/18
0530 Lt BRUCE 9th R,Innis Fus sent under cover of barrage to capture and hold Kote D.5 Later he reported that he reached the Easy side of the cutting and crossed the Railway Line himself reaching many of the enemy some established with M.gs and other digging in. He shot two with his revolver and threw a bomb amongst the remainder. He got back into the cutting and found what appeared to be an outlet of a big underground drain, entering this he travelled along until he found an opening which brought him out in the centre of the Town. His Platoon had meantime returned to K.34d 7.6

0830 Posts at Q2a 2.3 and touch gained with 30th Div in TRIANGLE.
The 4 Trench Mortars did useful work 2 with B.Coy and 2 with A, Coy The former was employed in clearing out M.Gs for the South Africans and the later one M.Gun nests in the Town.
Hand Grenades No.36 and Smoke Grenades No.27 were freely used in the mopping

Contd NO.5.

up of the Town.
Many Prisoners were sent back out of the Town without escort for which
receipts were not obtained. Receipt for Five only are in possession.
It was impossible to make an inventory of the captured materiel. At least
3 Motor Lorries were seen.

    Casualties - Officers 4 inc, M.O.
          O.Rks 81

Casualties to date

	K.	W.	M.	Total.
OFFICERS	2	15	0	17
O' Ranks	53	318	16	387.

       (Signed) J, Esmonde.
     Capt & ADJUTANT 2th Royal Dublin Fusiliers,

6th Lancs. Fus.
5th R. Innis. Fus.
6th R. Dublin Fus.
198th L.T.M.B.
No. 3 Signal Section.
198th Inf. Bde. H.Q.

The B.G.C. wishes to congratulate the Brigade on their performances of the last 12 days.

During that period they have advanced 13¾ miles on 10½ of which they were actually in touch with the enemy, have captured 484 prisoners, 23 field guns, 3 heavy howitzers and a large number of machine guns, in addition to inflicting heavy casualties on the enemy. Their final effort was to clear the town of LE CATEAU, East of the River SELLE, so liberating over 1000 French civilians who have been under German domination for over four years.

This result has been attained by the hard work and unselfishness of all ranks, coupled with a determination to do their duty and get to grips with the enemy in spite of all detriments.

The B.G.C. regrets the casualties sustained in fighting a stubborn enemy, but he knows that now the Brigade has got the measure of the enemy and that he can rely on them in future operations to do equally good work in bringing the war to a speedy and victorious conclusion.

21.10.18.
RHW

D.F.99

Guns captured by the 6th (s) Bn Royal Dublin Fusiliers.
October 6th – 10th 1918.

Ref No.	Nature.	German Reg No.	Place Captured	Remarks.
R.D.F.1.	77 mm.	221.	T22.c.8.7.	It was not possible to send to ascertain the Reg Nos. till 15.10.18 by this time the Guns had been removed, but very recently as the pick and Wheel marks showed G.O.C. Bde saw Nos R.D.F.13 & 14 during the Battle in company with O.C. 6th R.D.Fus.
R.D.F.2.	"	22846	T22.b.5.5.	
R.D.F.3.	"	A/697	T22.b.3.7.	
R.D.F.4.	"	52		
R.D.F.5.	"	2101		
R.D.F.6.	"	1152	T17.c.8.2.	
R.D.F.7.	"			
R.D.F.8.	"			
R.D.F.9.	"			
R.D.F.10.	"		B.3.d.3.9.	
R.D.F.11.	"			
R.D.F.12.	"			
R.D.F.13.	"			
R.D.F.14.	"		T17.a20.15	
R.D.F.15 } R.D.F.16 }	Light Trench Mortars		Mr Pettit Verger Farm	
R.D.F.17 } R.D.F.18 } R.D.F.19 }	Anti-Tank Rifles.		Petit Verger Farm and Morliches Farm.	

Machine Guns. No registered numbers taken nor were a fraction of the whole collected.

D.F. 99

Ville du Cateau.

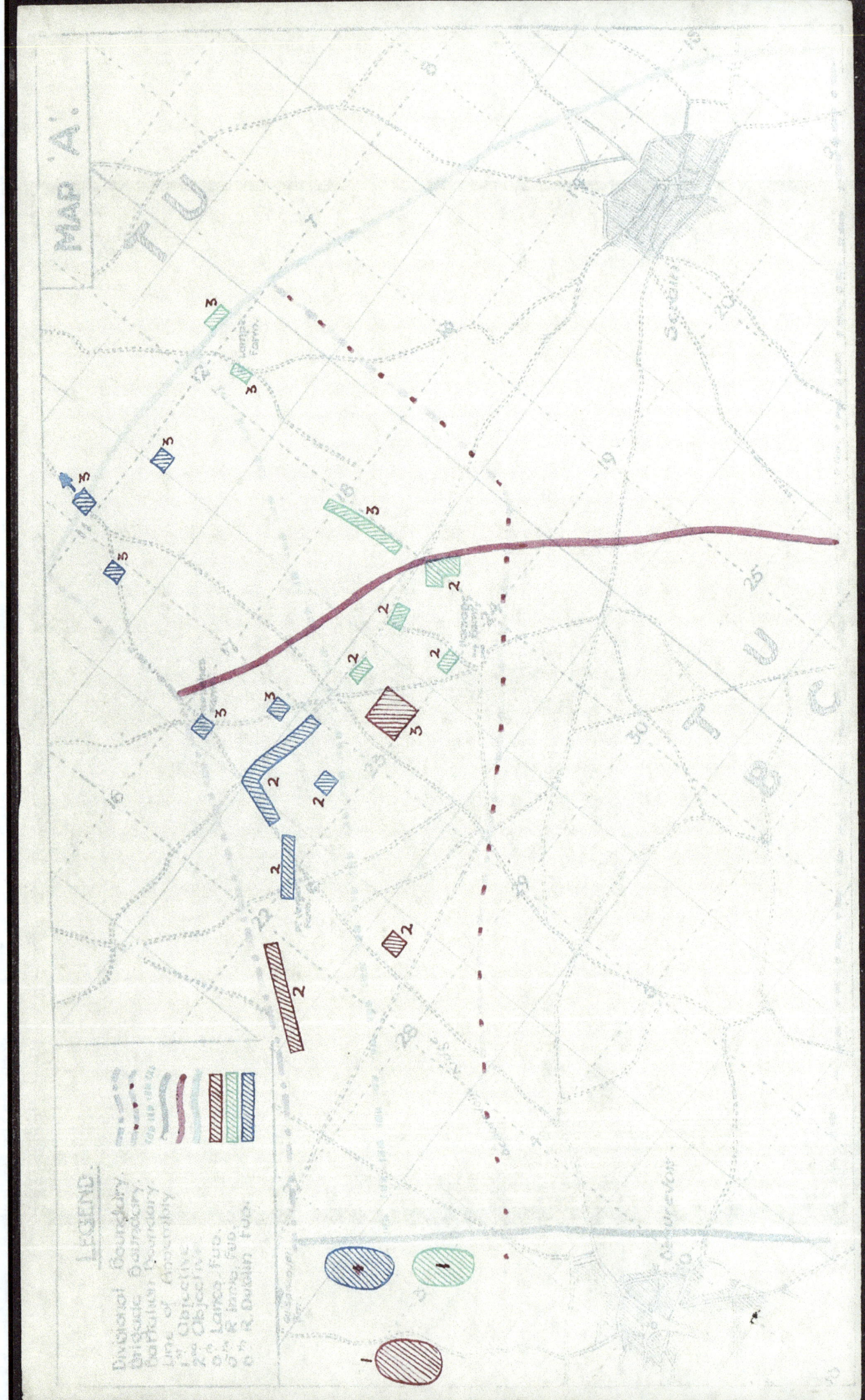

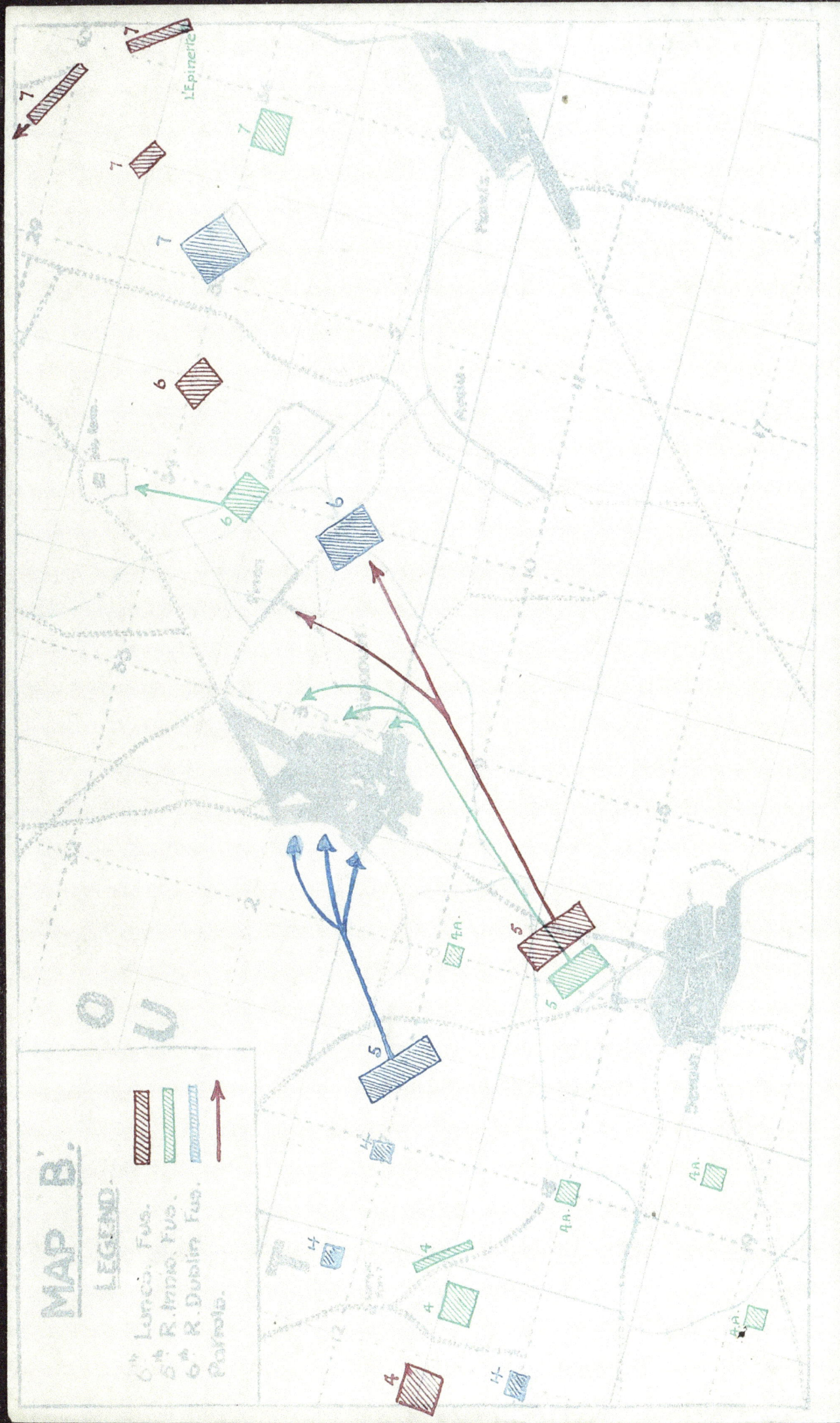

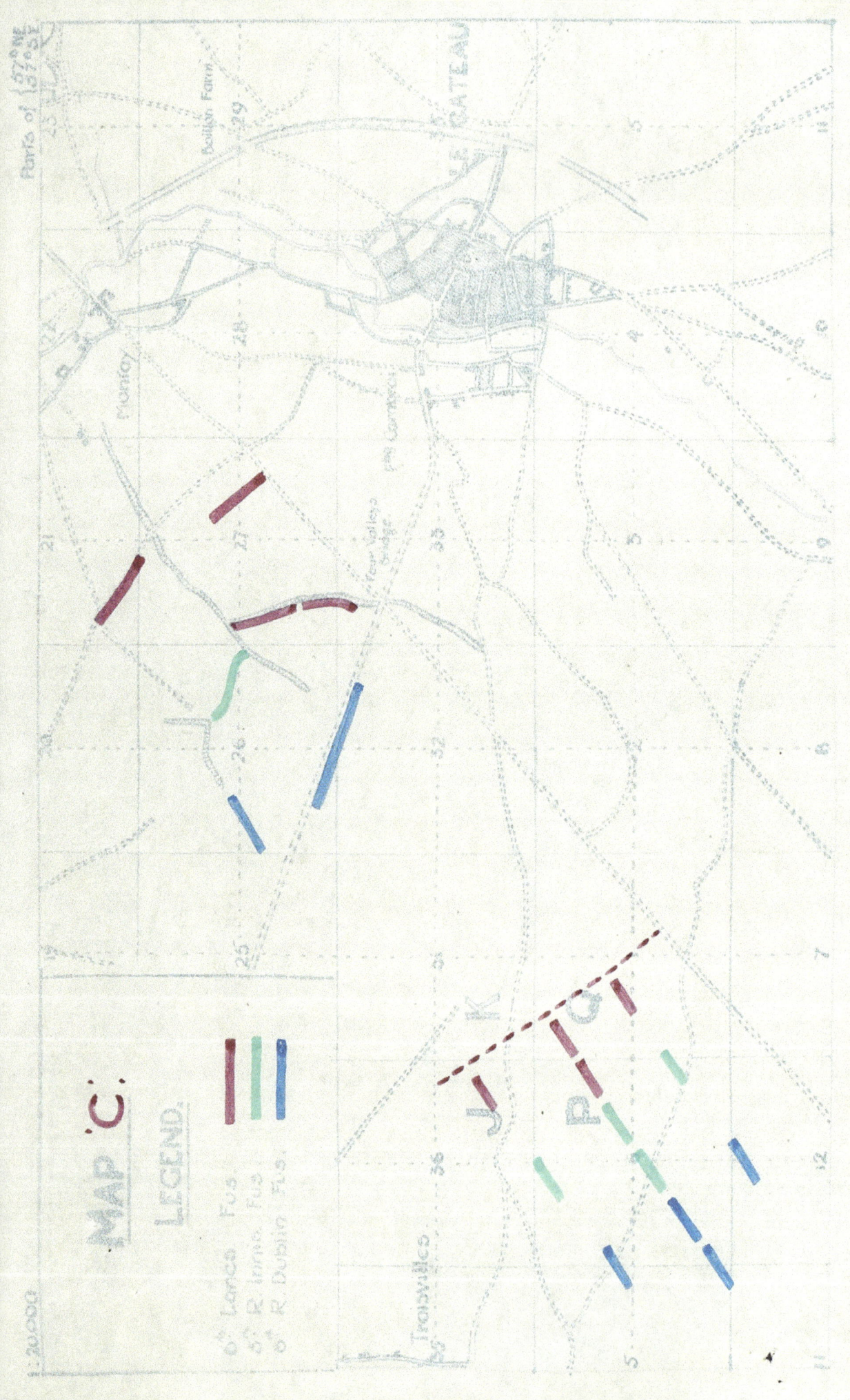

Army Form C. 2118.

WAR DIARY
INTELLIGENCE SUMMARY.
(Erase heading not required.)

6 R.D.F

Place	Date	Hour	Summary of Events and Information	Remarks and references to Appendices
PREMONT	1.11.18		1. Coy Training, movement order received. 2/Lt Featherstone to Div.H.Q.	
	2.		Bn moved by march route from PREMONT at 0900 arrived HONNECHY 1310.	After (1)
	3.		Bn moved to LE CATEAU at 1545 arriving 1840. G.O.C 198th Bde presented M.M. to N.C.O's and men of Battn.	After (11)
	4.		Bn moved to POMMEREUIL at 1600. "B" Teams remained at LECATEAU.	After 111
	5.		Bn moved to FONTAINE 0830 (halted for 3hrs) moved to LANDRECIES at 1515.	After (4)
	6.		Bn moved to BASSE NOYELLES at 1700, arriving in Billets 2145.	
	7.		Bn moved to DOMPIERRE and relieved 25th Div. in Line, 6th R.D.F. Bde Res.	After (6)
	8.		Bn moved to attack line K.3 6.8. 10.K.I.L. 5.0. la JONQUIRE FARM	After (6)
			6th R.D.F. in Bde Res.till reaching latter Farm when they relieved 5th R.Innis F. and became support to 6th Lanc Fus. Attack continued 6th Lanc F. unable to push forward owing to heavy hostile M.G.Fire. 1 Platoon "B"Coy under Lt Carrigg sent to reinforce their left flank owing to darkness attack discontinues at 1700.	
	9.		6th R.D.F. ordered to push through 6th L anc F. at 0600 and take final objective, the operation subsequently cancelled owing to enemy evacuating his line during the night.	After (7)

Army Form C.-2118.

WAR DIARY
or
INTELLIGENCE SUMMARY.

(Erase heading not required.)

Instructions regarding War Diaries and Intelligence Summaries are contained in F.S. Regs, Part II. and the Staff Manual respectively. Title pages will be prepared in manuscript.

Place	Date	Hour	Summary of Events and Information	Remarks and references to Appendices
le JONQUIERE FARM	11.11.18		Bn moved by march route to DOMPIERRE arriving 1100.	appx 8
	12.		Bn work filling in Mine Crater to enable supplies to get foreward Bn work filling in Mine Crater at Domp.Notification received at 0830 that hostilities to cease at 1100. Major A.H.Wodehouse and Capt.R.D.English rejoin from course.	9 appx 9
	13		Bn move to BAS LIEU at 1130 going into Billets.	" 10
	14		Bn move to SARS POTERIES.	A
			Guard of Honour consisting of 3 Officers & 46 O.Rs under Capt & Adjt, J.Esmonde M.C. proceed to SARS le CHATEAU for 4th Army Commander. 6 O.Rs of Battn presented with Military Medals.	A
	15.		Bn work improving Roads.	appx 11
	16		Bn move from SARS POTERIES to SOLRE le CHATEAU.	" 12
	17.		Bn move from SOLRE le CHATEAU to RANCE.	" 13
	19.		March to the RHINE commenced Bn acting as advance Guard to 66th Div. arrived at HELPIRNE 1445 going into Billets. "L"Coy outpost on main VOIECRE & FLORENNES Road.	
	23.		Bn moved to RO SSEE.	
HASTIERE	24.		Bn move to HASTIERE on River MEUSE.	
	30.		Bn in HASTIERE Billets since 24th reorganising,resting and cleaning Fighting Strength 30 Officers 573 O.Rs.	

~~Kriegsstammrolle~~

der

~~während der Mobilmachung~~

War Diary

Roy al Dublin Fusiliers

from 1 12/15 to 31 12/18

Volume 2

confidential

Laufende Nr.	Dienstgrad	Vor- und Familiennamen	Religion	Ort (Verwaltungsbezirk, Bundesstaat) der Geburt / Datum der Geburt	Lebensstellung (Stand, Gewerbe) / Wohnort	Vor- und Familiennamen der Ehegattin. Zahl der Kinder. Vermerk, daß der Betreffende ledig ist	Vor- und Familiennamen, Stand oder Gewerbe und Wohnort der Eltern	Truppenteil (Kompagnie, Eskadron)
1.	2.	3.	4.	5.	6.	7.	8.	9.

Anmerkung. 1. Reichen einzelne Spalten nicht aus, so sind die bezüglichen Angaben auf einer in Spalte 15 anzuklebenden Klappe weiter zu führen.
2. Die Kriegsstammrollen werden in gewöhnlichem Bogenformat angelegt. Für die Namen wird jede Seite in drei Querspalten geteilt.

Dienstverhältnisse: a) frühere, b) nach Eintritt der Mobilmachung	Orden, Ehrenzeichen und sonstige Auszeichnungen	Mitgemachte Gefechte. Bemerkenswerte Leistungen	Kommandos und besondere Dienstverhältnisse. Kriegsgefangenschaft	Führung. Gerichtliche Bestrafungen. Rehabilitierung	Bemerkungen
10.	11.	12.	13.	14.	15.
Dienstverhältnisse: a) frühere, b) nach Eintritt der Mobilmachung	Orden, Ehrenzeichen und sonstige Auszeichnungen	Mitgemachte Gefechte. Bemerkenswerte Leistungen	Kommandos und besondere Dienstverhältnisse. Kriegsgefangenschaft	Führung. Gerichtliche Bestrafungen. Rehabilitierung	Bemerkungen

198th Inf. Bde.
No. 1977/2/A.

6th Lanc. Fus.
5th R. Innis. Fus.
6th R. Dub. Fus.

Reference this office No 1977/2/A, d/d, 11.12.18.

2 baggage waggons only will be available for the move.

The four additional baggage waggons allotted for last move will not be available for this move.

2 lorries being allotted in their place.

Captain,
Staff Captain,
198th Infantry Brigade.

12.12.18.

6th Bn. Lancs. Fus.
5th Bn. N.Yorks.F.s.
6th Bn. R.Dublin Fus.
198th L.T.M.B.
2/2nd. Fld. Amb.

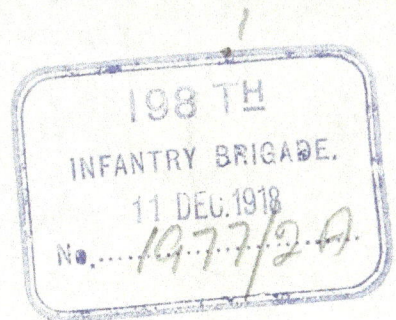

Reference Administrative Instruction No. 9

Lorries for the move will be allotted as under

Each Battalion: 2 lorries.
It is suggested that these lorries make the journey straight through to the new area on the 16th and 16th, thereby carrying four lorry loads in all.

L.T.M.B.   1 lorry, 15th.
2/2nd. Fld.Amb.   1 lorry, 16th. - *if required*

Guide // Guides for lorries will report Brigade Headquarters at 14.00 hours, 14th instant.

2/2nd. Field Ambulance guide will be rationed for 16th inst. and move with the L.T.M.B. lorry, guiding it back to the 2/2nd. Field Ambulance Headquarters.

Captain,
Staff Captain,
198th Infantry Brigade.

11.12.18.
HDC

March Table "B" to accompany 10th Div. O.O. by Oper.Order No.145.

Serial No.	Unit.	From.	Pass starting point at.	To.	Notes.
1.	29th Bde H.Q.	JAMBOUL Chateau.	09.30.	ROCHEFORT.	
2.	6th R..Ms.Fus.	CLERGNON.	09.35.	ON.	ROCHEFORT - JEMELLE.
3.	6th R.Dublin Fus.	HOUYET.	10.00.	JEMELLE.	CLERGNON - ROCHEFORT.
4.	5th R.Innis.Fus.	do.	10.15.	ROCHEFORT.	CLERGNON.
5.	199th L.T.M.B.	do.	10.30.	do.	do.
6.	2/2nd Field Amb.	VERPE.	10.35.	do.	do.
7.	545 Coy. A.S.C.	HOUYET.	10.40.	do.	do.

Starting point, for serial Nos.1 and 2.: Road junction ¼" S. of G in BOIS DES AUGES.

Starting point for serial Nos. 3,4,5,6,and 7: Cross road at 16th kilo. stone on HALMA - CRUPES Road.

12.10.18.
FJ.

MARCH TABLE "B" to accompany 198th Infantry Brigade Order No.148.

Serial No.	Unit.	From.	Pass Starting point at	To.	Route.	Remarks.
1.	6th Lancs.Fus.	ANSEREMME	09.30.	CLERGNON	CELLES.	
2.	2/2nd Fld.Amb.	do.	09.45	VEHRE.	do.	
3.	198th Bde.H.Q. Transport.	CELLES		Chateau JAMBJOUL.	CLERGNON.	To be clear of CELLES by 10.30.
4.	198th Bde H.Q. Less Transport.	Chateau 1" S. of A in ANSEREME.	10.05.	do.	ANSEREMME Rly. bridge - CELLES - CLERGNON.	
5.	5th R.Innis.Fus.	HASTIERE - PAR- DELA.	09.15.	HOUYET.	MESNIL - ST. BLAISE.	
6.	6th R.Dublin Fus.	HASTIERE - LAVAUX	09.30.	do.	do.	
7.	198th L.T.M.B.	do.	09.45	do.	do.	
8.	543 Coy. A.S.C.	do.	10.00	do.	do.	

Starting Point, for serial Nos.1, 2, and 4, : Road junction at 30th Kilo Stone on ANSEREMME - DINANT Road.

Starting point, for serial Nos 5, 6, 7, and 8: 8th Kilo. Stone on HASTIERE - MESNIL -St. BLAISE Road.

-2-

6. Brigade H.Q. will close at CHATEAU 1" S. of A in ANSEREMME at 09.00 on 15th and open at JEMBJOUL Chateau at 14.30 on same day.

A Report Centre will be maintained at the head of Brigade H.Q. column on the march for urgent messages.

Brigade H.Q. will close at JEMBJOUL Chateau at 09.00 on the 16th and open at ROCHEFORT on arrival.

7. ACKNOWLEDGE.

Captain,
Brigade Major,
198th Infantry Brigade.

Issued through Signals at 13.00.

DISTRIBUTION.

Copy No.	1.	66th Division, "G".
"	2.	66th Division, "Q".
"	3.	6th Lancs. Fus.
"	4.	5th R. Innis. Fus.
"	5.	6th R. Dublin Fus.
"	6.	198th L.T.M.B.
"	7.	No. 3 Signal Section.
"	8.	543 Coy., A.S.C.
"	9.	3/2nd Field Amboc.
"	10.	431 Field Co., R.E.
"	11.	South African Brigade.
"	12.	Staff Captain.
"	13.	B.I.O.
"	14.	B.T.O.
"	15,16,17.	War Diary.
"	18,19,20.	File.

SECRET.   Copy No.

108TH INFANTRY BRIGADE ORDER No. 14.

11th December, 1918.

Ref. Maps,
    NAMUR 8, 1/100,000.
    MARCHE 6, 1/100,000.

---

1. The 108th Infantry Brigade Group (less 431 Field Co., R.E.) will march on the 15th December to the HOUYET Area in accordance with March Table "A" (attached).

    The march will be continued to the ROCHEFORT Area on the 16th December, in accordance with March Table "B" (attached).

2. 108th Infantry Brigade H.Q. Transport will stage at CELLES on night 14th/15th December.
    Head of Column will not cross DINANT Bridge before 14.30 hours.

3. Billetting parties of Units staging in HOUYET will meet the Staff Captain at Cross Roads ½ mile S. of HOUYET Sta. at 10.00 hours on 15th December, where guides will also meet units on arrival.
    6th Lancs. Fus. and 2/2nd (E.L.) Field Amboc. will make their own arrangements for billets in CIERGNON and VERRE respectively.
    Billetting parties for ROCHEFORT Area will proceed on 13th instant in accordance with instructions already issued.

4. Owing to the bad hills to be crossed all waggons will be spaced 10 yards apart.

5. Baggage waggons will report to units by 13.00 14th instant, except Brigade H.Q. baggage wagon which will report by 14.00 hours on the 13th.

/6.

WAR DIARY or INTELLIGENCE SUMMARY

(Erase heading not required.)

Army Form C.2118

Instructions regarding War Diaries and Intelligence Summaries are contained in F.S. Regs., Part II. and the Staff Manual respectively. Title Pages will be prepared in manuscript.

Place	Date	Hour	Summary of Events and Information	Remarks and references to Appendices
HASTIERE.	1/12/18		Divine Service in Village Church at 0915.	
	4/12/18		Recreational training, Cleaning German Guns handed over in accordance with terms of the armistice.	
	8/12/18		Divine Service in Village Church at 0915.	
	12/12/18		Company and Recreational Training.	
	15/12/18		Battn. moved from HASTIERE at 0900 by march route, arrived at HOUYET at 1400, going into Billets.	
HOUYET	16/12/18		Battn. moved to JEMELLE by march route at 0815, Fighting strength 28.Off. & 549 Other Ranks. Lt.A.J.Carrigg arrived from FREVANT dump with Battn. Recreational Stores.	
JEMELLE	18/12/18		Battn. work Cleaning and organizing Billets.	
	19/12/18		Lt.Col.Little,D.S.O. M.C. proceeded to England on 14 days Special Leave	
	20/12/18		G.O.C. 198th Inf.Bde. inspected Battn. billets.	
	21/12/18		2/Lt. Corish & 199 Other Ranks joined from 66th Div.Reception Camp.	
	22/12/18		Lt.A.J.Carrigg & 50 Other Ranks proceeded to England for Demobilization.	
	24/12/18		Lt.W.O. Parish proceeded to England, Conducting Duty.	
	28/12/18		Recreational Training & repairing roads.	
	31/12/18		Two Companies work repairing JEMELLE & ROCHEFORT road. Two Companies practice Ceremonial drill. Fighting strength 34 Officers and 664 Other Ranks.	

Confidential

War Diary

Durham L. Infantry

From 1 2/19 to 28/2/19

Volume 4 4

6th Royal

WDF

34 Z

Army Form C. 2118.

WAR DIARY
or
INTELLIGENCE SUMMARY
(Erase heading not required.)

6 D F

33 Z

Place	Date	Hour	Summary of Events and Information	Remarks and references to Appendices
JEMELLE.	1.		Ceremonial Drill.	
	2.		Ceremonial drill, duty Coy. to work on road. Major A.H.Wodehouse to Leave U.K.	
	3.		Ceremonial Drill. Capt. R.E.English to U.K.Leave. Lt. S.E.Thornton to Hosp	
	5.		Ceremonial Drill, Capt. H.J.Hayes, M.C. to U.K.Leave.	
	6.		Parade under Company Commanders.	
	7.		Parade under Company Commanders. 2/Lt. J.J.Purcell rejoined from Hosp. 18 O.Ranks demobilized. 2/Lt.H.S.Scales demobilized.	
	8.		Ceremonial Drill, Major W.W.Vance,M.C. to Senior Officers Course-Aldershot Capt. Loveband & Lt.Levingston to U.K.Leave. Lt. A.A.Fitzgerald joined from Reception Camp.	
	9.		Ceremonial Parade-Capt Shadforth to Sen.Officers Course. Lt.Jowett demobilized, Capt.Watson (R.A.M.C.) to U.K.Leave.	
	11.		8 O.Ranks demobilized - Lt. C.W.Booth, 2/Lt.O.Moody, 2/Lt.Armstrong and 2/Lt. McMillan demobilized. Lt.Col.Little,D.S.O. M.C. rejoined from U.K.Leave. 2/Lt. Miller to U.K.Leave.	
	13.		Parade under Coy.Commanders. 24 O.Ranks demobilized. Lt. M. Carragher to Leave U.K.	
	14.		Ceremonial Drill.	
	15.		Ceremonial Drill. Capt. J.Esmonde M.C. to U.K.Leave	

WAR DIARY or INTELLIGENCE SUMMARY

Army Form C. 2118

(Erase heading not required.)

Instructions regarding War Diaries and Intelligence Summaries are contained in F.S. Regs., Part II. and the Staff Manual respectively. Title Pages will be prepared in manuscript.

Place	Date	Hour	Summary of Events and Information	Remarks and references to Appendices
JEMELLE	16.		Parade Coy.Commanders. 26.O.Ranks demobilized. 2/Lt. G.L.O'Hea to Paris, Leave.	
	17.		Parade under Coy.Commanders. Lt.Thornton rejoined from Hospital.	
	17-18		Brigade Platoon Competition. No.1.Platoon "A" Coy. represents Battalion. Lt.C.McCann to Leave, U.K. Lt.G.F.Larkin rejoined U.K.Leave.	
	20.		Battn. Route March. 41 O.Ranks demobilized. Result of Platoon Efficiency Competition:- 6th Royal Dublin Fusiliers----612 points. 6th Lancashire Fusiliers----571 " 5th Royal Inniskilling Fus----565 "	
	21.		Bde.Competition Cup Presentation by Brig.Gen.A.H.Hunter. Lt.W.Harney to U.K.Leave, Lt.Thornton to U.K.leave.	
	22.		Company Arrangements.	
	23.		Company Arrangements.	
	24.		Battn.parade for Brigade practice for the presentation of Union Flag.	
	26.		C.O's inspection of billets.	
	27.		Coy.arrangements. 2/Lts P.P. & J.J.Purcell to Leave U.K.	
	28.		Coy.arrangements. Capt.G.V.Loveband rejoined from Leave U.K. 2/Lt.G.L.O'Hea rejoined from Paris Leave.	
	29-30		Coy.arrangements. Lt.T.J.Byrne to Leave U.K. Major A.H.Wodehouse & Lt. W.O.Parish rejoined from Leave U.K.	
	31.		Bn.parade for Bde.practice for presentation of Union Flag.Strength Off. Capt.M.H.Irurry & 2/Lt.J.J.Young to Leave U.K. 36. Other Ranks 670.	

Army Form C. 2118.

Page 1.

WAR DIARY
or
INTELLIGENCE SUMMARY

(Erase heading not required.)

Instructions regarding War Diaries and Intelligence Summaries are contained in F.S. Regs., Part II. and the Staff Manual respectively. Title Pages will be prepared in manuscript.

Place	Date	Hour	Summary of Events and Information	Remarks and references to Appendices
JEMELLE.	1-2-19.		Company & Recreational Training.	
	6th		Lt. H.J. Oliphant to U.K. Leave. Lt. McGaffery, U.S.A. M.C. rejoined form duty.	
	10th		2 Officers & 100 Other Ranks detailed and held in readiness to proceed to 1st R.D.F.	
	11th		Lt. & Q.M. Unwin & Rev Burns to U.K. Leave.	
	13th		6th R.D.F. v 5th R.Innis.Fus. in semi final 66th Div.Football Competitn (6th R.D.F. lost 2.1.)	
	19th		Lt.Thornton & 2/Lt. J.J.Purcell to England conducting Demobilized men 6th Lancs. Fus.	
	21st		500 Other Ranks proceeded for Demobilization, conducted by Capt. H.J. Hayes, 2/Lieuts Miller, M.C. Win g, P.P.Purcell, G.D. O'Hea & Rooker.	
	26th		52 Other Ranks proceeded to England for Demobilization conducted by 2/Lt. Carragher.	
	26th		2/Lieuts Young & Manley rejoined from Leave.	

Capt.
Adjutant, 6th Royal Dublin Fus.

Confidential

War Diary

Vol 9

6th (S) Bn. The Royal Irish Fusiliers

Serial 1 3/19 to 31 3/19

Volume 4-6

352

66

Div Comdr

Herewith copy
of War Diary
for March 1919

J Esmonde Catt
for O/ GROS

31/3/19

WAR DIARY
or
INTELLIGENCE SUMMARY

Army Form C. 2118

Place	Date	Hour	Summary of Events and Information	Remarks and references to Appendices
TEMELLE BELGIUM	1/3/19		Fighting Strength 18 Officers 175 OR's. Orders Received known to close down C.E. camps 26-29 & move L & 77 OR's proceed to Join S/E R Rail Regt N for service at the RHINE	
"	4		The new Regimental transport moved from TEMELLE by motor lorries at 0900 arrived at BOHEME (96 kilos) at 1300. Village very dirty spent difficulty in finding billets for men. Left transport moved to next camp in morning at 1400	
BOHEME Belgium	5		10 OR proceeded for demobilyzation	
	8	14/61	Lieu Montgomery lectured to all Officers of the Bn, & other Battles wales RLM Shipm thor to England on Regimental leave remaining Officers 2Lts Henry & N Hawrice returned from Colonday duty in England Colo H. Hogue M.C. & Bayonet instructing course	
	12			
	13			
	16			
	17		Cadre School commencing at 1400 Brig Ew Hunt D.S.O M.C. mms 198 Bn Brig to complete Competition Br. Cadre sent to 437 Coy Rh 2.0 to demi share 16 Bn Cadre Co. completed 198 Infy B.Bn ceased to exist at mid night all moves if SS Bn to be known as 16 B.Bn Strength will RD Center	
	21		Fighting Strength 21 Officers 55 ORS. Effective 29 officers 74 OR. 6 capt Sg Command 2Lts WD Daniel, TH Hanby or turned & 17 longyuck Proceded to UK for demobilization	
	28		Strength 23 Officers 65 ORs Major AH Morehouse & 2Lt 64 Wing proceeded to U.K. with orders to report to War office on arrival	

J. Somervell Col—
Offr 16 R.D.F.

SECRET.   Copy No. 5

108th Infantry Brigade Order No. 147.

                                                    3rd March, 1919.

Ref. Sheet. MARCHE 2, 1/100,000.
----

1.   108th Infantry Brigade Group (Less 2/2nd E.
Lancs. Field Ambce) will move by lorry tomorrow, the
4th inst., in accordance with the attached March Table.

2.   Lorries will report at the H.Q. of Units concerned
at 09.30.

3.   Transport of units will march independently as
follows :-

Unit.	Time of passing Starting Point.
108th Brigade H.Q.	10.00.
5th R. Innis. Fus.	10.05.
8th R. Dublin Fus.	10.15.
6th Lancs. Fus.	10.30.

        Starting Point :-   ROCHEFORT Church.

4. ACKNOWLEDGE.

5.   Brigade H.Q. will close at ROCHEFORT at 09.30
on 4th instant, and open at SOVET on arrival.

                                            Captain,
                                        Brigade Major,
                                    108th Infantry Brigade.

Issued through Signals at ....

DISTRIBUTION.

Copy No. 1.	86th Division, "G".
" " 2.	86th Division, "Q".
" " 3.	6th Lancs. Fus.
" " 4.	5th R. Innis. Fus.
" " 5.	8th R. Dublin Fus.
" " 6.	5?? Coy., A.S.C.
" " 7.	2/2nd Field Ambce.
" " 8.	No. 3 Signal Section.
" " 9.	Staff Captain.
" " 10.	D.T.O.
" " 10, 11, 12.	War Diary.
" " 13, 14, 15.	File.

Table "A".

	Unit.	No. of Lorries.	From.	To.	Route.	Remarks.
1.	6th Lancs. Fus.	7	OM.	PAYS.	Any.	
2.	5th R. Innis. Fus.	8	ROCHEFORT.	SOVET.	CINEY Station - BRAIBANT - 2nd Class Road to the South bet een 15th & 16th Kilo. Stone on BRAIBANT-SPONTIN Road.	
3.	6th R. Dublin Fus.	9.	JEMELLE.	ACIENE.	Any.	
4.	198th Brigade H.Q.	4.	ROCHEFORT.	SOVET.	As for Serial No. 2.	
5.	545 Coy., A.S.C.	1.	ROCHFORT.	ACHENE.	Any.	Column to be clear of ROCHEFORT by 10.00 a.m.

Supplies

"Confidential"

War Diary

6th Royal Dublin Fusiliers

Period 1/4/19 to 30/4/19

Volume #6

Army Form C. 2118

WAR DIARY
or
INTELLIGENCE SUMMARY
(Erase heading not required.)

Instructions regarding War Diaries and Intelligence Summaries are contained in F.S. Regs., Part II. and the Staff Manual respectively. Title Pages will be prepared in manuscript.

Place	Date	Hour	Summary of Events and Information	Remarks and references to Appendices
Retest	17/9/19		Lt. A.R. Wade returned from 14 days leave. Strength 21 officers 532 O.R.	
Belgium	6/9/19		Lt. McJann DCM rejoined from Londonderry duty at Depot	
	8/9/19		Capt. J.J. Hayes rejoined from ordinary duty in the UK	
	9/9/19		2/Lt. G.T. Lunyon returned admitted to 53 Casualty Clearing Station	
	4/9/19		Lt. Col. W.M. Ware RAMC & 2/Lt. J.G. Halliday RAMS proceed to UK for 8 days and relief of the Strength accordingly	
	10/9/19		2/Lt. C. Richardson admitted 53 Casualty Clearing Station	
	15/9/19		Lt. Col. Sigginet rejoined from leave and returned to resume command	
	16/9/19		Lt. Col. Whittle DSO MC proceed to Army to take over command vice Lieut. Col. Brig Gen Kennet DSO MC. Call is at Major R.C. Adamson command of Bn. Cadre vice A.H. Little	
	19/9/19		Lt. Col. Seligman & 2/Lt. Richardson reported from Hospital	
	22/9/19		Cadre proceed to NAMUR for duty with A.D.E.S.	
	29/9/19		Lt. T.J. Byrne Adam proceed to HO 66 Div Cadre for Duty	
			Total admissions to date 15 officers 569 O.R.S.	
			Strength 18 officers 58 O.R.	

Adjutant, 6th (S.) Bn. Roy. Dublin Fus.

6 R D F
96 3

292

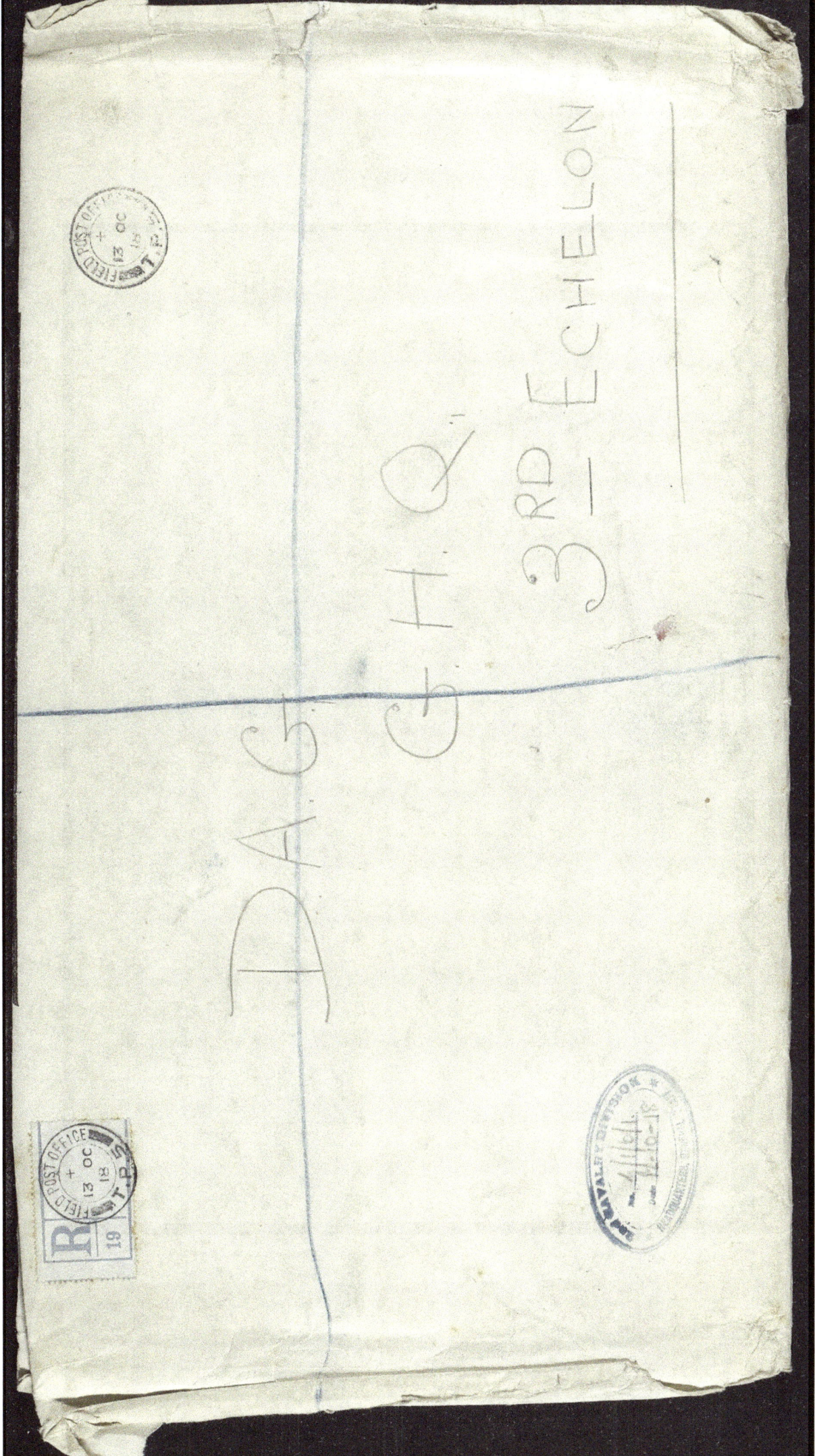

SECRET Appx I DM/36

O.C. 6th R Dublin Fus.

1. On receipt of further orders the 6th R. Dublin Fus will be substituted for the 6th Leinsters in 198 Inf Bde.

2. All English personnel in 6th R.D.F. will be transferred to 9th Glos: Regt & will be replaced by personnel of 6th Leinsters which is being broken up.

3. The 198 Inf Bde (including 6th R.D.F.) will leave the 66 Div. temporarily about Sept. 12th

4. Lt. Col. Little DSO will report at Bde HQ. at 10.30 a.m. tomorrow 9th inst., & will proceed by car with the Bde. to a conference at 198 Inf Bde So & He will bring statement of present strengths, & details of number of personnel referred to in para. 2.

Acknowledge.   R M Bond
                        Capt
                    Bde maj 197 Inf Bde

SECRET.   Copy No...5....

ADDENDUM TO 198th INFANTRY BRIGADE ORDER NO. 167.

                                              29th September, 1918.

        Brigade H.Q. will close at OPPY(?) at 1.0 p.m.
today, and re-open at MARQUILLIES on arrival.

                                              [signature]
                                                Captain,
                                              Brigade Major,
BM.O.B.   198th Infantry Brigade.

Copies to all recipients of 198th Infantry Brigade
Order No. 167.

MARCH TABLE.

Unit.	Time of passing Starting Point.	Route.	From	To	Remarks.
5th R.Inis.Fus.	1-0 p.m.	HAMPIGNY - ALMICOURT - BAYONVILLERS		HARBONNIERES.	1. Intervals will be observed in accordance with S.S.751. para. 10, 1.c., 100 yds between Companies. 100 yds between Battalion and Transport. 600 yds between battalions. 50 yds between each section of L2 vehicles.
108th. L.T.M.B.	1.15 p.m.	--do--		--do--	
6th Innis. Fusrs.	1.20 p.m.	--do--		--do--	
108 Inf.B.de.H.Q.	1.35 p.m.	--do--		--do--	
6th R.Dublin Fus.	1.40 p.m.	--do--		BAYONVILLERS.	2. Transport will move behind their own battalions.
548 Company, A.S.C.	2-0 p.m.	--do--		HARBONNIERES.	
2/2nd. E.C.Fld.Ambce.	2.10 p.m.	--do--		--do--	3. Guides from billeting parties will meet units at entrance to respective villages.

Starting Point is Cross-roads E. of first Q in EQUILLOY.

SECRET.   Copy No......

198TH INFANTRY BRIGADE ORDER No. 102.

                                                    10th Sept.1918.

1. The 198th Infantry Brigade, consisting of

        5th Bn.R.Inniskilling Fus.
        9th Bn.Gloucester Regt.
        6th Bn.R.Dublin Fus.
        No.3 Sig.Section.
        545 Coy. A.S.C.,

    will leave the Division temporarily on the 12th Sept. 1918.

2. All personnel of 5th Inniskilling Fus., 9th Gloucester Regt.,
    6th R.Dublin Fus., and 5th Leinster Regt., with the
    exception of those mentioned in para.3, will be returned
    from Divisional Signal, Lewis Gun and P.& B.T. Schools
    on the 10th instant.

3. Following Signallers of 6th Leinster Regt., are being
    transferred to 5th Connaught Rangers and will remain at
    Divisional Signal School.

        5123 Pte Halpin.   10208 Pte Kavanagh.
        5843 " Bombo.   8141 " Horine.
        1812 " Furlong.   5617 " Lynn.
        4075 " Mansfield.   5586 " Potch.
        5665 " Frande.   5833 " Lee.
        5131 " Seadon.   8030 " Gilmore.
         996 " Davies.   5100 " Leafe.

4. Personnel of 6th R.Dublin Fus. will rejoin their unit
    at ADANCOURT Camp.

5. Trench Mortar personnel of 6th R.Dublin Fus. will be
    transferred from 107th L.T.M.B., to 198th L.T.M.B.

6. Trench Mortar personnel of 6th Leinster Regt. less Lieut
    P.J.Roe, will be returned to their unit by lorry which will
    report at T.M.School by 12 noon 10th instant.

7. Lieut.P.J.Roe will remain at the School in Command of the
    198th L.T.M.B.

8. Limber of 5th R.Inniskilling Fus. now at T.M.School, will be
    sent on 10th Sept. by road to rejoin unit at ADANCOURT Camp
    staging night 10/11th Sept. at LONDINIERES or CLAIS.

9. 198th L.T.M.B. will probably remain at the Brigade T.M.
    School, after the departure of 198th Infantry Brigade.

                                            Captain,
                                            Brigade Major,
                                        198th Infantry Brigade.

Issued through Signals at:........

                                                    /DISTRIBUTION.

DISTRIBUTION.

66th Division "G"	Copy No.1.
66th Division "Q"	" No.2.
5th R.Inis.Fus.	" No.3.
9th Gloucester R.	" No.4.
6th R.Dublin Fus.	" No.5.
5/6th Loin.R.	" No.6.
543 Coy. A.S.C.	" No.7.
No.3 Sig.Sec.	" No.8.
Staff Captain.	" No.9.
Camp Commdt.	" No.10.
2/2nd H'Brian Fld.Amb.	" No.11.
War Diary.	" No.12, 13, 14.
File.	" No.15, 16, 17.

SECRET

Copy No. 5

ADMINISTRATIVE INSTRUCTIONS ISSUED IN REFERENCE TO 198th INFANTRY BRIGADE ORDER NO. 102.
-o-o-o-o-o-o-o-o-

11th Sept., 1918.

1. Lists of billets in the new area and instructions as to advance parties have already been issued.

2. Rations for the 12th instant will be carried on the man. Rations for the 13th instant will be carried on the supply wagons. Rations for the 14th instant will be delivered to FORMERIE station and handed over to units under arrangements to be made by train.
   Rations for consumption 15th instant and following will be drawn in the new area and delivered by Train Company to the respective unit headquarters.
   The Supply Railhead in the new area is FREVENT.

3. Baggage wagons will report to units at 12-0 Noon 11th inst. Supply wagons, carrying supplies for the 13th, on the afternoon of the 11th instant.
   3 lorries per battalion will report at battalion headquarters 6 hours before actual time of entrainment. These will be used for one journey only.

4. 1 blanket per man only will be taken to the new area. Other blankets will be handed in to the Camp Commandant and receipts obtained.

5. Practice ammunition will be returned to Brigade Headquarters to-day.

6. All Camp equipment will be handed over to the Camp Commdt. Tents will not be struck.
   Receipts for stores handed over will be obtained from the Camp Commandant and a certificate, in duplicate, that there are no deficiencies in handing over and that the lines have been left clean. One copy of this certificate will be forwarded to Brigade Headquarters.

7. Detailed instructions as to entrainment will be issued later. Place of entrainment is FORMERIE station.
   The first train, carrying 198th Inf. Bde. Hdqrs and Signals and 543 Company, A.S.C., leaves at 4-0 p.m. 12th instant. Other trains follow at 4-hour intervals.

P. Ingleson

Captain,
Staff Captain,
198th Infantry Brigade.

Copy sent to O.M. LRDT

Issued through Signals at.....

Issued to all recipients of 198th Inf. Bde. Order No. 102.

5th Inniskilling Fus.
9th Gloucester Regt.
6th R.Dublin Fus.
543 Coy. A.S.C.
No.3 Signal Sect.

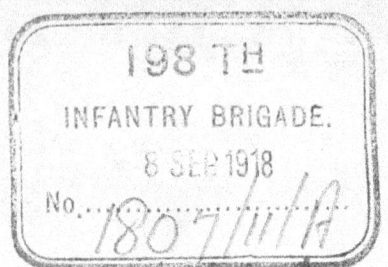

The following billeting parties will be detailed by Units, to proceed by lorry as under, to-morrow, to the new area.

    Each Battalion, 1 Officer 6 N.C.Os.) To report at Camp
    543 Coy. A.S.C. 2 O.R.   ) Commandants office
                                                              at 7.30 a.m. 11th in
                                                              for lorry.

    No.3 Sig.Sec.   2 O.R.   ) Lorry will
    Bde H.Q.,   1 Officer to represent the) collect at
                  Staff Captain, and 2 O.R.) Bde H.Q. at
                                                           7.0 a.m. on
                                                                     11th inst.

    All the above personnel should take a Bicycle.

    Officers and O.R., should if possible, have a workable knowledge of French.

    Interpreters at present with units will proceed with advance parties.

                                                                               Captain,
                                                                           Staff Captain,
                                                                198th Infantry Brigade.

10.9.18.
RV

BILLETING LIST.   66th Division.
                   7068/Q.

Serial No.	Unit.	Where billeted.	Application to	Remarks.
1.	Brigade H.Q. and Sig. Sect.	AUXI LE CHATEAU. MAISON-PONTHIEU	Town Major.	If Cav.Corps returns good Bde. H.Q. at MAISON PONTHIEU.
2.	'A' Battn. H.Q. and 1 Coy.	BERNATRE.	Sub Area Cdt. at MAISON PONTHIEU.	
3.	1 Coy.	FROUVILLE.	Area Cdt. at BERNAVILLE.	
4.	" "	WAVANS.	Area Commdt. WAVANS.	
5.	'B' Battn. B.H.Q 48 H.Q. and 2 Coys.	MAISON PONTHIEU	Sub Area Cdt. at MAISON PONTHIEU.	Good Chateau and pond for horse watering. Billet Warden in village.
6.	1 Coy.	LE PONCHEL.	(Sub Area Cdt. (at BUIRE AU (BOIS.	
7.	" "	QUOEUX.	(	
8.	'C' Battn. H.Q. and 2 Coys.	GUESHART.	MAIRIE.	There is no Area Cdt. at present, but Mayor is making out list of billets. Interpreter 2nd. Cav.Res. Park in GENNE IVERGNY can give all information.
9.	1 Coy.	GENNE IVERGNY.	Sub Area Cdt. FONTAINE L'ETALON.	
10.	" "	VACQUERIETTE.	Sub Area Cdt. WAIL.	
11.	Company of Divl. Train.	AUXI LE CHATEAU.	Town Major.	

N.B. - Area and Sub Area Commandants have all been warned as to arrival of above units, and asked to prepare full information.

198TH INFANTRY BRIGADE
6 SEP 1918
No. 18077/8/11

5th. Royal Inniskilling Fusiliers.
5th. Gloucester Regt.
6th. Royal Dublin Fusiliers.
545 Coy. A.S.C.

Forwarded with reference to this office
No.E07/198A dated 10.9.1918.

This or a copy of same should be given
to the officer in charge of your billeting party.

Captain,
Staff Captain,
10.9.1918.   198th. Infantry Brigade.

SECRET.   66th Division.
                                                           7068/Q.

197th Infantry Bde.   A.D.M.S.,
198th   do.   D.A.D.V.S.
199th   do.   A.P.M.
    'G'.   D.A.D.O.S.
C.R.E.   S.C., (D.C.G's Dept.)
Signals.   Camp Commdt. ABANCOURT Camp.
Div. Train.   Headquarters, ABANCOURT Area.
----

1.   The 198th Infantry Bde. including Signal Section
and No. 543 Coy. of the Train, will leave the Division
shortly; probable date 12th September.

2.   Further instructions will be issued as to actual
date and time of entrainment.

3.   Probable place of entrainment, ABANCOURT FORMERIE Station.

4.   The Brigade will be billeted in the neighbourhood of
AUXI-LE-CHATEAU.
        List of billets in the new area is attached. (Will be for-
This List cancels the one already issued.   warded later).

5.   Rations will be taken for the days up to, and including,
the 14th instant.
        Rations for consumption 15th instant will be drawn
in the new area.

6.   Two blankets per man will be taken to the new area.

7.   All tents and camp equipment will be handed over by
Units to Camp Commandant, ABANCOURT, before departure.

8.   Details as to lorries etc. for transporting blankets
etc. to the station, will be notified later.

9.   Instructions have been received for the disbandment
of the 6th Bn. The Leinster Regiment forthwith.

10.   The following numbers of Other Ranks will be forthwith
transferred from the 6th Bn. The Leinster Regt. to
the Battalions stated :-

To the 9th Bn. Gloucester Regt.

        185 (to include 5 Corporals) (English personnel).

To the 6th Bn. Royal Dublin Fusiliers.

        105 (to include 5 Corporals).

To the 5th Bn. Connaught Rangers.

        245 (to include 5 Corporals).

(2)

10. With the exception of the 5 Corporals per Battalion, no N.C.O. of, or above, the rank of Sergeant will be transferred.

11. All Warrant Officers, N.C.Os. and men of the 6th Bn. The Leinster Regt., surplus, after the above transfers have taken place, will be sent to the Base Depot; nominal rolls being forwarded direct by the Unit to the D.A.G., 3rd Echelon.

12. Nominal Rolls, in quadruplicate, of all Officers of the 6th Bn. The Leinster Regt. will be forwarded to Divisional Headquarters, for forwarding to the A.G., G.H.Q., and instructions will be issued as to their disposal.

13. 1st Line Transport, with drivers, of 6th Bn. Leinster Regt. will proceed to Advanced Horsed Transport Depot, ABBEVILLE, under orders which will be issued later.

14. The Officer Commanding the 6th Bn. The Leinster Regt. will take immediate steps to effect the settlement of all outstanding accounts; will cause a Balance Sheet to be prepared, and will be responsible for the safe custody of any funds until the Army Trustee has been appointed (G.R.O. 4505 dated July 13th 1918).

15. All regimental equipment (including bicycles) of the 6th Bn. The Leinster Regt. will be collected at the Headquarters of the 6th Bn. The Leinster Regt. for handing over to the D.A.D.O.S., 66th Division.

16. The O.C., 6th Bn. The Leinster Regt. will retain such Officers and staff as he may require for settling all details of the disbandment, and for receiving and despatching any personnel returning from leave.
    Personnel of this staff will, on completion of their duties, be sent to their respective Battalions, or the Base, as the case may be.

Major.
D.A.A.G.
66th Division.

10.9.18.

SECRET?

198th Inf,Bde.
No. 1207/0/A

5th Inniskilling Fus.
9th Gloucester Regt.
6th Leinster Regt.
6th R.Dublin Fus.

Attached is forwarded for information.

6th Leinster Regt. will forward nominal rolls in quintruplicate, in accordance with para.12, to reach this office by 9.0 a.m. to-morrow, 11th instant.

Captain,
Staff Captain,
198th Infantry Brigade.

10.9.18.
RV.

197th. Inf. Bde.   66th. Divn.
                                                          7068/Q.

    Reference 66th. Div. G.X. 22 dated 9/9/18. Move of
6th. Royal Dublin Fusrs. from 197th. Infantry Brigade to 198th.
Infantry Bde.

1.   Two lorries will report at Battalion H.Q., 6th. Royal Dublin
Fusrs. at 7 a.m., 10/9/18. These lorries may be used to make two
journeys, if necessary.

2.   All Camp equipment and Camp stores will be handed over to
Camp Commandant, SERQUEUX before departure.
    One blanket per man may be taken, and will be struck off
charge Camp Commandant, SERQUEUX, and taken on charge of Camp
Commandant, ABANCOURT Camp.

                                        (Sd.) D.V.M. BALDERS.
                                                    Major.
                                                D.A.A.G.,
9/9/18.   66th. Division.

6th. Royal Dublin Fusrs.   2589/Q.

                    For information and necessary action.

                                                    Captain.
                                               Staff Captain.
B.H.Q.   197th. Infantry Brigade.
9/9/18.

18th. (L.H.Y) The King's.
10th. Black Watch.
6th. Royal Dublin Fusrs.

B.M.L.28/3/2

1. 198th. Brigade, including Signal Section, will leave the Division temporarily about 12th. September.

2. All personnel of 6th. R. Dublin Fus. will be returned from Divisional Signal, Lewis Gun and P & B.T. Schools on 10th. September.

3. Captain MURPHY and his batman will remain at Divisional Schools.

4. Transport for conveyance of Officers kit etc. will be sent by Brigade to report at L.G. & P & B.T. Schools at 12.30 p.m., 10th. instant.

5. Personnel of 6th. Royal Dublin Fus. will rejoin their Unit at ABANCOURT CAMP.

6. Personnel, as under, will be detailed to relieve that now at Schools at 12.30 p.m., 10th. September :-

Signal School.

18th. The King's......1 Cook & 1 Camp Fatigue man.
10th. Black Watch....1 Camp Fatigue man.

L.G. & P & B.T. School.

10th. Black Watch....1 Q.M.S.

7. T.M. personnel of 6th. R. Dublin Fus. will be transferred from 197th. T.M. Battery to 198th. T.M. Battery.

8. 198th. T.M. Battery will probably remain at the School after the departure of the 198th. Brigade.

B.H.Q.
9/9/16.

Captain.
Staff Captain.
197th. Infantry Brigade.

SECRET.　　　　　　　　　　　　　　　　　　　　COPY NO. 5.

197th. INFANTRY BRIGADE
OPERATION ORDER NO. 98.

Reference :- Sheet DIEPPE. 16.　　　　　　9th. Septr. 1918.
　　　　　　1/100,000

1. 6th. Bn. Royal Dublin Fusiliers will be transferred from the 197th. Infantry Brigade to the 198th. Infantry Brigade on the 10th. September, and will take over the camp at present occupied by the 2/24th. London Regt., ABANCOURT Camp. Move will be completed by 4.00 p.m.

2. 2 Lorries will report at Battalion H.Q. at 7.00 a.m., 10th. instant.

3. 2 Baggage wagons will report at Battalion H.Q. at 6.a.m., 10th. instant.
   Supplies for consumption, 11th. inst. will be drawn by 542 Coy., A.S.C. on Supply wagons, which will then move with the column.
   Supplies for consumption, 12th. instant will be drawn from the Refilling Point in the new area.
   After completion of move, all wagons will report back to 542 Coy., A.S.C.

4. Arrangements will be made direct by 6th. Royal Dublin Fusiliers with the Camp Commandant, SERQUEUX for the handing over of all Camp Stores, Equipment etc.

5. ACKNOWLEDGE.

　　　　　　　　　　　　　　　　　　　　　Captain.
　　　　　　　　　　　　　　　　　　　　Brigade Major.
　　　　　　　　　　　　　　　　　　　197th. Infantry Brigade.

DISTRIBUTION.

Copy No. 1......B.G.C.
　　　　 2......Bde. Major.
　　　　 3......Staff Captain.
　　　　 4......Bde. Gas Officer.
　　　　 5......6th. Royal Dublin Fusrs.
　　　　 6......18th. (L.H.Y) The King's.
　　　　 7......10th. Black Watch.
　　　　 8......542 Coy., A.S.C.
　　　　 9......2/2nd. Northumbrian Fld. Amb.
　　　　10......H.Q., 198th. Infantry Bde.
　　　　11......H.Q., 66th. Division 'G'.
　　　　12......H.Q., 66th. Division 'Q'.
　　　　13......Camp Commandant, SERQUEUX.
　　　　14......War Diary.
　　　　15...... do.
　　　　16......File.

Appx II

5th Bn. R. Inisk'g. Fus.
5th Bn. Gloucester Regt.
6th Bn. Leinster Regt.
5th Bn. R. Dublin Fus.   Copy to 66th Div. "A".

In continuation of Administrative Instruction No. 102, issued to-day.

1. 198th Infantry Brigade Group will entrain at FORMERIE Station on the 12th and 13th instants in accordance with the attached table.

2. On arrival in the new area, the Brigade will come under the Third Army.

3. C/Lieut. HAMBLEN, 5th Bn. R. Inisk'g. Fus. is detailed as entraining officer. He will report to R.T.O. FORMERIE at Noon, 12th instant.

4. An officer from each unit will report to the Brigade Entraining Officer on arrival at the station and hand him a written marching-out state giving number of officers, other ranks, L.D. and H.D. horses and axles for entrainment.
   This state to be given by the Brigade Entraining Officer to the R.T.O.

5. An officer from Divisional Headquarters will be at the entraining station throughout the entrainment.

6. Loading and unloading parties will be detailed as under :-

Loading Parties.

Unit.	Number of Party.	To report at;	To Load Trains Nos.	Remarks.
5th Glosters.	1 Offr. 50 O.R.	FORMERIE Stn at Noon, 12th.	1 & 2.	To travel on Train No.3.
5th R. Inis.Fus.	1 Offr. 50 O.R.	FORMERIE Stn at 6 p.m. 12th.	3 & 4.	To travel on Train No.4.

Unloading Parties.

Dublin Fus. 1 officer and 50 O.R. to travel on Train No. 1 and unload Trains Nos. 1 and 2.
   Units travelling on trains 3 and 4 will provide their own unloading parties.

P. Hughes
Captain,
Staff Captain,
198th Infantry Brigade.

11.8.18.
TDC

66th Divn.
7068/Q

TABLE.

Train		Station of Entrainment and time of departure.	Station of Detrainment and time of arrival. (approx.)	Transport report R.T.O. FORMERIE.	Personnel report R.T.O. FORMERIE.	
1.	198 Inf. Bde. H.Q. Bde. Signal Sect. 543 Coy. A.S.C.	FORMERIE. 16 hours 12.9.18.	AUXI LE CHATEAU 21 hours 12.9.18	12 hours 12.9.18.	2 hours 12.9.18.	A loading party of 1 Officer and 50 Other Ranks will be detailed by 198th Inf. Bde. to report R.T.O. FORMERIE, 4 hours before departure of each Train, for loading vehicles etc.
2.	6th R.Dublin.Fus.	FORMERIE. 20 hours 12.9.18	AUXI LE CHATEAU. 1 hour 13.9.18	16 hours 12.9.18.	18 hours 12.9.18.	
3.	9th Gloucester.R.	FORMERIE. 24 hours 12.9.18.	AUXI LE CHATEAU. 5 hours 13.9.18.	20 hours 12.9.18.	22 hours 12.9.18.	
4.	5th R.Inniskilling Fusiliers.	FORMERIE. 4 hours. 13.9.18.	AUXI LE CHATEAU. 9 hours 13.9.18.	24 hours 12.9.18	2 hours 13.9.18.	

SECRET.   Copy No.

ADMINISTRATIVE INSTRUCTION ISSUED IN REFERENCE TO
198TH INFANTRY BRIGADE ORDER NO. 103.

16.9.18.

1.   Battalions of 198 th Infantry Brigade will be re-grouped as follows on September 17th and 18th, 1918.

5th R. Innis. Fus.

   Battalion Headquarters, BERNATRE. (in billets vacated by
              an M.T. Coy. A.S.C.)
   2 Coys, RAINCOURT.
   2 Coys, HERMONT.
   Transport, HERMONT.

9th Gloucester Regt.

   Battalion Hdqrs and 2 Coys, MAISON PONTHIEU.
   1 Coy, FEUILLY-LE-DIEU.
   1 Coy, ACQUET.
   Transport, MAISON PONTHIEU.

8th R. Dublin Fus.

   Headquarters and 4 Coys, GUESCHART.
   Transport, GUESCHART.

2.   Companies billetted in the AUTHIE Valley will move on September 17th as outlined in 198th Infantry Brigade Order No. 103.
   548 Company, A.S.C. will detail 2 baggage wagons to report at Battalion Headquarters of units at 2-0 p.m. on that day.

3.   Companies North of the River AUTHIE, i.e.,
   One Coy. of 5th R. Innis. Fus, at ROUGEFAY.
   One Coy. of 9th Gloucesters at QUOEUX.
   One Coy. of 8th R. Dublin Fus. at VACQUERIETTE
will move on September 18th.

   One lorry per battalion will be allotted for the completion of the re-grouping of battalions on that day. Battalions will send a guide for their lorry to be at Brigade Headquarters at 9-0 a.m.

4.   ACKNOWLEDGE.

                                              P. Nylson
                                              Captain,
                                              Staff Captain,
                                         198th Infantry Brigade.

Issued to all recipients of 198th Infantry Brigade Order No. 103.

SECRET   Copy No. 3

198TH INFANTRY BRIGADE ORDER NO. 104.

19th October, 1918.

Ref. Sheet 11, 1/100,000.

1. The 198th Infantry Brigade will move by March Route to the BOYIERES Area on the 20th inst. in accordance with attached March Table "A".
   On the 21st inst., 198th Infantry Brigade will move to the LIECOURT Area in accordance with instructions to be issued later.

2. No troops will halt in AUXI-LE-CHATEAU.

   6th R. Dublin Fus. will halt short of the town before 9.50 a.m. if necessary.

   9th Gloucester Regt. and 198th Infantry Brigade H.Q. will clear the town before halting, 9th Gloucester Regt. leaving sufficient space for 198th Inf. Bde. H.Q. to halt clear of the town.

3. Units will report arrival in billets.

4. Units of this Brigade to acknowledge.

                                    Captain,
                                    Brigade Major,
                                    198th Infantry Brigade.

DISTRIBUTION.

    Copy No. 1.   5th R. Inniskilling Fus.
    "   "   2.   9th Gloucester Regt.
    "   "   3.   6th R. Dublin Fus.
    "   "   4.   Staff Captain.
    "   "   5.   No. 3 Signal Section.
    "   "   6.   543 Coy. A.S.C.
    "   "   7.   Inspector of Training, GRECY.
    "   "   8.   66th Division, "G".
    "   "   9.   66th Division, "Q".
    "   " 10.   Third Army, "G".
    "   " 11.   "   " , "Q".

Copy No 3

ADMINISTRATIVE INSTRUCTIONS ISSUED IN REFERENCE TO
198th INFANTRY BRIGADE ORDER NO. 104.

-o-o-o-o-o-o-

19th September, 1918.

1. Locations.

On arrival in the new area, battalions will be billeted as follows:-

5th Bn. R. Innis. Fus.	BARLY.
9th Bn. Gloucester Regt.	Battn. H.Q. and 3 Companies, BONNIERES.
	One Company, BEAUVOIR.
6th Bn. R. Dublin Fus.	BONNIERES.
198 Inf.Bde.HQ & Signals	BONNIERES.
543 Company, A.S.C.	BEAUVOIR.

2. EXTRA TRANSPORT.

Two baggage wagons per battalion will report to units in the afternoon of the 19th instant.
Battalions are each allotted 2 lorries to be retained for the 20th and 21st. Guides to be sent to Brigade Headquarters at 7-0 a.m. 20th instant.

3. SUPPLIES.

Supplies for the following day's consumption will be delivered to units' Headquarters by supply wagons on the evening of the 20th and 21st. instant.
Supply wagons will move with 543 Company, A.S.C; baggage wagons with the transport of units.

4. BILLETING PARTIES.

Instructions as to billetting parties for the first day have already been issued. as under
Billetting parties for the LIENCOURT Area will report to the Staff Captain or his representative at LIENCOURT cross-roads at 6-0 p.m. 20th instant.
Battalions should send these billetting parties on one of their lorries, which should be loaded with stores which will not be required on the journey.

Battalions,	1 officer, 6 O.R.
Brigade Headquarters,	1 O.R.
543 Coy. A.S.C.	2 O.R. to proceed on lorry of 9th Glosters.
Signals	1 O.R.

5. CLEANLINESS OF BILLETS.

Commanding officers will ensure that the billets at present occupied and the billets occupied on the night 20/21st. Sept. are left clean. Certificates to this effect will be obtained from the Area Commandants concerned, and copies forwarded to Brigade H.Q.

6. ACKNOWLEDGE.

Captain,
Staff Captain,
198th Infantry Brigade.

Copies to all recipients of 198th Infantry Brigade Order No. 104.

5th Bn: R: Innis Fus:
9th Bn: Gloucester Regt:
6th Bn: ~~Leinster Regt:~~ Dub Fus
543 Company, A:S:C.
No: 3 Signal Section:
Staff Captain.

Reference 198th Inf: Bde: Order No: 104.

The following distances will be maintained on the march:-

    Between Battalions, 500 yards;
    Between Companies, 100 yards,
    Between last Company and transport, 100 yards;
    Between each six vehicles or pair of animals, 25 yards.

The following will be the order of march for transport in this brigade;

    Pack Animals.
    Spades
    Mess Cart.
    Maltese Cart.
    Limbers.
    Water Cart.
    Cookers.
    G:S: Wagons.

Only one brakesman will march with each vehicle; Remainder of personnel will march as a formed company body in rear of the transport.

Clock hour halts will always be observed; i.e., from X plus 50 minutes till X plus 60 minutes.

The first time units pass the G:O:C:, they will come to attention. Otherwise, they will march at ease unless ordered to the contrary.

                                            Captain,
                                     Brigade Major,
                            198th Infantry Brigade.

19:9:18;

Appendix "A" to accompany 198th Infantry Brigade Order No. 104.

Serial No.	Unit.	From.	To.	Starting Point.	Route.	Remarks.
1.	5 R. Innis. Fus.	BEL AIRE (Battalion H.Q.) LATIGCURT. (2 Coys.) HEIRIC. (2 Coys.)	B.RIN.	Cross Roads in LATIGCURT.	ROVITE - BELLOCURT - FROUEN-LE-GRAND - BEL AIR. IL.	Head of column to pass Starting Point at 8.30 a.m.
2.	9 Glouc. Regt.	LAIBOC FONILIEN. (Bn. H.Q. & 2 Coys.) MAGNY-L-DILS. (1 Coy.) AC UET. (1 Coy.)	BO IRES. (Bn. H.Q. & 3 Coys.) BEAUVOIR. (1 Coy.)	Cross Roads in AC UET.	AUKI-LE-CHATEAU - AVA S - VILLERS-l'Hopital.	Head of Column to pass Starting Point at 8.30 a.m.
3.	198th Inf.Bde.H.Q.	MAISON POSTIEU.	BO IRES.	As for Serial No. 2.	As for Serial No. 2.	Head of Column to pass Starting Point at 8.45 a.m.
4.	6 R. Dublin Fus.	GUESCHARS.	BO IRES.	As for Serial No. 2.	As for Serial No. 2.	Head of Column to pass Starting Point at 9.0 a.m.
5.	543 Coy. A.S.C.	ST. IOT.	BEAUVOIR.	As for Serial No. 2.	As for Serial No. 2.	Head of Column to pass Starting Point at 9.15 a.m.

"A" Form.
MESSAGES AND SIGNALS.

Army Form C. 2121.
(In pads of 100.)

TO: 6 R Dublin Fus.

Sender's Number: 46
Day of Month: 19

AAA

[message illegible]

SECRET.   Copy No. 3

198TH INFANTRY BRIGADE ORDER NO. 105.

20th September, 1918.

Reference Map. IM'S 11, 1/100,000.

----

1. The 198th Infantry Brigade will move by March Route to the LIU COURT Area tomorrow, 21st instant, in accordance with attached March Table "A".

2. Units will report arrival in billets.

3. Units of this Brigade to ATTLE LODGE.

                                                R.A. Eden
                                                Captain,
                                            Brigade Major,
                                        198th Infantry Brigade.

Issued through Signals at ....

DISTRIBUTION.

Copy No.	1.	5th R. Inniskilling Fus.
" "	2.	9th Gloucester Regt.
" "	3.	6th R. Dublin Fus.
" "	4.	543 Coy., A.S.C.
" "	5.	66th Division, "G".
" "	6.	66th Division, "Q".
" "	7.	No. 3 Signal Section.
" "	8.	Staff Captain.
" "	9,10,11.	War Diary.
" "	12,13,14.	File.

TABLE "A" to accompany 188th Infantry Brigade Order No. 105.

Srl No.	Unit.	From.	To.	Starting Point.	Route.	Remarks.
1.	5 R.Innis.Fus.	BARLY.	GRAND RULLECOURT.	Cross Roads at Church in NEUVILLETTE.	BEAUDRICAURT - LE SOUICH - IVERGNY pass - SUS ST. LEGER.	Head of Column to pass Starting Point 8.30 a.m.
2.	6 R.Dublin Fus.	BONNIERES.	LIENCOURT.	Cross Roads ½ mile N. of Mon. LEBLOND.	REBREUVIETTE - LE CAUROY.	Head of Column to pass Starting Point 8.45 a.m.
3.	2/5 Gloucester Regt.	BONNI`ERS. (1 Coy. 1 Cov.) 1 Co., BEAUVOIR.	BEL-BOURT. LIGNEREUIL.	As for Serial No. 3.	REBREUVIETTE - LE CAUROY. ETREE-WAMIN BERLENCOURT	Head of Column to pass Starting Point 9.0 a.m.
4.	193 Inf.Bde. H.Q.	BONNIERES.	GRAND RULLECOURT.	As for Serial No. 2.	As for Serial No. 3.	Head of Column to pass Starting Point 9.15 a.m.
5.	543 Coy., A.S.C.	BEAUVOIR.	DENIER.	As for Serial No. 2.	REBREUVIETTE - EREE - ART - BERLENCOURT.	Head of Column to pass Starting Point 9.0 a.m.

Appx (5)   Copy No. 5

ADMINISTRATIVE INSTRUCTIONS ISSUED IN REFERENCE TO
198th INFANTRY BRIGADE ORDER NO.106.

27th Sept. 1918.

1. 198th Infantry Brigade will entrain on September 28th, 1918 in accordance with the attached table.

2. Each unit on arrival at the Station will hand to the entrainment officer an accurate entrainment state for transmission to the R.T.O.

3. (a) D.A.A.G., 66th Division will generally supervise the entrainment.
(b) 6th Bn. R. Dublin Fus. will detail an officer not below the rank of Captain to report to R.T.O. CORBIE immediately on arrival. This officer will act as Detrainment Officer for 198th Infantry Brigade Group.

4. Rations for consumption on 28th will be carried on the man. Rations for consumption on 29th will be issued in CORBIE Area.

5. Units will entrain with waterbottles full.

6. A MOTOR ambulance will be at each station of entrainment.

7. Billets in CORBIE Area will be notified at the station of detrainment.

7. Lorries for the conveyance of surplus baggage and blankets are allotted as under:-

Each Bn. & Bde.H.Q.   1½ lorries.
198th L.T.M.B.   1   "

Guides (2 per Bn), for lorries will report at Bde. H.Q. at 7 a.m., when lorries will be despatched as under :-

No.of lorries.	Unit to which sent.	Remarks.
2	6th Lancs. Fusrs.	One lorry to be loaded with half a load only and then despatched to 6th R.Dub.Fus. by their second guide who will accompany lorry from Bde.HQ.
1	6th R.Dub.Fus.	
1	5th R.Innis.Fus.	Extra ½ lorry from Bde.H.Q. later.
1	198th L.T.M.B.	

Lorries immediately on being loaded will assemble at LIENCOURT Cross Roads whence they will proceed in convoy direct to CORBIE, reporting on arrival to D.A.A.G., 66th Division at the Station for instructions.
A small off-loading party will accompany each lorry.

9. Units will report by 6 p.m. to-night the number of men unable to walk to the station. Arrangements will then be made to transport them to the station.
2/2nd. Field Ambulance will hold one Daimler ambulance in reserve for this service.

10. ACKNOWLEDGE.

P. Nykoza
Captain,
Staff Captain,
198th Infantry Brigade.

Copies to all recipients of 198th Infantry Brigade Order No. 106.

> 198TH INFANTRY BRIGADE.
> 20 SEP 1918
> No. 1593/12 A

5th Bn. R. Innis. Fus.
9th Bn. Gloucester Regt.
6th Bn. R. Dublin Fus.
543 Company, A.S.C.
No. 3 Signal Section.

1. On arrival in the new area, units will be billetted as follows :-

    198th Inf. Bde. H.Q. & Signals.   GRAND RULLECOURT.
    5th Bn. R. Innis. Fus.   -do-
    9th Bn. Gloucester Regt.   -do-
    6th Bn. R. Dublin Fus.   LIENCOURT.
    543 Company, A.S.C.   DENIER.

2. Immediately on completion of the move, battalions will instruct lorry drivers to report to Brigade Headquarters, GRAND RULLECOURT, not later than 4-0 p.m.

3. Railhead in the new area will be TINQUES.

4. ACKNOWLEDGE.

                          Captain,
                       Staff Captain,
               198th Infantry Brigade.

20.9.18.
HBC

SECRET.   Copy No. 5

AMENDMENT TO ADMINISTRATIVE INSTRUCTION ISSUED IN REFERENCE TO 198th INFANTRY BRIGADE ORDER NO. 106.

-o-o-o-o-o-

27th Sept. 1918.

Para. 3 (a). For "entrainment", read "detrainment".

Para. 7. The allotment of lorries is amended as follows:-

    198 Inf.Bde.HQ.   1 lorry.
    2/2nd Fld.Ambce.   ½ "

2/2nd. Field Ambulance will send the necessary guide to Brigade Headquarters. The lorry will be half filled by 5th Bn. R.Innis. Fus. and despatched to the Field Ambulance.

All lorries will re-assemble on being loaded, at Brigade Headquarters, GRAND RULLECOURT, and not at LIENCOURT Crossroads as previously stated.

Para. 9. Men unable to march will, as far as possible, be sent as unloading parties on the lorries. The remainder will be sent on ahead to the station under a competent N.C.O. who will endeavour to get lifts for them on the road. Men unable to move will be evacuated as sick under Divisional arrangements. The numbers of such men will be notified to Brigade Headquarters not later than 7-0 a.m.

No motor ambulances are available to take men to the station.

ACKNOWLEDGE.

                                          P.
                                          Captain,
                                         Staff Captain,
                                    198th Infantry Brigade.

SECRET.   Copy No. 5

198th INFANTRY BRIGADE ORDER NO. 107.

28th Sept. 1918.

1. 198th Infantry Brigade Group (less 431 Field Company, R.E.) will move by march route in accordance with the attached table to-morrow, 29.9.18.

2. Units will be located as under :-

    6th Lancs. Fusrs.   )
    5th R. Innis. Fus.   )
    198th L.T.M.B.   )   HARBONNIERES.
    198 Inf. Bde. H.Q.   )
    2/2nd. Fld. Ambce   )

    8th R. Dublin Fus.   BAYONVILLERS.

3. Billetting parties (less 8th R. Dublin Fus) will report to the Staff Captain at the Church (in ruins) HARBONNIERES, at 10 a.m. 8th R. Dublin Fus. will make their own arrangements to billet in BAYONVILLERS.
    Completion of billetting arrangements to be reported by them to the Staff Captain at Church, HARBONNIERES.

4. Guides for lorries will report at 198th Inf. Bde. H.Q. at 8-0 a.m.

5. ACKNOWLEDGE.

                                                    Captain,
                                                  Staff Captain,
28.9.18.   198th Infantry Brigade.

DISTRIBUTION.

    66th Division, "G".   Copy No. 1.
    66th Division, "Q".   2.
    6th Bn. Lancs. Fusrs.   3.
    5th Bn. R. Innis. Fus.   4.
    8th Bn. R. Dublin Fus.   5.
    198th L.T.M.B.   6.
    545 Company, A.S.C.   7.
    2/2nd. E.L. Fld. Ambce.   8.
    No. ? Sig. Section   9.

ENTRAINMENT PROGRAMME "A".

Train No.	Unit.	Strength. Officers.	Strength. O.R.	Entrain.	Time.	Remarks.
1.	6th LA.CS.FUSRS. South African Bde.HQ. 4 S.A. Regt. S.A.I.L.H.	30 5 27 2	970 80 849 45	TI OGHES.	13.30 22.9.18.	1. Troops will arrive at Station of Entrainment 1 hour before departure of train. 2. Probable length of journey 4 to 5 hours. 3. Station of Detrainment, COMBLE.
		64	1843	ENTRAINMENT PROGRAMME "B" PETIT MOUVT.		
2.	17th Fld.Coys R.E. Divnl. HQ. Divnl. Signals 6th L. DUBLIN FUSRS.	17 30 1 40	412 250 80 874		12.25 22.9.18.	
		88	1556			
3.	199th INF.BDE.H.Q. 5th R.I. RIS FUSRS. 198th L.T.M.B. 2/2nd S.M. FIELD AMBCE. Mob.Vet.Section.	7 38 5 5 2	70 765 60 180 26	PETIT MOUVT.	14.25 23.9.18.	
		58	1101			

Church Fire 198
Och. 18 /66

302

Appendix I

Copy No. 5

198th INFANTRY BRIGADE ORDER NO. 108.

30th September, 1918.

Ref. Map. SHEET 17, 1/100,000.

----

1. The 198th Infantry Brigade will move by March Route tomorrow, the 1st October, to the CAPPY Area, in accordance with the attached March Table.

2. Two Field Ambulances will follow at least ½ mile in rear of the column.

3. The following distances will be observed on the march:-

   100 yds. between Companies.
   100 yds. between Battalion and Transport.
   500 yds. between Battalions.
   50 yds. between each section of 12 vehicles.

4. ACKNOWLEDGE.

                       Captain,
                       Brigade Major,
                       198th Infantry Brigade.

Issued through Signals at 01-00

DISTRIBUTION.

Copy No.	Recipient
1.	66th Division, "G".
2.	66th Division, "Q".
3.	6th Lanc. Fus.
4.	5th R. Inniskilling Fus.
5.	6th R. Dublin Fus.
6.	198th L.T.M.B.
7.	543 Coy., R.E.
8.	2/2nd Field Ambulance.
9.	O.C., No. 3 Signal Section.
10.	Staff Captain.
11.	Brigade Transport Offr.
12, 13, 14.	War Diary.
15, 16, 17.	File.

Appendix I

Serial No.	Unit.	From.	To.	Route.	Time of passing Starting Pt.	Remarks.
1.	6 Lancs. Fus.	HARBONNIERES	CAPPY Area.	PROYART - FROISSY - Southern Bank of Canal - CAPPY.	11.00	Not to enter PROYART before 12.00
2.	198 Inf. Bde. H.Q.	HARBONNIERES	CAPPY Area.	As for Serial No.1.	11.15.	
3.	5 R.Innis. Fus.	HARBONNIERES	CAPPY Area.	As for Serial No.1.	11.20.	
4.	198 L.T.M.B.	HARBONNIERES	CAPPY Area.	As for Serial No.1.	11.35.	
5.	6 R.Dublin Fus.	BAYONVILLERS	CAPPY Area.	As for Serial No.1.	11.40.	
6.	2/2 E.Lancs. Fld. Ambce.	HARBONNIERES	CAPPY Area.	As for Serial No.1.	12.00	
7.	543 Coy., A.S.C.	HARBONNIERES	CAPPY Area.	As for Serial No.1.	12.05	

Starting Point - Bend in road at junction of HARBONNIERES - PROYART Road and track from VAUVILLERS.

6th LANCS FUS
5th INNIS FUS   198 LFMB
6th R. Dub. Fus   2/2nd F.A   1630/2/A

Appendix D

Reference 198 I.B. Order 108.

I. Detail billetting parties to proceed by bicycle & report to Staff Capt at AREA COMMANDANT'S billet CAPPY (billet at C in CAPPY) at 9.45 a.m without fail.

II. 2/2nd F.A. will detail two horse ambulances to follow in rear of Brigade Column on move tomorrow to pick up men who fall out on the march.

III. No sick other than hospital cases will be evacuated. 2/2nd F.A. will make necessary arrangements to transport men unable to march to new area by motor ambulance or otherwise.

IV. Lorry allotment will be notified later.

V. Acknowledge

30-9-18.

P. Nyleron
Capt
Staff Capt
198. I.B.

appendix (2)

6TH ROYAL DUBLIN FUSILIERS
TACTICAL SCHEME NO. 1

Ref. Maps-
        LENS 1:100,000
        AMIENS 17. 1:100,000

Information 1. The enemy is holding the high ground
    (a) Between MONTAUBAN and GUILLEMONT and the valley of HARDECOURT in strength.

    (b) The G.O.C. 66th Division has orders to seize the village of HARDECOURT and push on and capture the high ground about B de BERNAFAY and B des TRONES.

    (c) The 198 Inf. Bde. has been detailed to act as Advanced Guard and will be distributed as follows.
        Vanguard   6th R.D.F.
                          (5th R.I.F.
        Mainguard   (198 L.T.M.B.
                          (6th L. Fusrs.

Intention 2. The 6th R.D.F. in it's capacity as Vanguard will push on with all possible speed and make good the high ground WEST of HARDECOURT

Instructions 3. "D" Coy will furnish two platoons as point
    (1) Remainder will march in following order, "D" Coy less two platoons., A., B., C., Coys, H. Qrs.
    (2) Flank guards will not be put out until orders are given by O.C. Van guard.
    (3) Two Cyclist orderlies will report to O.C. Point at Starting Point.
    (4) Starting Point - Church CAPPY.
           Time - 10 a.m.

                Route - SUZANNE - MARICOURT - HARDECOURT

    (5) Lewis Gun Limbers and Packs will accompany Coys. Remainder of Transport will be brigaded and march under orders of B.T.O.
    (6) Further instructions will be given to O.C. Coys at C.O's Conference at 8.45 a.m.
    (7) "B" Teams will not take part in the exercise but will form up as a separate body and march at the head of the Transport.

                                              Captain.

              Adjutant to 6th Royal Dublin Fusiliers.

Copy 1 to Major Vance.
     2   O.C. "A" Coy
     3   "B"
     4   "C"
     5   "D"
     6   H.Q. to warn all concerned.
     7   Transport Officer.
     8   File.

SECRET.

Appendix (2)

Reference Addendum No. 1 to 198th Infantry Brigade Order No. 110.

Route. After "SUZANNE - MARICOURT" add "HARDECOURT - TRONES WOOD".

                            Captain,
                        Brigade Major,
1.10.18.   198th Infantry Brigade.

Copies to recipients of 198th Infantry Brigade Order No. 110.

Appendix (2)

6th Lancs. Fus.
5th R. Inniskilling Fus.   198th Inf. Bde.
6th R. Dublin Fus.   No. G. 1/27

Notes in connection with tactical scheme on 2/10/18.

1. Lewis Guns will remain in limbers until Commanding Officers consider it necessary to take them out in view of the tactical situation.
   When this is done L.G. teams will be fully armed with guns and drums.
   Nos. 1 & 2 only may put their packs in the limber - all remaining personnel will wear dress laid down for the march.

2. Stokes Mortars will be imaginary, but the teams will be present.

3. The Senior Officers in charge of 'B' teams and spares will take command of the column of 'B' teams as detailed in March Table to accompany 198th Infantry Brigade Order No. 110, Addendum No. 1 (Serial No. 5).

4. Commanding Officers will create any minor tactical situations they may desire for the training of their command.

5. The G.O.C. will meet Commanding Officers at cross Roads on South Eastern outskirts of MARICOURT, A.22.a.0.4, at 11.0 a.m.

6. One copy of Sheet 57c. (layered) and Sheet 62c (layered) are enclosed.

7. Rifle Grenade dischargers may be carried mounted on the rifle.

                                              Captain,
                                              Brigade Major,
1.10.18.   198th Infantry Brigade.
NHW

NARRATIVE.

Appendix (2)

193th Infantry Brigade as detailed in previous orders is an advance guard to a Division moving from SUZANNE - MARICOURT - HARDECOURT - TRONES WOOD - GUILLEMONT - GINCHY - LES BOEUFS.

The cavalry have been detailed on a special mission.

Aeroplanes report enemy consolidating in A.6, also apparently in S.29 and S.30 and T.25. Considerable enemy movement in a N. and N.E. direction.

The Divisions on our right and left are moving parallel with us.

That on the right via MAUREPAS - T.20.c. - T.21.c. on MORVAL.

That on the left via CARNOY - MONTAUBAN and LONGUEVAL on FLERS.

SENT TO TROOPS IV.   (Appendix (2))
------

2. Leading Battalions of 74th Brigade have been moved by valley
South of LUDENCOURT to attack spur in B.1. Have reached the E.
end . line through .7.central.   8th R. Dublin Fus. at the
base tire reached on E. and . line through A. 12.central.
Concealed .edge turn in LUDECORT to open on their flank.

*near

Reserve Battalion is ordered to mop up LUDECORT.

SITUATION REPORT.   I. Offensive (2)

On reaching the southern end of BOIS DE PETTICOURT the Vanguard is shelled from the direction of JUBLAINS COD, only field guns and howitzers.

Appendix 2

SITUATION REPORT. III.
-------------+--------------

Message received from advanced guard of Division on right saying they have gained MAUREPAS, but are under M.G. fire from the spur in F.1.

SITUATION REPORT.   II.

Appendix (2)

In passing between BOIS D'EN HAUT and BOIS ?????, vanguard
comes under machine gun fire from the high ground 1000 yds.
? of ?RDECOURT.

SITUATION REPORT.   V.
                                          Appendix (2)

Battalion have gained spur in B.1 and high ground in a.6.
HARDECOURT has been cleared of enemy.
    Patrols have pushed forward to the line HDQ WOOD -
ARROWHEAD Copse. Southern edge of TRONES WOOD report no
sign of the enemy. Aeroplanes drops a message saying small
bodies of enemy and some motor busses going N.E. along the GINCHY -
LES BOEUFS road.
    March of the advanced guard is resumed as follows :-

        Vanguard, under Lt.Col. A. S. PATTERSON, D.S.O.
                                        5th R. Inniskilling Fus.
                                        ~~Details, 5th Lancs. Fus.~~
                                        Details of 198 I.T.M.B.
                                        5 Lancs Fus Less [?]

    Main Guard,
        in order of march

                6th R. Dublin Fus.
                19th Inf. Bde. H.Q.
                198 I.T.M.B. less detachment 5 R. Inniskilling
                6th Lancs. Fus.
    "B" team and transport having been halted in MARICOURT
are ordered to move forward.

SECRET.   Appendix (2)
                                                     Copy No. 5

198TH INFANTRY BRIGADE ORDER No. 110.

1st October, 1918.

Reference Maps, LENS 11, 1/100,000.
              AMIENS 17, 1/100,000.

1. The enemy is holding the high ground between MONTAUBAN and GUILLEMONT and the valley of HARDECOURT in strength.

2. It is the intention of G.O.C., 66th Division, to seize the village of HARDECOURT and pushing on to capture the high ground about B. de BERNAFAY and B. des TROYES.

3. The 198th Infantry Brigade has been detailed to act as advanced guard and will be distributed as follows :-

   Van Guard.   6th R. Dublin Fus.

   Main Guard.   5th R. Inniskilling Fus.
                           198th L.T.M.B.
                           6th Lancashire Fusiliers.

4. Head of the Main Guard will pass CAPPY Church at 10.30.

   Route. SUZANNE, MARICOURT.

5. ACKNOWLEDGE.

                                    Captain,
                                for Brigade Major,
                                198th Infantry Brigade.

Issued through Signals at 18.30.

DISTRIBUTION.

          Copy No. 1.   66th Division, "G".
          "   " 2.   66th Division, "A".
          "   " 3.   6th Lancs. Fus.
          "   " 4.   5th R. Inniskilling Fus.
          "   " 5.   6th R. Dublin Fus.
          "   " 6.   198th L.T.M.B.
          "   " 7.   543 Coy., A.S.C.
          "   " 8.   2/2nd Field Ambulance.
          "   " 9.   O.C., No. 3 Signal Section.
          "   " 10.   Staff Captain.
          "   " 11.   Brigade Transport Officer.
          "   " 12,13,14. War Diary.
          "   " 15,16,17. File.

SECRET.   Copy No. 5

198TH INFANTRY BRIGADE ORDER No. 109.

1st October, 1918.

Reference Maps. AMIENS 17, 1/100,000.
             LENS 11, 1/100,000.

---

1. 198th Infantry Brigade Group will move to the GUILLEMONT Area tomorrow, 2nd instant.

2. A tactical exercise in accordance with O.O. No. 110, will be carried out by the Brigade tomorrow, 2nd instant.

3. Transport will be Brigaded and will march under orders of Brigade Transport Officer, except that Pack Animals and Lewis Gun limbers will proceed with their Companies.

4. ACKNOWLEDGE.

                                               Captain,
                                        for Brigade Major,
                                        198th Infantry Brigade.

Issued through Signals at 18.30.

DISTRIBUTION.

    Copy No. 1.   66th Division, "G".
      "   " 2.   66th Division, "Q".
      "   " 3.   6th Lancs. Fus.
      "   " 4.   5th R. Inniskilling Fus.
      "   " 5.   6th R. Dublin Fus.
      "   " 6.   198th L.T.M.B.
      "   " 7.   543 Coy., A.S.C.
      "   " 8.   2/2nd Field Ambulance.
      "   " 9.   O.C., No. 3 Signal Section.
      "   " 10.   Staff Captain.
      "   " 11.   Brigade Transport Officer.
      "   " 12,13,14. War Diary.
      "   " 15,16,17. File.

Units will be required to move from No. 1 to No. 1 in the order shown on order o. 11.

Serial No.	Unit	From	Route	Time of passing start point	Remarks
1.	183th I.L. Bde. H.Q. CAPPY.	do.	GUILLEMONT Area.	30th S - BARLEUX.	10.25.
2.	5 R.I.ish-Mill ps.	do.	do.	do.	10.30.
3.	190th I.M.G.B. (less 1 Sect. 2 guns).	do.	do.	do.	10.45.
4.	6th Lances.Fus.	do.	do.	do.	11.00.
5.	B teams and sources of units in above order of march.	do.	do.	do.	11.15.
6.	Remainder and scout of Battns. in above order of march.	do.	do.	do.	11.20.	Under orders of Brigade ave Sport Officer.
7.	2/2 d. Ld. Fus.	do.	do.	do.	11.30.
8.	5/3 of.,...	do.	do.	do.	11.35

N.B. Dress; full marching order. Steel helmets to be worn. S.B.R's in alert position.

SECRET.   Copy No. 5

ADDENDUM No. 1. to 198th INFANTRY BRIGADE ORDER No. 110.

1st October, 1918.

----

1. Reference para. 3. Units comprising the Main Guard, 2/2 E.L. Field Amboc., and 543 Coy. A.S.C. will pass the starting point in accordance with attached March Table.

2. Starting Point - CAPPY Church.

3. "B" Teams and spares will not accompany their units but will march behind the Main Guard.

4. 6th R. Dublin Fus. Section of 198th L.T.M. Battery will be under the orders of O.C., Vanguard.

5. ACKNOWLEDGE.

                                          Captain,
                                      Brigade Major,
                                  198th Infantry Brigade.

Issued through Signals at 22.30

DISTRIBUTION.

As for 198th Infantry Brigade Order No. 110.

SECRET.   66th DIVISION.   66th Divn.
                                                           7171/A

ORDER OF BATTLE AND COMPOSITION.

G.O.C.,	Major General	H.K.BETHELL,C.M.G.,D.S.O.
A.D.C., & Camp Commdt.	Captain.	A.HOFMAN.
A.D.C.	2nd Lieut.	J.H.C.WILSON.
G.S.O.1.	Lieut.-Colonel.	F.P.NOSWORTHY,D.S.O.,M.C.,
G.S.O.2.	Lieut.-Colonel.	The Hon.W.E.GUINNESS,D.S.O.,
G.S.O.3.	Captain.	J.C.O.MARRIOTT,D.S.C.,M.C.
A.A.& Q.M.G.	Lieut.-Colonel.	F.J.LEMON,D.S.O.
D.A.A.G.	Major.	D.V.H.BALDERS,M.C.,
D.A.Q.M.G.	Major.	R.E.OTTER,M.C.,
A.D.M.S.	Colonel.	J.MACKINNON, D.S.O.,
D.A.D.M.S.	Major.	W.H.ROWELL.
D.A.P.M.	Captain.	G.H.JENNINGS.
D.G.O.	Captain.	C.E.PRICE,M.C.,
D.A.D.V.S.	Major.	R.G.ANDERSON.
D.A.D.O.S.	Major.	A.W.BREHAUT.
Div. Claims Officer.	Lieut.	C.T.STEWART.
Div. Salvage Officer.	2nd Lieut.	F.T.W.SAUNDERS.
254 (Div.) Employ. Coy.	Captain.	L.CHATFIELD.
Div. Signal Coy.	Major.	E.H.EVELEGH,D.S.O.,M.C.,
Div. Intelligence Officer	Lieut.	C.DAVIS.

66th Divl. R.A.

C.R.A.,	Brigadier-General	A.BIRTWISTLE,C.M.G., D.S.O., T.D.,
Brigade Major.	Captain.	J.A.B.LOMAX,M.C.,
Staff Captain.	Captain.	R.CARPENTIER,M.C.,
S.O. for reconnaissance.	Lieut.	R.W.BELL.
O.i/c D.A. Sigs.	Captain.	C.C.VALDER
330 Bde. R.F.A.		
Commander.	Lieut.-Colonel.	A.P.BOXALL.
Adjutant.		
A Battery.	Major.	F.X.S.CARUS,M.C.,
B do.		
C do.	Major.	V.H.DICKSON.
D do.	Major.	A.R.KENWORTHY.
331 Bde. R.F.A.		
Commander.	Lieut.-Colonel.	R.J.ADAMS.
Adjutant.	Captain.	L.A.GODFREE.
A Battery.	Major.	E.J.NIXON,D.S.O.,M.C.,
B do.	Major.	H.HOWDEN.
C do.	Major.	J.D.BELL,M.C.,
D do.	Major.	F.W.WHITE,M.C.,
66th D.A.C.		
Commander	Lieut.-Colonel.	T.P.RITZEMA.
Adjutant.	Captain.	D.COOPER.
No. 1 Section.	Captain.	E.S.BICKHAM.
No. 2 do.	Captain.	T.NUTTALL.

66th Divl. R.E.,

C.R.E.	Lieut.-Colonel.	O.S.DAVIES, D.S.O.;
Adjutant.	Captain.	S.SKADDOCK.
430th Field Co., R.E.	Major.	G.H.MORGAN,M.C.
431st Field Co. R.E.,	Major.	P.H.SHARPE.
432nd Field Co. R.E.	Major	R.L.GRACEY,D.S.O.,
9th Bn. Glouc.R.(Pioneers)	Lieut.-Colonel.	E.P.NARES,M.C.,

P.T.O.,

(2)

198th Inf. Bde.		
G.O.C.,	Brig.-General.	A.J.HUNTER,D.S.O.,M.C.,
Brigade Major.	Captain.	R.A.EDEN,M.C.,
Staff Captain.	Captain.	P.INGLESON,M.C.,
6th Bn. Lan. Fus.	Lieut.-Colonel.	R.F.CROSS,D.S.O.,
5th Bn. R. Innis. Fus.	Lieut.-Colonel.	A.W.S.PATERSON,D.S.O.
6th Bn. R.Dub. Fus.	Lieut.-Colonel.	F.B.LITTLE,D.S.O.,M.C.,
198th L.T.M. Battery.	Lieut.	P.J.ROE.
199th Inf. Bde.		
G.O.C.	Brig.-General.	G.C.WILLIAMS,D.S.O.
Brigade Major.	Captain.	R.J.P.WYATT, M.C.,
Staff Captain.	Captain.	J.S.FOX.
18th Bn.(MY)K.(L'pool)R.	Lieut.-Colonel.	J.F.P.MORRELL,MVO.
9th Bn. Manch. Regt.	Lieut-Colonel.	V.M.B.SCULLY, O.B.E.,
5th Bn. Connaught Rangers.	Captain.	F.RUDDY,M.C., D.C.M.,
199 L.T.M.Battery.		
South African Bde.		
G.O.C.	Brig.-General.	W.E.C.TANNER,C.M.G.,DSO.
Brigade Major.	Captain.	E. BARLOW.
Staff Captain.	Captain.	S.W.E.STYLE,M.C.,
1st South African Regt.	Major.	H.H.JENKINS.
2nd " " "	Lieut.-Colonel.	H.W.M.BAMFORD,O.B.E. M.C.,
4th " " "	Lieut.-Colonel.	D.M.L.McLEOD,DSO. MC. DCM.
S.A.L.T.M.Battery.	Captain.	M. WOOLF.
Train A.S.C.,	Lieut.-Colonel.	A.ENGLAND,D.S.O.
541 Coy A.S.C.		
542 Coy.A.S.C.	Captain.	F.T.CLARKE.
543 Coy. A.S.C.	Captain.	A.W.BALL.
544 Coy.A.S.C.	Captain.	J.L.SANDILANDS.
Field Ambulances.		
2/2nd (East Lancs.) Fld.Amb.	Lieut.-Colonel.	A.BAXTER.
2/3rd. (East Lancs)Fld.Amb.	Lieut.-Colonel.	E.H.COX.
S.A.Fld. Amb.	Lieut.-Colonel.	R.N.PRINGLE,D.S.O.,M.C.

66th, D.H.Q.
30.9.18.

SECRET.   Copy No. 5

198TH INFANTRY BRIGADE ORDER No. 113.

Appendix (3)

5th October, 1918.

Reference Sheet, 62c.

---

1. 198th Infantry Brigade will move by road today 5th October to ST. EMILIE, in accordance with the attached March Table.

2. Transport will march in rear of their own units. Distances will be the same as the march on the evening of 4.10.18 (see 198th Infantry Brigade Order No. 112).

3. <u>Dress.</u> Battle Order with greatcoats.

    One blanket per man will be taken on by lorry. Greatcoats will also be taken by lorry unless units are notified to the contrary.

4. All surplus kit will be dumped at Brigade H.Q., MOISLAINS. 6th R. Dublin Fus. will detail an officer to look after this kit with 1 N.C.O. and 3 men to be detailed by Major VANCE from spares.

5. B teams and spares will remain at MOISLAINS under the orders of Major VANCE, M.C., 6th R. Dublin Fus. All men unable to march ten miles owing to bad feet will be included among those to be left at MOISLAINS, the A.D.M.S. is arranging for medical attention. Personnel left behind at MOISLAINS will be rationed up to and including the 5th inst.

6. Lorries will report to units as under unless notified to the contrary.

    2 lorries per Battalion.
    2/3 lorry.   198th L.T.M.B.
    1/3 "   2/2nd Fld. Ambce.
    1   "   198th Infantry Brigade H.Q.

7. Brigade H.Q. will close at MOISLAINS at 09.00 and re-open at ST. EMILIE on arrival.

8. ACKNOWLEDGE.

                                        Captain,
                                        Brigade Major,
                                        198th Infantry Brigade.

Issued through Signals at ....

<u>DISTRIBUTION.</u>

    Copy No. 1.   66th Division, "G".
    "   "   2.   66th Division, "Q".
    "   "   3.   6th Lancs. Fus.
    "   "   4.   5th Lancs. Fus.
    "   "   5.   6th R. Dublin Fus.
    "   "   6.   543 Coy., A.S.C.
    "   "   7.   2/2nd Field Ambulance.
    "   "   8.   198th L.T.M.B.
    "   "   9.   O.C., No. 3 Signal Section.
    "   " 10.   199 Infantry Brigade.
    "   " 11.   Staff Captain.
    "   " 12.   D.A.C.
    "   " 13,14,15. War Diary.
    "   " 16,17,18. File.

MARCH TABLE TO ACCOMPANY 198TH INFANTRY BRIGADE ORDER No. 113.

Serial No.	UNIT.	FROM.	TO.	ROUTE.	Time of passing Starting Point.	Remarks.
1.	5th R.Irish. Fus.	MOISLAINS.	ST. EMILIE.	TEMPLEUX-LA-FOSSE - LONGAVESNES - VILLERS FAUCON.	09.45.	
2.	6th Leinster Fus.	do.	do.	do.	10.05.	
3.	198 I.C. Edo.T.C.	do.	do.	do.	10.15.	
4.	6th R.Dublin Fus.	do.	do.	do.	10.20.	
5.	198th L.T.M.B.	do.	do.	do.	10.35.	
6.	2/2 H.Fl.Ambce.	do.	do.	do.	10.40.	
7.	545 Coy. A.S.C.	do.	do.	do.	10.45.	

Starting Point - Road junction D.20.d.0.4.

Appendix (3)

66th DIVISION INSTRUCTION No. 1.

Distribution :- down to Company Commanders.

INTELLIGENCE ARRANGEMENTS DURING BATTLE.

The following procedure will be adopted.

1. Summaries. No Summary will be called for, but a short general outline of the day's operations will be either wired or telephoned to D.H.Q. by 6 p.m. each evening. This outline will include the action taken by enemy artillery and aircraft; movement on rail and road; any work on defences observed.

2. Identifications. Early information as to identity of prisoners is essential. As batches of prisoners arrive at Bde. H.Q., men from different units will be given slips (as attached) to fill in. Number of prisoners, approx:, identification, time and place of capture will then be wired to Division and Corps "I" by priority wire.

An identification wire should read as follows :-

"20 prisoners 6th Coy. 1st I.R. 185 Divn captured in "G.16.a. about 10 am."

3. Disposal of Prisoners. Prisoners will be sent down to Divl. P.O.W. Cage as soon as possible after capture for examination by the D.I.O.
In the case of a number of prisoners being employed in carrying down our stretcher cases from the front line, samples of each unit will be detached and sent down to the Cage at once - the stretcher bearing party arriving later.

4. Escorts. Regimental escorts are responsible for conducting prisoners as far back as Bde. H.Q. where they will be given signed receipts for the numbers taken over from them. The disposal of prisoners in rear of Bde. H.Q. will be carried out under Divisional arrangements.

5. Documents. (a) Officers and N.C.Os will be searched immediately after capture. All documents found on them will be sent down by the escort who will hand them over to the Bde. Intelligence Officer at Bde. H.Q.

(b) Documents will not be taken from other ranks until arrival at Corps Cage.

(c) Paybooks, identity discs and personal belongings will NOT be taken from prisoners.

(d) THE RETENTION OF ANY CAPTURED DOCUMENTS IS STRICTLY FORBIDDEN. Documents of interest will be returned to units if desired, after they have been examined. Individuals desiring the return of any document should write their name and unit on the back or envelope of the document.

(e) Escorts and guards should be warned to take special precautions to prevent prisoners from destroying papers.

/6. Separati

-2-

6.
Separation of Officers, N.C.Os and men.
Care will be taken that officers, N.C.Os and privates are separated at once, and no communication allowed to pass between the groups.

7.
Searchers.
Each Brigade will detail two searchers who will systematically search the battlefield, enemy positions, H.Q., dead, etc., for papers, documents, maps, etc., have them packed in sandbags, and forwarded as quickly as possible to the Divisional Cage.

This personnel should be armed with handy weapons and carry torches.

8.
General.
It is most important that the transmission of prisoners and documents back to Corps Cages should proceed as rapidly as possible. Detailed examination of prisoners and documents is undertaken at Corps H.Q. Examination by lower formations is to be confined strictly to items of immediate tactical importance, i.e., Enemy Intentions, dispositions, and the location of supports and reserves.

No attempt should be made to examine any other documents but MAPS.

F.P. Ewsworthy
Lieut-Colonel,
General Staff,
66th Division.

D.H.Q.,
WD 5.10.18.

SECRET.   Appendix (4)   Copy No. 5

198TH INFANTRY BRIGADE ORDER No. 114.

6th October, 1918.

Reference Sheets, 62c and 62b, 1/40,000.
 LOMBREMAIN Special Sheet, 1/20,000.
---

1. 198th Infantry Brigade Group will move by March Route on 7th Oct. to the vicinity of LE CAMELET in accordance with the attached March Table.

2. <u>Distances.</u>

   Fourth Army distances will be observed as far as ROWSSOY. East of ROWSSOY, 100 yards distance between platoons.

3. <u>Dress.</u>   Battle Order.
   Greatcoats will be carried in the pack.

4. <u>Transport.</u>

   Lewis Gun limbers will march in rear of their Companies. Remaining transport will move under the orders of the Brigade Transport Officer.

5. <u>Light Trench Mortars.</u>

   5th R. Inniskilling Fus. and 6th R. Dublin Fus. will each detail two pack animals with drivers and the Staff Captain will detail eight pack animals with drivers to report to 198th L.T.M.B. at 7am ~~tomorrow~~, 7th inst.

   A gun and 20 rounds will be loaded on to every three pack ~~mules~~ animals.

   O.C., 198th L.T.M.B. will detail

   1 Section with one gun to report to O.C., 5th R.Innis. Fus.
   1 Section with one gun to report to O.C., 6th R.Dublin Fus.
   1 Section with one gun to report to O.C., 6 Lancs. Fus.
   1 Section with one gun to be in Brigade Reserve and to be attached to 6th Lancs. Fus.

   Sections will as far as possible be attached to units from which their personnel was drawn, and will report to the units to whom they are to be attached before leaving camp 7th instant

6. 2/2nd E. Lancs. Field Ambulance will remain in Camp near ST. EMILIE.

7. Brigade H.Q. will close at ST. EMILIE at ~~11.00~~ 10.30, and re-open at A.11.a.15.20 on arrival.

8. <u>ACKNOWLEDGE.</u>

                                         Captain,
                                         Brigade Major,
                                         198th Infantry Brigade.

Issued through Signals at ..01.30......

   <u>DISTRIBUTION.</u> (Overleaf).

DISTRIBUTION.

Copy No.	1.	66th Division, "G".
" "	2.	66th Division, "Q".
" "	3.	6th La[n]c. Fus.
" "	4.	5th L[a]n[c]s. Fus.
" "	5.	6th R. Dublin Fus.
" "	6.	198th L.T.M.B.
" "	7.	523 Coy., A.S.C.
" "	8.	2/2nd Field Ambulance.
" "	9.	431 Field Co., R.E.
" "	10.	O.C., No. 3 Signal Section.
" "	11.	199 Infantry Brigade.
" "	12.	S.A. Brigade.
" "	13.	Staff Captain.
" "	14,15,16.	War Diary.
" "	17,18,19.	File.

Secret   WARNING ORDER Appendix (5)

5th R. Irish Fus.   198 L.T.M.B.
6th R. Dublin Fus.   431 Fld. Coy. R.E.
6th Leins. Fus.   Capt Grey.

1. Track to assembly area as
   follows:

   A.11.c.7.7.
   along bank to stream at
   A.11.b.5.5.
   Bridge over stream A.11.b.57
   thence along railway to road at A.12.d.7.8.
   Cross Roads B.1.c.5.1.
   Road Fork B.7.b.2.9.

2. All units will proceed by
   this track.
   Then 6th Leins. Fus. and attached
   troops to track in B.3.c. under
   guidance of O.C. 6th Leins. Fus.

   6th R. Dublin Fus. and 5th R. Irish Fus.
   along track to B.2.b.6.1. Thence
   by track to the centre of
   assembly position B.3.b.3.8.

3. Capt Grey will collect battalion taping
   parties and R.E. and start work the
   moment the tape arrives.
   Tape being got.

4. Heads of units will pass Bridge at M.H.L.5.7. at the following times:—

   6' R. Dublin Fus at 22.00 o'clock
   5" Inniss Fus at 23.00 o'clock
   6' Leins R at 00.01 o'clock

5. All units will reconnoitre the beginning part of the track detailed in para 1. as far as the LOOP (CRANK) road at once and make the necessary arrangements for guides.—

6. ACKNOWLEDGE

           R. S. [?] Capt.
             Bde Major
                196th [?] Bde

7.9.18
3 pm

Appendix (S)

G60/1

1. 6th Bn Lancs Fus.
   5th Bn R. Innis Fus.
   6th Bn R. Dublin Fus.
   491 Field Coy. R.E.

Reference this office G60/1
dated 6.10.18. para 5.

Corrections:
 For centre line B.3.a.1.5
read B.3.b.1.5.

Acknowledge by wire.

D. Sheln
Captain
Bde Major
7.10.18   19th Inf Bde

SECRET.

INSTRUCTION NO. 2 ISSUED UNDER 198th INFANTRY BRIGADE ORDER NO.115.

MACHINE GUNS.

1. 50th Division are co-operating with 16 machine guns on LES LARLIERES Farm, T.17.c.

2. The following guns of 25th Machine Gun Battalion (attached 66th Division) will be disposed as under :-

   (a) 4 guns will deal with LA SABLONIERE.
   (b) 4 guns will deal with Copse and Dugouts N. of LA SABLONIERE.
   (c) 4 guns will deal with T.28.d. and T.29.c.
   (d) 4 guns will deal with PETIT VERGER Farm (T.22.d.)

   These guns will co-ordinate their barrage with artillery programme allowing necessary clearances.
   They will be in position by midnight Y/Z night.

   After ceasing fire on above targets these 16 guns and 4 additional guns will concentrate in the valley B.5.Central and be in Divisional Reserve. They will then be prepared to deal with any counter attack from a Northerly direction.

   (b) 16 guns will concentrate at B.13.b.3.0. by 1900 on Y/Z night, sending liaison officer to MUSHROOM QUARRY to keep in touch with assembly of infantry.
   After Zero they will advance with the infantry of South African and 198th Bdes. and will take up positions from which they will be able to deal with the following points by direct fire :-

   4 guns on LE HAMAGE FARM (T.24.c.)
   4 " " PETIT POLIE FARM (U.19.c.0.3.)
   4 " " LES FOLIES (U.19.d.)
   4 " " Redoubt about U.25.central.

   On capture of RED Line these guns will remain laid on above targets until further orders.

   (c) 4 guns are allotted to 6th R. Dublin Fus.
   2 of these guns will assist O.C. 6th R. Dublin Fus. in the capture of PETIT VERGER FARM and 2 in the capture of LARLIERES FARM.
   After the capture of these localities these guns will be withdrawn:

   2 to about T.22.b.0.7.
   2 to about T.23.c.7.5.

   There they will be available to assist in the defence of the Red line in the event of a hostile counter-attack.
   Special attention must be paid to the Northern flank, but care must be taken to ensure that all troops moving South from VILLERS OUTREAUX or from just ___ of the village are hostile before fire is opened.

   (d) 2 guns are allotted to 5th R.Innis.Fus..
   These guns will assist in the capture of LE HAMAGE FARM. After the capture of the Red Line they will be withdrawn to about T.24.a.3.5. when they will be available to assist in the defence of the Red Line in the event of a hostile counter-attack.

3. ACKNOWLEDGE.

G. Eden.
Captain,
Brigade Major,
198th Infantry Brigade.

7.10.18.

DISTRIBUTION.

66th Divn. "G",	Copy No.1.
6th Bn. Lancs.Fus.	2.
5th Bn. R.Innis.Fus.	3.
6th Bn. R.Dublin Fus.	4.
'C' Coy. 25th M.G.Bn.	5.
431 Fld.Coy. R.E.	6.
199 Inf.Bde.	7.
South African Bde.	8.

Appendix (5)

SECRET.   Issued down to Platoon Commanders.

INSTRUCTION No. 2.   Issued under Divl. Order No. 97.

AIRCRAFT.-

1.   Contact aeroplanes of 35th Squadron R.A.F. will fly along the line at each objective and will call for flares by sounding a succession of "A's" on the Klaxon Horn, and by firing a White Very light.
     If the aeroplane fails to mark the line accurately, it will repeat its call ten minutes later.

2.   Troops in the advanced line will answer these calls as follows :-

   (a) By lighting Red ground flares, 3 of which in tin are to be carried by every N.C.O. and section commander.
   (b) By firing Very lights, if possible, 3 in succession.
   (c) By flashing pocket torches in a westerly direction.
   (d) By using as reflectors pieces of tin sewn inside flap of box respirator, or carried separately.
   (e) By waving ground sheets or helmets.

3.   The urgent importance of replying to calls of contact aeroplanes must be impressed on all troops. By this means only can formations be furnished with information enabling them to deal with hostile resistance and to exploit success.
     Failure to respond to calls also forces aeroplanes to fly so low as to suffer heavy casualties in pilots and machines. It may also lead to artillery fire being turned on to localities which though occupied by our troops are supposed to be hostile owing to lack of information. At the same time it must be understood that THOSE IN REAR POSITIONS ARE NEVER TO ANSWER CALLS FOR SIGNALS.

4.   Red flares show best against dark backgrounds such as the shadow at the bottom of a shell hole or trench.

5.   COUNTER ATTACK PLANES.

   (a) From Zero hour, counter-attack planes will be constantly in the air with the object of observing hostile concentrations or abnormal movement.

/(b) In the event

(b) In the event of an enemy concentration indicating a counter-attack, the counter-attack aeroplane will signal this information to the artillery by wireless. In the case of counter-attack actually developing a white PARACHUTE flare will be fired by the aeroplane in the direction of the troops moving for the impending counter-attack, for the information of the infantry.

Red lights fired from counter-attack machines indicates targets for artillery and other aircraft and must not be confused with the above.

6. MARKINGS ON PLANES.

The following will be the markings of machines allotted to special duties :-

(a) Contact patrol machine - Rectangular panels 2 foot by 1 foot on both lower planes about 3 feet from the fuselage and a streamer on the tail.

(b) Machines working with the Tanks - Black band under the tail.

7. Smoke bombs may be dropped from aircraft to screen the advance of our infantry and tanks.

Walter Guinness
Lieut-Colonel,
General Staff,
66th Division.

D.H.Q.,
6.10.18.

SECRET.   Issued down to Platoon Commanders.

INSTRUCTION No. 2.   Issued under Divl. Order No. 97.

AIRCRAFT.

1. Contact aeroplanes of 35th Squadron R.A.F. will fly along the line at each objective and will call for flares by sounding a succession of "A's" on the Klaxon Horn, and by firing a White Very light.
    If the aeroplane fails to mark the line accurately, it will repeat its call ten minutes later.

2. Troops in the advanced line will answer these calls as follows :-

    (a) By lighting Red ground flares, 3 of which in tin are to be carried by every N.C.O. and section commander.
    (b) By firing Very lights, if possible, 3 in succession.
    (c) By flashing pocket torches in a westerly direction.
    (d) By using as reflectors pieces of tin sewn inside flap of box respirator, or carried separately.
    (e) By waving ground sheets or helmets.

3. The urgent importance of replying to calls of contact aeroplanes must be impressed on all troops. By this means only can formations be furnished with information enabling them to deal with hostile resistance and to exploit success.
    Failure to respond to calls also forces aeroplanes to fly so low as to suffer heavy casualties in pilots and machines. It may also lead to artillery fire being turned on to localities which though occupied by our troops are supposed to be hostile owing to lack of information. At the same time it must be understood that THOSE IN REAR POSITIONS ARE NEVER TO ANSWER CALLS FOR SIGNALS.

4. Red flares show best against dark backgrounds such as the shadow at the bottom of a shell hole or trench.

5. COUNTER ATTACK PLANES.

    (a) From Zero hour, counter-attack planes will be constantly in the air with the object of observing hostile concentrations or abnormal movement.

/(b) In the event.

-2-

(b) In the event of an enemy concentration indicating a counter-attack, the counter-attack aeroplane will signal this information to the artillery by wireless. In the case of counter-attack actually developing a white PARACHUTE flare will be fired by the aeroplane in the direction of the troops moving for the impending counter-attack, for the information of the infantry.

Red lights fired from counter-attack machines indicates targets for artillery and other aircraft and must not be confused with the above.

6. MARKINGS ON PLANES.

The following will be the markings of machines allotted to special duties :-

(a) Contact patrol machine - Rectangular panels 2 foot by 1 foot on both lower planes about 3 feet from the fuselage and a streamer on the tail.

(b) Machines working with the Tanks - Black band under the tail.

7. Smoke bombs may be dropped from aircraft to screen the advance of our infantry and tanks.

Walter Guinness
Lieut-Colonel,
General Staff,
66th Division.

D.H.Q.,
6.10.18.

6th L.N. Lancs Fus.
6th L. Dub. Fus.
5th R. Innis "

198TH INFANTRY BRIGADE.
No. G.60/2

Appendix (5)

Herewith 25 copies of 198 Infantry Brigade instruction No 5. in connection with ~~...~~

198 Inf Bde Order No 115 which will be issued later —

7.10.18

Capt.
Brigade Major
198 Inf Bde

"A" Form.
MESSAGES AND SIGNALS.

Army Form C. 2121.
(In pads of 100.)

Prefix... Code... ...Words. Charge. Office of Origin and Service Instructions.	Sent At... ...m. To By	This message is on a/c of: ...Service. Uffen (S-) (Signature of "Franking Officer.")	Recd. at... ...m. Date... From... By...

TO 5th R. Innis Fus
    6 Dublin Fus
    6 Leins Fus

Sender's Number.	Day of Month.	In reply to Number.	AAA
E 75	7		

In	continuation of	E.72
units	must	assist	units
who	covering	them	to
withdraw	and	see	that
they	withdraw	by	zero
must	has	now	are
Units	must	be	in
position	without	fail	by
Zero	~~delay~~	two	~~out~~
~~units~~	will	hours	The
fact	that	they	are
in	position	at	once
to	Brigade HQ.	~~and~~	~~...~~
~~...~~	~~...~~	~~...~~	~~...~~

From 198 Bde
Place
Time

(Z) [signature] Capt.
Censor. Signature of Addressor or person authorised to telegraph in his name.

*This line, except A A A, should be erased if not required.
Wt. W 3253/P511. 500,000 Pads. 1/18. B. & S. Ltd. (E2389.)

Aff main 5

"A" Form.
MESSAGES AND SIGNALS.
Army Form C. 2121.

TO	Lancs Fus	4.31 75 C
	Dub Fus	
	Innis Fus	

Sender's Number: HX72 Day of Month: 7 AAA

The strong points mentioned in ~~para~~ Preliminary Instructions will be constructed by RE + Lancs Fus. 1 RE + 1 Platoon for each strong point. aaa 40 RE will move with Lancs Fus for their purpose aaa On Innis Fus & Dublins gaining GREEN LINE they will inform Lancs Fus direct, repeating to Bde. Lancs Fus will then send up the Consolidating party. Innis Fus + Dub Fus will be responsible for manning these points in their own sectors. Lancs Fus + RE

Appendix (5)

"A" Form.
MESSAGES AND SIGNALS.

Army Form C. 2121.
(In pads of 100.)

will return to their units when strong points are completed.

Location of strong points is approximately as follows.

No 1 MARLICHES FARM
No 2 T 11 central
No 3 T 11 c 6.2
No 4 T 12 6 22.

Inns Fus are responsible for siting No 4 - Aus Fus for 1, 2 + 3. RE for the trace of the works + the plan Corps LF that the work is carried out.

From: 198 Inf Bde

(Z) A Hunter BG

"A" Form.
MESSAGES AND SIGNALS.

Army Form C. 2121.
(In pads of 100.)

TO
- 5th R. Innis. Fus.
- 6th Lancs. Fus.
- 6th R. Dublin Fus.
- 198 L.T.M.B.
- 431 Field Co. R.E.
- Captain GREY.

Sender's Number.	Day of Month.	In reply to Number.	AAA
B 3	7		

Assembly will take place in accordance with warning order already issued aaa Acknowledge.

From SUHU

Captain.

"A" Form.
MESSAGES AND SIGNALS.

Army Form C. 2121.
(In pads of 100.)

Prefix	Code	Words	Charge	This message is on a/c of:	Recd. at ... m.
Office of Origin and Service Instructions.		Sent At ... m. To ... By ...		Offen. (S) Service. (Signature of "Franking Officer.")	Date From By

Secret & Confidential

TO 5 R Inskn Fus
    C Lancashn Fus
    6 R Dublin Fus

Sender's Number.	Day of Month.	In reply to Number.	AAA
E.72	7		

At zero minus two hours all covering troops & now out in front of your assembly position will be withdrawn are always Although units their own responsible for precautions must protection special be taken during them two hours

From Place 198 Inf Bde
Time

The above may be forwarded as now corrected. (Z)

Censor. Signature of Addressee or person authorised to telegraph in his name.

*This line, except AAA, should be erased if not required.
Wt. W 3253/P511. 500,000 Pads. 1/18. B. & S. Ltd. (E2389.)

"A" Form.
MESSAGES AND SIGNALS.

Army Form C. 2121.
(In pads of 100.)

TO
430 Field Co. R.E.
6th Lancs. Fus.)
5th R. Innis. Fus.) For information.

AAA

Please detail a sapper to report to each Battalion to act as booby trap finder. He will report to O.C. Battalion immediately on receipt of this order.

From SUHU.

"A" Form.
MESSAGES AND SIGNALS.

Army Form C. 2121.
(In pads of 100.)
No. of Message..........

Prefix	Code	m.	Words.	Charge.			
Office of Origin and Service Instructions.					This message is on a/c of:		Recd. at ...... m.
			Sent				Date........
			At........ m.		.........Service.		From......
			To........				
			By........		(Signature of "Franking Officer.")		By......

TO 6th R. E Dublin Fus.

Sender's Number.	Day of Month.	In reply to Number.	AAA
E.B.	7		

50 Div: report enemy in
gas shelling GOUZEANCOURT FARM
T.27.c.0.5.

From 19th Hy Bde
Place
Time 6 pm

The above may be forwarded as now corrected. (Z)

"A" Form.
MESSAGES AND SIGNALS.

Army Form C. 2121.
(In pads of 100.)

TO: 8th Lancs. Fus.
6th R. Dublin Fus.
5th R. Innis. Fus.
431 Field Co.

Sender's Number.	Day of Month.	In reply to Number.	
B. 4.	7.		AAA

Please send an officer representative with a watch to these H.Q. at once to synchronise watches.

aaa This officer will take back Zero hour and must know the exact position of his unit aaa He must report not later than 9 p.m.

From: SUHU

Capt.

...ND SIGNALS.

TO: 5th Innis Ins, 6th Lancs Ins, 6th Dubs Ins, 66 Div G, O.C. 3 Sect Co, 198 L.T. M.G. Co

Sender's Number: E 71
Day of Month: 7

Copy of 66 Div instruction No 6 is attached aaa The following are approximate bounds of Bde HQ and Bde Report centre

Time at which office will open at earliest	Bde Hq	Advanced report centre
O	B8 a 3.8	B 3 c 8.2
O + 45	B 3 b 4.1	T 29 d 6.7
O + 1hr/15min	"	T 28 b 5.3
O + 1hr/50min	"	T 29 b 2.7
O + 2h/30	T 29.b.2.7	T 22 b 3.8

All moves will be by the Bde

Capt
6 Bde

axis of ~~liaison~~ liaison i.e.
B8 a 2.2 — GOUY BEAUREVOIR road
across country — B3 d 8.2 — B3 b 4.1
— across to BEAUREVOIR — VILLERS
OUTRIEUX road at B3 b 9.3 —
X roads T 29 b 6.1 — X roads T 28 b 5.8
— road junction T 39 b 2.7 — road
junction T 33 b 3.8
Messages coming along this
road should always come
across B.A.R.C. whose duty
it is to transmit
to bde

From 198 Inf Bde
Place
Time 3.50 pm

7. Appendix (5)

"A" Form.
MESSAGES AND SIGNALS.

Army Form C. 2121.
(In pads of 100.)

TO { R I F / R D F / L F   C Co No 1 Tank Bn

Sender's Number: Hx 74
Day of Month: 7

AAA

On Oct 8th tanks will move 1500 yards in rear of front line till RED LINE is reached. aaa For exploitation to the Green line Mark 5 Tanks are allotted as follows:-

3 Tanks Capt Symon R D F
2 Tanks Capt Robinson R Irish F

Each Battn will provide one OR to go in each Tank, to report at JILL COPSE.

On Green line being taken tanks will return to Div Reserve

From
Place 198 Bde
Time

"A" Form.
MESSAGES AND SIGNALS.

Army Form C. 2121.
(In pads of 100.)

Prefix	Code	m.	Words	Charge	This message is on a/c of:	Recd. at ... m.
Office of Origin and Service Instructions			Sent At ... m. To ... By ...		*Uppen* (signed) ...... Service. (Signature of "Franking Officer.")	Date ...... From ...... By ......

TO: 6" Dublin Fus
5 R. Irvin Fus
6 Lan Fus

Sender's Number.	Day of Month.	In reply to Number.	AAA
* E 74	7		

Zero hour will be ~~five am~~ aaa Acknowledge
0510 aaa
Five am

From: 148 Inf Bde
Place:
Time: 8 pm

Signature: A.R. du Cafe

"A" Form.
MESSAGES AND SIGNALS.

Army Form C. 2121.
(In pads of 100.)

Prefix	Code	Words	Charge	This message is on a/c of:	Recd. at ... m.
Office of Origin and Service Instructions.		Sent At ... m. To By		Afkin (S) Service. (Signature of "Franking Officer.")	Date From By

TO { 5 Innis Fus
     6 Dubl Fus
     6 [Leins] Fus

Sender's Number.	Day of Month.	In reply to Number.	AAA
E 76	7		

Third Army carried out a successful attack to-day and the Division Commander further out to B/C the close support and to old keeping close to the squash which the troop of Third Army did to-day

From 198 Inf Bde
Place
Time 8.20 pm

SECRET. Appendix (5) Copy No. 5

198TH INFANTRY BRIGADE ORDER NO. 115.

Reference attached 1/20,000 combined sheets (Secret).

7.10.18.

1. In accordance with instructions already issued, 66th Division will attack and capture the line shewn in green on the attached map. ×

 7th Infantry Brigade, 25th Division, will attack on right of the 66th Division and 149th Infantry Brigade, 50th Division on left.

 The task of the latter Brigade is to co-operate with the 5th Corps and capture VILLERS OUTREAUX at the same time protect the Northern flank of 66th Division.

2. The attack will be carried out on the morning of the 8th October. Zero hour will be notified later.
 The final objective will be reached in two bounds.
 First objective; RED Line.
  Practice Trench, U.25.central -
  U.19.c.6.5,
  U.19.a.1.6.
  T.18.a.1.1.
  T.17.d.4.4.
  MARLICHES FARM inclusive.

 (a) 66th Division will attack and capture RED Line with South African Brigade on Right and 198th Infantry Brigade on Left. The dividing line between Brigades is shewn on the attached map.
 The attack will be preceded by a strong artillery barrage and will be supported by tanks.
 As soon as the barrage ceases, 5th R.Innis.Fus. and 6th R.Dublin Fus. will push forward and capture remainder of the WALINCOURT - AUDIGNY Line as far North as T.11.central. They will secure high ground by T.11.central.
 Infantry jumping off line will run from

 B.4.c.0.3. in straight line to T.27.c.7.8.

3. Barrage will come down at Zero 200 yards in front of that line.
 Assaulting troops will be formed up on jumping off line. Infantry Posts in front of this line will be withdrawn during the night 7/8th October under arrangements made by 25th and 50th Divisions.

4. The attack of the Division will be covered by 18th Divisional Artillery Group consisting of
 82nd and 83rd Brigades, 18th Div. R.F.A.
 290th and 291st Brigades, 58th Div. R.F.A.
 65th, 64th and 150th Army Brigades, R.F.A.
 also by 76th Brigade, R.G.A. and 89th Brigade, R.G.A.
 82nd, 84th, 290th and 291st Brigades will cover Left of the Division.
 83rd, 65th and 150th Brigades will cover Right of the Division.
 Arrangements have been made for one gun to fire on the dividing line between attacking Brigades to fire one smoke shell every other lift.

5. ACKNOWLEDGE.

× Map to Battalions only.

R.H.d..
Captain,
Brigade Major,
198th Infantry Brigade.

Issued at 12.0.

DISTRIBUTION.

Copy No. 1.		66th Divn. "G".
" " 2.		66th Divn. "Q".
" " 3.		6th Lancs. Fus.
" " 4.		5th R.Innis.Fus.
" " 5.		6th R.Dub. Fus.
" " 6.		198th L.T.M.B.
" " 7.		543 Coy. A.S.C.
" " 8.		2/2nd. Field Ambce.
" " 9.		431 Field Coy. R.E.
" " 10.		O.C. No.SSignal Section.
" " 11.		199th Infantry Bde.
" " 12.		S.A. Brigade.
" " 13.		Staff Captain.
" " 14,15,16,		War Diary.
" " 17,18,19,		File.

10. TANKS.   Eight Tanks, Heavies, Mark V, have been allotted to this Brigade.   Details will be issued later.

11.   431 Field Co., R.E. are attached to this Brigade from 17.00 October 7th.   They will assist in the construction of strong points (Details in para. 8.)
Detailed instructions will be issued later.

12.   The following instructions are being issued with 108th Infantry Brigade Order No. 115.

(a) Orders for marching to assembly tapes.
(b) Information concerning enemy.
(c) Artillery arrangements.
(d) Smoke.
(e) Machine Guns.   x
(f) Aircraft.   x
(g) Tanks.

x Have already been issued.

13.   ACKNOWLEDGE.

Thomas P. McIntosh Lt.
for Captain,
Brigade Major,
108th Infantry Brigade.

DISTRIBUTION.

Copy No.		
" "	1.	36th Division, "G".
" "	2.	36th Division, "Q".
" "	3.	6th Lancs. Fus.
" "	4.	5th R. Innis. Fus.
" "	5.	6th R. Dublin Fus.
" "	6.	108th L.T.M.B.
" "	7.	549 Co., A.S.C.
" "	8.	2/2nd Field Ambulance.
" "	9.	431 Field Co., R.E.
" "	10.	O.C., No. c Signal Section.
" "	11.	10 Infantry Brigade.
" "	12.	South African Brigade.
" "	13.	Staff Captain.
" "	14,15,16.	War Diary.
" "	17,18,19.	File.
" "	20.	B.I.O.

SECRET.

6th Bn. Lancs. Fusrs.
5th Bn. R.Innis.Fus.
6th Bn. R.Dublin Fus.
431 Field Coy. R.E.

Appendix (5)

198 IC
INFANTRY BRIGADE
No. ....

1. A reconnaissance will be carried out by Commanding Officers and any officers they may select, on the morning of the 7th inst.
   Route of approach will be reconnoitred and the position of any tracks required will be noted.
   The approximate position of the tape line and approach tapes will also be decided upon.

2. The following are the proposed routes to assembly positions, which will be adhered to unless the reconnaissance to-morrow makes any changes necessary.

   5th R.Innis. Fus.

   Across Canal about A.11.d.8.9.
       Railway   A.12.a.
                 to A.12.d.6.8.
                 to B.1.c.5.1.
                 to B.8.b.7.4.
                 to B.3.c.8.2.
   thence to assembly positions.

   6th R.Dublin Fus.

   Across Canal about A.11.d.8.9.
       Railway   A.12.a.
                 to A.12.d.6.8.
                 to B.1.c.5.1. *B.7.b.20.95*
                 to B.2.b.8.1.
   thence to assembly positions.

   6th Lancs. Fusrs.

   Across Canal about A.11.d.8.9.
       Railway   A.12.a. - *A.12.d.6.8. - B.1.c.5.1. - B.7.b.20.95*
   thence to assembly position to be chosen by Officer Commanding 6th Bn. Lancs. Fusiliers in the valley in B.2.d. and B.3.c.

3. Units will report to Brigade Headquarters at LE CATELET by 1 p.m 7th instant the results of the reconnaissance as laid down in para. 1 above.

4. Commanding Officers will select approximate positions of Battalion Headquarters at each stage of the attack and will notify this office of positions selected by 4 p.m. 7th instant.

5. The following bearings give the general direction of the attack.

   Left boundry, left battalion, 34° to red line, T.16.d.3.7.
   Centre of Assembly Line, B.3.a.1.5. 44° to red line, T.23.b.2.8.
   Right boundry, right battalion, 53° to red line, T.24.b.6.2.
   True bearings in each case

   Since the conference of Battalion Commanders this afternoon, certain alterations have been made in the Red Line.
   The red line now runs along the Switch Line in T.24.b. - T.24.a. - T.23.b. - T.23.a. - T.16.d.
   5th Bn. R. Innis. Fus. and 6th Bn. R. Dublin Fus. will now both exploit success to the Green Line. LE HAMAGE Farm (T.24.c) is now inclusive to 5th R. Innis. Fus.

                                                 Captain,
                                               ~~Staff Captain~~,
                                               Brigade Major,
                                               198th Infantry Brigade.

7.10.18.
HBC

SECRET.   Appendix (5)   Copy No. 5.

198TH INFANTRY BRIGADE PRELIMINARY ORDER No. 1.

7th October, 1918.

Reference Sheets, 63o & 63b, 1/40,000.
MONTBREHAIN Special Sheet, 1/20,000.

----

1. **GENERAL PLAN.** With a view to increasing the breach in the enemy's defences, major operations are about to be taken in a general north-easterly direction by the Third and Fourth Armies; the object and tactical boundaries of XIII Corps are as shown on the attached map.
   38th Division (V Corps) will be operating on the northern flank, and 30th American Division (American 2nd Corps) on the southern flank of the XIII Corps.
   The attack will probably take place on the morning of the 8th October.

2. **CORPS PLAN.** It is presumed that by the above day our front line will run approximately East of VILLERS FARM (xxxB) (T.30.b), East of GOUZEAUCOURT Farm (T.28.d) and East of BEAUREVOIR.

   (a) The attack on the RED LINE will be made by the 66th Division on a two Brigade front in conjunction with one Brigade from 25th Division on the right, and one Brigade from the 6th Division on the left.
   The task of the latter Brigade will be to protect the left flank of the Corps, and to co-operate with the 38th Division in the capture of VILLERS OUTREAUX.

   (b) After the capture of the RED LINE the intention is to exploit the situation northwards from LES HARLICHES (T.17.c) along the spur T.11.central, also to capture SERAIN, in conjunction with the 2nd American Corps, who will take PREMONT. If, therefore, the operation is successful, the position at the end of the day should be as shown by the GREEN LINE.

3. **DIVISIONAL PLAN OF ACTION.** 66th Division will attack with South African Brigade on the right and 198th Infantry Brigade on the left, each Brigade being on a two Battalion front. The 199th Brigade will follow up the attack, and after capture of the RED LINE will pass through the 198th and South African Brigades in order to seize SERAIN and secure the high ground in U.7, U.14, U.15 and U.21.

   After the capture of the RED LINE 198th Infantry Brigade will push forward on the left and secure the high ground about T.11.

4. **BRIGADE PLAN OF ACTION.** The 198th Infantry Brigade will attack with the 6th R. Dublin Fus. on the left and the 5th R. Inniskilling Fus. on the right.
   The 6th Lancs. Fus. will be in Brigade Reserve.

5. **DIVIDING LINES.** (a) Between S.A. Brigade and 198th Infantry Brigade. B.2.c.3.3 (BELLEVUE F'RM) T.28.1.4.1 (Cross Roads) — T.24.b.35.15.

   (b) Between 198th Infantry Brigade and 30th Division. T.27.c.8.5 — T.22.1.1.9 — T.17.c.4.3.

/(c) PREMONT

-2-

(c) Between 5th R. Innis. Fus. and 6th R. Dublin Fus.
B.3.b.3.2 (Centre of Assembly Line) - T.22.d.3.0 -
T.23.b.3.0 - B.12.b.0.0. - B.12.a.4.3.

6. Bearings for line of advance given in this office
No. G. 60/1 (issued to Battalions only) will hold
good except that bearing for Left Boundary Left
Battalion will read $\frac{8}{43}$ to Red Line T.16.d.8.3.

7. By 14.00 on Y day the Brigade will be disposed
as follows :-

    5th R. Innis. Fus.   LE CATELET - N'URCY Line,
                          A.17.a.9.9 - Rly. A.11.c.6.4.

    6th R. Dublin Fus.   LE CATELET - N'URCY Line,
                          Rly. A.11.c.6.4 - Road A.11.c.6.5.

    5th Innes. Fus.   Rly Cutting. A.11.a.
                        A.10.d.

8. CONSOLIDATION.   Each objective or line gained will be consolidated
by the assaulting troops at once.

Strong points will be constructed by Battalions
about the following positions :-

    6th R. Dublin Fus.   (i) LES MARLICHES Farm,T.17.c.3,7.
                        (ii) T.11.b.2.1.
                        (iii) T.11.c.7.3.

    5th R. Inniskg.Fus.   T.12.b.3.2.

199th Infantry Brigade are constructing strong
points about the following positions :-

    U.7.central.
    U.8.c.4.3.
    Mill, S.14.b.9.8.

South African Brigade are establishing the
following strong points :-

    U.19.c.3.3.
    U.19.b.8.1.

ARTILLERY.   The attack to the RED LINE will be preceded by
a strong barrage. This barrage will come down and
rest for three minutes 100X in front of the
enemy outpost line. It will then move forward by
lifts of 100 in three minutes for 1800 yards. It
will then slow down to 100X in four minutes until it
reaches the line 500 in front of the first objective
(Red Line). The barrage will then dwell for 30
minutes when it will lift and the second phase of
the attack will commence.

The attack from the RED LINE will be supported by
mobile Field Artillery which will move forward with a
view to supporting the infantry over open sights.
Details of the Field Artillery Barrage and employment
of Corps H.A. will be forwarded later.

One Battery of the 112th Brigade, R.F.A. has been
attached to this Brigade. One section of this Battery
will be attached to 6th R. Dublin Fus. and one section
to 5th R. Inniskilling Fus.

/10. TANKS.

Sent   Appendix 5

198TH INFANTRY BRIGADE.
REPORT OF OPERATIONS.
7.10.18 - 12.10.18.

PART I.
7.10.18 - 18.00 8.10.18.

---

1. **ASSEMBLY.**

   On 7th October the 198th Infantry Brigade Group moved by march route to the vicinity of LE CATELET and occupied their assembly position in the LE CATELET - NAUROY line.

   Battalions were distributed as follows :-

   5th R. Inniskilling Fus.   RIGHT.
   6th R. Dublin Fus.   LEFT.
   5th Lancs. Fus.   RESERVE, in the GOUY - BELLICOURT railway cutting.

   198th Infantry Brigade H.Q. RAILWAY RIDGE.

2. **DEPLOYMENT.** see Map A. position 1.

   On the evening of 7th October units began their march to position of deployment at 23.00. Rain began about 19.00 and fell heavily till 22.00. The 'going' was as a result very slippery. In spite of this all units moved forward very well and were approaching their tapes in good time.

   At 01.00 an attack on VILLERS OUTREAUX resulted in a heavy hostile barrage being put down on our positions of deployment.

   The 6th R. Dublin Fus. were lining up on their tapes and the 5th R. Inniskilling Fus. were just nearing them when the barrage came down.

   Both battalions suffered considerable casualties and were correspondingly disorganised.

   /Heavy shelling continued

Heavy shelling continued throughout the period of deployment.

At 04.45 however, both battalions were in position on their tapes ready to advance.

The 6th Bn. Lancashire Fus. had meanwhile assembled in Reserve without ~~any~~ much difficulty.

One Section of 198th L.T.M.B. was allotted to each Battalion, and the guns with 28 rounds of ammunition were brought up on pack mules and off loaded at the positions of deployment.

3. ATTACK.

At 05.10 our barrage opened and the infantry advanced to the attack.

On the whole the enemy showed little tendency to fight, and often ran away before our troops could get to grips with him, with the exception of M.G. nests which fought stoutly.

From the earliest stages of the attack the 6th R. Dublin Fus. were troubled by machine gun fire on their left flank.

As the attack progressed this became more serious as VILLERS OUTREAUX was not taken and the enemy had therefore a perfect target for enfilade M.G. fire. In spite of these difficulties the 6th R. Dublin Fus. pushed on and captured PETIT VERGER Farm and MARLICHES Farm. The latter they were unable to hold owing to enfilade M.G. fire.

The 6th R. Dublin Fus. then established a defensive flank along the ridge in T.22.b. This flank was further extended by four posts which were established by the 6th Bn. Lancashire Fus. in T.23.c.

On the right the 5th R. Inniskilling Fus. continued their advance and established themselves on the RED LINE.

There was some fighting in HAMAGE FARM and HAMAGE WOOD but, with the assistance of tanks, the wood was soon cleared and a battery of 77 mm. was captured.

/The position at 09.15

PART II.

16.00 8.10.18 - 18.00 9.10.18.

----:----

1. RELIEF OF PORTION OF 199th Infantry Brigade FRONT.

About 17.00 on 8th October orders were received from the Divisional Commander that the Brigade would take over a portion of the front of 199th Infantry Brigade who were carrying out a minor operation with a view to re-adjusting their front before an attack the next morning.

Unfortunately G.O.C., 199th Infantry Brigade and his Brigade Major were both in the line arranging for this minor operation, and details for relief could not be arranged till 19.00. It was then decided that the 5th R. Innis. Fus. should relieve the 9th Manchester Regt., less 1 Coy. in U.7.central and LYPE POST, to be relieved by 6th R. Dublin Fus. *which was.*

The latter portion of the relief was carried out, but owing to a misunderstanding the three Coys., 9th Manchester Regt., were not relieved by 5th R. Inniskilling Fus. *(see map B. position 4. 4a shows position intended)*

2. ORDERS FOR ATTACK ON 9TH OCTOBER.

About 00.15 on 9th October orders were received for an attack the next morning.

It was decided that the 6th Lancs. Fus. would lead the attack with 5th R. Inniskilling Fus. in Support and 6th R. Dublin Fus. in Reserve.

3. ATTACK.

6th Lancs. Fus. were formed up at 04.50 and advanced at 05.20 clearing the eastern outskirts of ELINCOURT.

Two Coys. of 5th R. Inniskilling Fus. followed up and entered ELINCOURT from the South and East. The remaining Companies were late reaching their assembly position.

It soon became evident that the enemy had withdrawn and would offer no serious resistance in ELINCOURT.

/The 6th R. Dublin Fus. entered

The position at 09.15 was approximately as shown on attached map. (Map A. position 2)

At 09.15 the enemy counter attacked N. of HAVRE FARM. This counter attack was repulsed with the assistance of two tanks.

During the next hour there were several minor actions along the MALINCOURT - AUDIGNY Line, the enemy attempting to debouch from there to counter attack our troops establishing themselves on the RED LINE. All these local counter attacks were repulsed with loss to the enemy.

At 10.30 the 6th R. Dublin Fus. established touch with the battalion on their left the 4th K.R.R.C. of the 50th Division.

As our troops advanced along the S.E. side of VILLERS OUTREAUX the 6th R. Dublin Fus. advanced again and captured MARLICHES FARM (11.30) and established themselves along the line of their final objective (Green Line on attached Map "A"). At the same time the 5th R. Innis. Fus. continued their advance, captured LAMPE FARM, and established themselves on the Green Line. (Map A. position 3)

The 8th R. Dublin Fus. entered the village from the West and with the assistance of the 5th R. Inniskilling Fus. rapidly cleared the village capturing some dozen prisoners. (see map B. position 5)

A section of R.E. were detailed to search for booby traps and mines in ELINCOURT.

They discovered an unexploded charge under the Railway Crossing at the Southern exit of the village.

Considerable delay was caused by a very dense fog which lasted from 06.00 to 07.15 when the 6th Lanc. Fus. continued their advance without meeting any opposition, captured the BOIS DE PINON and IRIS COPSE and reached their final objective - the M'METZ-CL'RY Road at 10.50, sending patrols to S. exit of CL'RY to gain touch with Brigade on our left. *organized*

The 5th R. Inniskilling Fus. then moved up into Support sending one Company to IRIS FARM to secure their left flank, and the 6th R. Dublin Fus, into Reserve.

The South African Brigade who had been following up close in rear of the Brigade then passed through the 6th Lancs. Fus. and continued the advance.

At 12.00 the Brigade was therefore distributed in accordance with attached map "B". (position 6)

4. BRIGADE IN DIVISIONAL RESERVE.

Orders were received at 13.00 that the Brigade was in Divisional Reserve and would hold the RED LINE (final objective of 198 and 199 Infantry Brigades) in the event of a hostile counter attack.

All units were ordered to be prepared to move at 2 hours notice, and O.C., "A" Coy., 25th M.G. Battalion was ordered to place eight guns in position covering the southern portion of the Red Line in addition to the eight already in position in the Northern Sub-sector. (map B. position 7)

PART III.

18.00 9.10.18 - 05.00 11.10.18.

----:----

1. ORDERS FOR ATTACK.

At 00.30 the Divisional Commander dictated to the G.O.C. on the telephone orders for attack at 06.00 10th October.

2. APPROACH MARCH.

At 03.30 10th October the Brigade marched through MARETZ and MAUROIS to REUMONT.

3. ADVANCE.

East of REUMONT the Brigade deployed at 06.15 N. of REUMONT - LE CATEAU Road. The advance was carried out on a one battalion front with three Companies in the line.

The 6th Lancs. Fus. again led the attack with the 5th R. Inniskilling Fus. in Support and the 6th R. Dublin Fus. in Reserve.

Touch was obtained with 199th Infantry Brigade on the right, and with the 2nd Argyle and Sutherland Highlanders of the 33rd Division on the left. 199th Infantry Brigade were deployed before this Brigade as they led the march to the position of deployment. 199th Infantry Brigade accordingly advanced slowly in order to allow this Brigade to get into line with them.

Owing to the very short time available in which to make arrangements for this attack it was impossible to arrange for artillery co-operation.

The Brigade advanced accordingly without artillery Support.

At the outset of the attack little opposition was encountered either from hostile shell or machine gun fire, but as our troops neared LE CATEAU the shelling became heavy.

The enemy had evidently several batteries, chiefly 5.9, ready in position, and the 6th Lancs. Fus. in particular suffered casualties from shell fire.

/77 mm. firing over open sights

77 mm. firing over open sights on the forward slopes in K.21 and K.27 were particularly troublesome.

In spite of these difficulties the 6th Lancs. Fus. pushed on and captured the high ground in K.27.b. and d.

The high ground and the line of the INCHY – LE CATEAU Railway were very heavily shelled and it became evident that a further advance without more artillery support and without counter-battery work would be difficult.

The enemy was holding the line of the River SELLE in strength.

The situation at 12.00 was as shown on attached map "C".

4. ATTACK ON MONTAY.

At 16.25 verbal orders were received by the G.O.C. from the Divisional Commander that the Brigade would attack and capture MONTAY at 17.00.

This order was communicated verbally to O.C., 6th Lancashire Fus. by the Brigade Major at 16.45 and at 17.30 the 6th Lancs. Fus. advanced on MONTAY.

The advance came under heavy machine gun fire from the Eastern bank of the river.

In spite of this the 6th Lancs. Fus. pressed on and entered MONTAY supported by two Coys. 5th R. Inniskilling Fus.

Touch was established with 18th K.L. on the right but it was found impossible to cross the river as the bridges were broken and the river was unfordable. (22.55).

Our line then ran as shown on attached map "D".

5. Throughout the 11th the situation remained approximately unchanged. Some casualties were suffered from the enemy's shell fire which was still very heavy.

Arrangements were made for the relief of the 6th Lancs. Fus. and the 6th R. Dublin Fus. during the night 11th/12th and instructions were given to

/O.C., 6th R. Dublin Fus.

O.C., 6th R. Dublin Fus. to endeavour to cross the river SELLE, and get into touch with troops of the 33rd Division on the high ground East of the river.

At 17.00 orders were received that the Brigade would be relieved that night by a portion of the South African Brigade.

The relief was effected without incident, though the shell fire was heavy, and the Brigade concentrated in billets in REUMONT.

To sum up the Brigade were in action practically continuously from dawn 8th Oct. to dawn 12th Oct. During this period the Brigade advanced 13 miles, 9 miles of which were realised fighting.

26 guns and a number of prisoners were captured and two villages were liberated.

Total captures made during this period were :-

77mm. Guns.	5.9" How.	Anti-Tank Rifles.	T.Ms.	A.A. Guns.	M.Gs. counted.
23	3	3	2	1	48.

Prisoners - 342 O.R.

Total casualties during this period were :-

Officers.		O.R.			
K.	W.	K.	W.	NYD.	M.
4	26	71	579	1	125 ⊗

⊗ Practically all these have been accounted for, either K, W, or M, i.e.,

K.	W.	M.
13	59	53x.

x. All these 53 must be either killed or wounded in our hands. No men fell into enemy hands as far as is known.

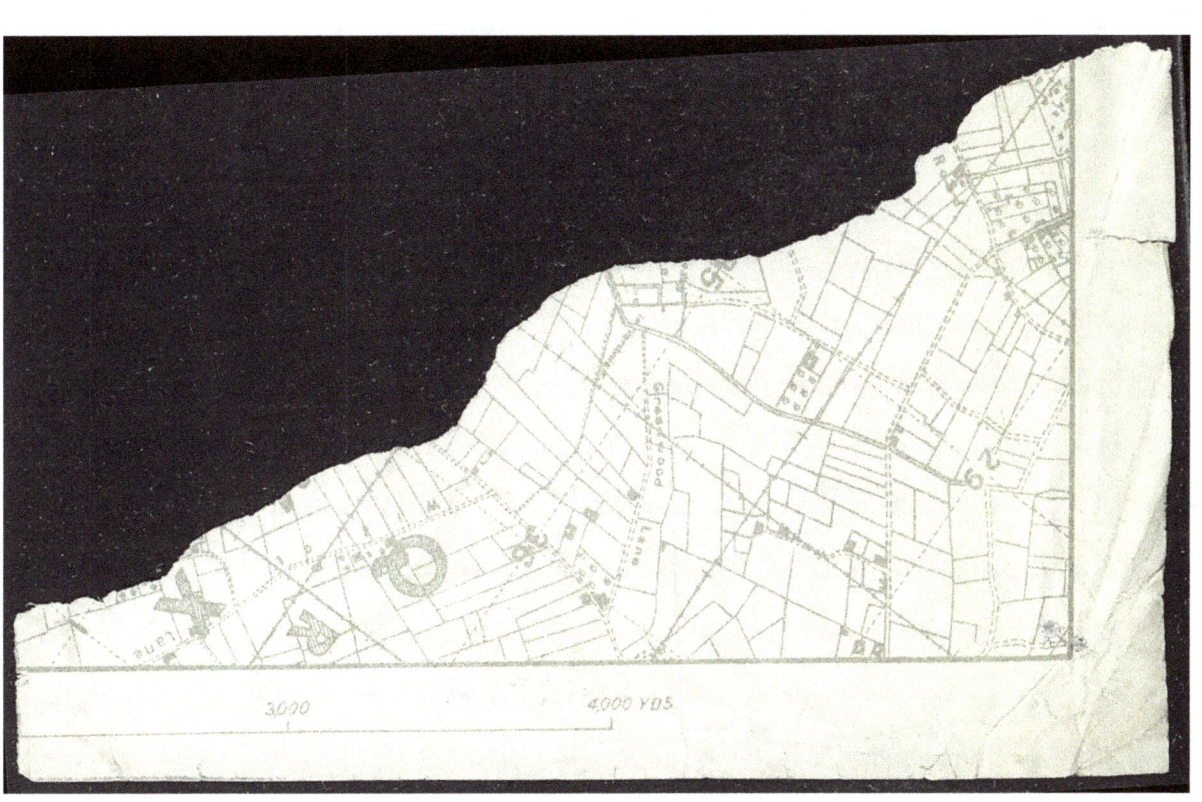

198TH INFANTRY BRIGADE.

Brigade Commander.	Brigadier General A.J. HUNTER, D.S.O., MC.
Brigade Major.	Captain R.A. EDEN, M.C.
Staff Captain.	Captain P. INGLESON, M.C.
Brigade Intell. Offr.	Captain T.H.G. GREY, M.C.
Signalling Officer.	Lieut. A.T. TERRY.

6th LANCASHIRE FUSILIERS.

Commanding Officer.	Lieut. Colonel R.F. GROSS, D.S.O.
Second-in-Command.	Major J.S. TOWNSHEND, M.C.
Adjutant.	Captain F. FRANKS, M.C.
O.C., "A" Coy.	Captain R.A.V. WHITE.
O.C., "B" Coy.	Captain J.S. RUTHERFORD.
O.C., "C" Coy.	Captain L.B.L. SECKHAM, M.C.
O.C., "D" Coy.	Captain C.H. POTTER, M.C.

5TH R. INNISKILLING FUS.

Commanding Officer.	Lieut. Colonel A.W.S. PATERSON, D.S.O.
Second-in-Command.	Major G.M. KIDD, M.C.
Adjutant.	Captain H.J. EASTWOOD, M.C.
O.C., "A" Coy.	Captain G.R. ROCHE-KELLY.
O.C., "B" Coy.	Captain W.C.G. BOLITHO.
O.C., "C" Coy.	Captain W.R. GALLWAY.
O.C., "D" Coy.	Captain T.T.H. VERSCHOYLE.

6TH R. DUBLIN FUSILIERS.

Commanding Officer.	Lieut. Colonel W.B. LITTLE, D.S.O., M.C.
Second-in-Command.	Major W. VANCE, M.C.
Adjutant.	Captain J. ESMONDE, M.C.
O.C., "A" Coy.	Captain H.J. Hayes.
O.C., "B" Coy.	Captain H.A. SHADFORTH.
O.C., "C" Coy.	Captain H.J. GAFFNEY, M.C.
O.C., "D" Coy.	Captain W.B. ENGLISH.

198TH L.T.M.B.

Officer Commanding.	A/Captain P.J. ROE.

6th Lancs. Fus.
5th Innis. Fus.
9th R. Dub. Fus.
108th Inf. Bde.
66th Division "G".

108th Inf. Bde.
No. B.M. 205

Appendix (6)

1 Copy

1. 9th R. Dub. Fus. will relieve one Company 9th Manch. Regt., dispositions as follows, to-night :-

    H.Q., and 3 Platoons, U.7. Central.
    1 Platoon, LAMPE POST, T.12.b.5.2.

Guides will be at LAMPE FARM, T.12.d.25.70 at 10 p.m.

2. 5th Innis. Fus., will relieve H.Q., and 3 Coys. 9th Manch. Regt. in the following dispositions:-

    1 Coy. U.13. Central.
    1 "   U.8.c.4.3.
    1 "   LA FOLIE FARM.
    1 "   as may think best (in reserve)

Guides will be at Headquarters 9th Manch. Regt., at U.19.c.8.6., at 10 p.m.

3. 9th R. Dub. Fus. will continue to keep in touch with the Lincolns of the 21st Division in T.6.a.

4. 5th Innis. Fus. will push forward patrols to the general line T.12.b.5.2. - U.7.a.9.2. - U.2.a.0.5.- U.8.b.0.5. - U.8.d.95.50.

5. 6th Lancs. Fus. will remain in Brigade Reserve and will be concentrated in T.12., East of the AUDIGNY - WALINCOURT Line

108th L.T.M.B. will be withdrawn into Brigade reserve and will concentrate with the 6th Lancs. Fus.

6. O.C., 9th R. Dub. Fus. will move his Battalion H.Q. and reserves to the area West of the AUDIGNY - WALINCOURT Line in T.18.b.

7. Brigade Headquarters will close at LA SABLONNIERE at 8.0 p.m. and open at PETIT VERGEN FARM at 8.50 p.m. tonight.

8. ACKNOWLEDGE.

Captain,
Brigade Major,
108th Infantry Brigade.

8.10.18.

9. In view of future events it is essential that Battn HQ should be easily found by runners.

C. Dub Lus.

6. R. Dub. Fus.

Appendix 6

SECRET.   Copy No. 3.

198TH INFANTRY BRIGADE ORDER No.116.

                                                8th October, 1918.

Division
1.   &&&&&& was successful in capturing all
objectives today. Line now runs LA LAMPE Farm -
U.7.Cent. - U.8.b.0.5. - Windmill, U.8.d.9.3.
     The advance will be continued to-morrow, 9th
October with 199th Inf.Bde. on right and 198th Inf
Bde on left.
     It is understood that other troops are operating
on our left flank.

     Boundaries :- Northern Boundary, T.13.Cent. - N. corner
of BOIS DE PINON - T.19.c.0.0. thence prolonged in
a straight line.
     The Southern Boundary of 198th Inf.Bde. is line
running through Mill in U.14.b. and P.31.a.1.2.
Stream at this point inclusive to 198th Inf.Bde.
     Objectives of 199th Inf.Bde. and 198th Inf.Bde.
is a line joining O.30.Cent.-Point 150 on ROMAIN -
CHAUSSE Road in V.1.b.
2.   ⊗ 8th Lancs.Fus. will form up in U.14.b. and will
advance so as to clear the Eastern outskirts of
ELINCOURT after which, capture BOIS DE PINON
and so to the first objective.
     ⊗ 5th Innis.Fus. will follow close behind 8th
Lancs.Fus. and will attack and mop up ELINCOURT
from the South and South West.
     6th Dublin Fus. will form up in U.7. and 8. and
attack and mop up ELINCOURT from the West.

     When ELINCOURT has been dealt with, ⊗5th Innis.Fus.
will push forward as support to ⊗8th Lancs.Fus.
     ⊗ Dublin Fus. are drawn into Bde. Reserve in O.35v
     ⊗ (These Battns. may spread into 199 Bde. area, provided
3.   ARTILLERY. C.R.A. is arranging for shelling of (they do
ELINCOURT and high ground in U.10 and U.16 from (so in
Zero minus 30 to Zero.   (rear of
     Barrage will come down 300 yds in front of present (199
front line from Zero to Zero plus 3.   (Bde.
     The operation must be in the nature of open
warfare but the ~~further~~ artillery will be
for our advance at the following rates:-
     First 1000 yds.- 100 yds in 5 minutes.
     From 1000 yds to objective, 100 yds in 4 minutes.

     The Artillery will arrange for a protective Barrage
to stand beyond the first objective for 30 minutes,
South African Brigade will then go through with their
own Artillery.

4.   Machine Guns are allotted special action.
     It is hoped to get the assistance of some tanks.
     198th Inf.Bde H.Q. will be at PETIT VERGER Farm.
     Advance Report Centre will be, at Zero, where trench
crosses road at T.24.b.1.9. Further positions will
be notified later.   R.E.
     198th L.T.M.B. and M.G.Coy. will be in Bde. Reserve
and will receive special instructions.
     Zero hour , 05.30 on 9th October, 1918.

5   ACKNOWLEDGE.

                                              Captain,
                                          Brigade Major 198 Inf Bde

9.10.18

198 Inf Bde
No. B.M. 201.

~~6 Lanc Fus~~
~~5 Innis Fus~~
6 R Dub Fus

Passed

6 R Dub Fus will arrange to get into
touch with troops on their left. They will
push out patrols and endeavour to get into
touch with the enemy, but will not exploit
success further than T.6.c.

5 Inniskilling Fus will get into touch
with the troops on their right. They will
push out patrols and will endeavour to
get into touch with the enemy, but will
not advance beyond U.1 without orders.

Your casualties have been noted
and forwarded to Division.

Captain,
Brigade Major
8.10.18   198 Infantry Brigade

MESSAGES AND SIGNALS.

TO	6 R	Out	Feb

Sender's Number: 58
Day of Month: 8th
AAA

Am	holding	sunken	road
T 17 C	0 0	to	T 23 B 2.8
aaa	my	left	flank
is	open	to	enfilade
fire	from	VILLERS	OUTREAUX
aaa	Hun	machine	gunners
seem	to	be	working
back	in	that	direction
aaa	Have	no	Stretcher
bearers	&	several	men
to	be	evacuated	aaa
L G	drums	also	required
aaa	We	stormed	MARLICHES
Farm	and	high	ground
beyond	but	owing	to
heavy	machine	gun	fire
from	N	and	E

From
Place
Time

1 K 6 wounded
2 s/tt 43 OR
4 Mar 5 nov 76

MESSAGES AND SIGNALS

had to evacuate again aaa had many casualties from our own smoke shells aaa Have with me 1 Officer 43 OR KRR. 4 officers 176 OR 6th R Dub Fus aaa Am reorganising Corps aaa Did you receive my S6 aaa What is the situation in VILLERS OUTREAVY aaa Acquaint few more Hours

Day of Month: 5 Sept

From: B Coy
Time: 09.45

A Shadforth Capt

10   Appendix 7

Bde
198TH INFANTRY/INSTRUCTION No.1.

Ref.1/80,000 or 1/40,000 Ordnance Map.

1. The objectives of the Division to-morrow, are K.16.Cen.-
   K.23.Cen. - K.29.
   Northern Corps Boundary, P.11.Cent. - K.15.Cent.
   Southern Boundary P.33.Cent. - K.29.Cent.

2. The Inter-Brigade Boundary, Roman Road inclusive to
   198th Inf.Bde.   Northern Boundary onwards, Roman Road
   exclusive to 198th Inf.Bde.

3. Posts on the line at present, are on the line P.12.b -
   P.18.d. - Q.7.c. - Q.13.a and b.

4. The Cavalry Corps are reported in Q.1., Q.2., Q.3., and
   Q.31. (that is in a North Easterly direction).

5. Bde. will move at 3.0 a.m. and will move through South
   African Brigade outposts at 6.0 a.m. The advance will
   be on a one Battalion front, each Battalion having 2 Coys.
   in the line.

6. The following **Artillery** are attached to each Brigade
   1 troop Yeomanry,
   3 Sections Cyclists
   1 Bde Artillery.
   1 M.G.Coy.

7. The idea is to push well forward and secure the Canal
   crossings at LE CATEAU before the Germans expect attack
   there.

8. Order of march, 6 Lancs. Fus. and one Section M.G.Coy.
   also if allotted, one section R.Es.
                      198th Inf.Bde. H.Q. and Sig.Sec.
                      8th Innis.Fus.One Coy. M.Gs. plus one
                      section/8.Dub.Fus.
   X.   198th L.T.M.B.
                      82nd Bde. R.F.A.

9. Instructions re transports will be issued later.
                                    ed
10. The 8th Lancs.Fus. with attach/troops will move in
    artillery formation. Leading Units will pass starting
    point L'EPINETTE at a time to be detailed later, but
    not before 3.0 a.m.

11. M.G.Section, will join 8th Lancs.Fus. at the starting
    point.

12. ACKNOWLEDGE.

10.10.18.
                                          Captain,
                                          Brigade Major,
                                          198th Infantry Brigade.

13. Brigade Axis of liaison, L'EPINETTE, REUMONT Church,
    Q.1.Cent., Point 150 in K.27.d., K.23.a.Cent. This line
    is the same as the Divisional Axial Line.

"A" Form.
MESSAGES AND SIGNALS.

TO — C R Dublin Fus

Sender's Number.	Day of Month.	In reply to Number.	AAA
Bm 224	10	—	

On the objective being captured the main line of resistance will be the high ground K.27 and the spur in K.21 aaa only one Coy of 6 Lan Fus will be East of the river on this Bde front aaa This Coy will act as an outpost line

From 198 Inf Bde
Place HQ
Time —

Form C. 2121.

Prefix	Code				This message is on a/c of:		Recd. at	m.
Office of Origin and Service Instructions.		Sent				Service.	Date	
		At	m.		*appended*		From	⑦
		To						
		By			(Signature of "Franking Officer.")		By	

TO	O C R Dublin Fus

Sender's Number.	Day of Month.	In reply to Number.	AAA
	10		

The situation on 66 Div front
was as follows on 9/
2nd Bde held posts at K 21 a Cen
K. 27. d. 3.3. and K. 27. d. 5. .
There is also a possible for or
five men in K. 27 d 2 1. of a
non of Kings Liverpool Regt
who was left of 199 Bde. NCO
reports that he was with a num
of the Lan Fus there are Kings
Liverpool Regt who from up with
right of 198 Bde on main road
at K. 27. d. 7. 6. an 198 Bde line
runs over to K. 27. b. 0. 7. and
from K. 21. d. 0 1. to cross roads
in K. 21. c. where they join
up with Argyle & Sutherlands

From			
Place			
Time			

The above may be forwarded as now corrected. **(Z)**

Censor. Signature of Addressor or person authorized to telegraph in his name.

* This line, except **A A A**, should be erased if not required.

MESSAGES AND SIGNALS.

Prefix	Code	Words	Charge	This message is on a/c of:	Recd. at ... m.
Office of Origin and Service Instructions		Sent			Date
At ... m.				Appendix	From
To				Service.	⑦
By				(Signature of "Franking Officer.")	By

TO — 2.

Sender's Number	Day of Month	In reply to Number	AAA
Bm 226	10		

of 33rd Div will Law Fus hold front line of 198 Bde and possibly a few men in farm K.21.a.9.8 and the cottages on the Montay–NEUVILLY Road as (2) Battalions will consolidate positions they are in depth on O.C 6 the Fus will arrange to withdraw tonight as many of his men as possible and replace them with the 2 Sections Vickers guns which are attached to him and he will also, by means of patrols push forward and lay to form posts the cottages on the MONTAY–

From
Place
Time

The above may be forwarded as now corrected. (Z)

Censor. Signature of Addressee or person authorized to telegraph in his name.

* This line, except A A A, should be erased if not required.

MESSAGES AND SIGNALS.

TO	3 Officers (7)

Sender's Number	Day of Month	In reply to Number	
Bm 226	10		AAA

– NEUVILLY Road and to gain touch with 199 Bde who are pushing forward towards MONTAY from LE CATEAU aaa The Patrols of Scouts will secure the crossing of the river and report if bridges are in tact or not aaa These positions when established will be consolidated aaa (?) Rations, water etc for tonight will come up to La NEUMONT-MONTAY Road aaa Battalions will send guides and carrying parties to be at cross roads K 3 d 6.4 at 6pm aaa If our front is being heavily shelled guides and carrying parties will move further west and intercept limbers

From	
Place	
Time	

The above may be forwarded as now corrected. (Z)

AND SIGNALS.
Army Form C. 2121.
(In pads of 160.)

No. of Message.......

Prefix	Code...... m.	Words.	Charge.	This message is on a/c of:	Recd. at ...... m.
Office of Origin and Service Instructions.		Sent			Date
		At........ m.		............Service.	From
		To			
		By........		(Signature of "Franking Officer.")	By........

TO   4   Appendix (7)

Sender's Number.	Day of Month.	In reply to Number.	AAA
BM 256	10	—	

(4) 1 Coy 100 M.G. Bn less 2 sections and 198 L.T.M.B. will be in Bde reserve in the neighbourhood of Bde HQ aaa

(5) Battn HdQrs of 198 Inf Bde are as follows:—
5 Lan Fus (Right Bn) K.27.c.9.5
5 Lewis Fus (Support) K.27.a.1.1
(2/5 Lanc Fus (Reserve) K.32.b.20.95
Rfl. Bde HQ at Q 1 a Cent.
2/4 Kings Liverpool Regt (198 Bde) are in quarry K.33.a.9.2

(6) Acknowledge

From 198 Inf Bde
Place HQ
Time ——

(Z)

The above may be forwarded as now corrected.

Censor.   Signature of Addressor or person authorised to telegraph in his name

* This line, except A A A, should be erased if not required.

O.C. B Coy. C.O. 14

Appendix (7)

At 17.50 the Lancashire Fusiliers are proceeding to attack MONTAY pass The 6th D. F. will remain in present location until further orders

16.40

15/10 [signature] MC

"A" Form.
MESSAGES AND SIGNALS.

Army Form C. 2121.
(In pads of 160.)

Prefix	Code	m	Words.	Charge.	This message is on a/c of:	Recd. at	m
Office of Origin and Service Instructions.			Sent			Date	
			At	m.	*[signature]* Service.	From	⑦
			To			By	
			By		(Signature of "Franking Officer.")		

TO — ~~Cav~~ ... 6th Div ... 199 Bde

Sender's Number.	Day of Month.	In reply to Number.	A A A
	10		

Tw[o] ~~Norman's~~ Bns 199 Bde will complete the capture of LE CATEAU and then operat[e] against spur ... K.35 a + b ~~...~~ NE of the town aaa 6th ~~Can~~ Div will seize MONTAY and cross[ing] river SELLE [to] obt[ain] touch with 199 Bde on right and 33rd Div on left on K.17 e aaa Ack aaa Confirming verbal orders issued by me ... this afternoon aaa Zero ...

From 199 Bde
Place
Time

The above may be forwarded as now corrected. (Z)

[signature]

Censor. Signature of Addressor or person authorized to telegraph in his name

* This line, except A A A, should be erased if not required.

"A" Form.
MESSAGES AND SIGNALS.

Army Form C. 2121.
(In pads of 100.)

Prefix	Code	Words	Charge	This message is on a/c of:	Recd. at ... m
Office of Origin and Service Instructions.		Sent At ... m To By		*Appendix* Service. (Signature of "Franking Officer.")	Date From ⑦ By

TO { O Sqn A. & 195 L T M B
      6 F A Bde O C N 3 F A 62 Bde MGC
      O Sqn 16 Hy 16 Hy 5 M B

Sender's Number.	Day of Month.	In reply to Number.	AAA
M 218	10		

You	will	pass	during
point	at	LA PANETTE	at
03.15	aaa	Orders	will
be	issued	you	at
starting	point	aaa	guns
will	not	pass	during
point	until	you	notify
these	orders		

From SUNU
Place
Time 03.45

This line, except AAA, should be erased if not required.

199th Inf.Bde
No. B.M. 234.

66th Division "G".
5th Inns. Fus.
6th Innis. Fus.
6th R. Dublin Fus.
"A" Coy. 66th M.G.Bn.
199th L.T.M.B.
Troop Northd Yeomanry.
No 3 Sig. Sec.
2nd Bde. R.F.A.

Appendix (8)

The following is the scheme of defence of the Brigade group :-

(i) The front line Battalion has a proportion finding the outpost line; the remainder for immediate counter-attack.

(ii) The Support Battalion, and 2 sections "A" Coy., 66th M.G.Bn., for the defence of the main line of resistance, the companies in reserve, being used for local counter-attack at the discretion of the Commanding Officer.

(iii) The reserve battalion is in Brigade reserve, as are "A" Coy. 66th M.G.Bn. less 2 Sections, 199th L.T.M.B., and Troop Northumberland Yeomanry.

The role of the Reserve may be,

(a) Counter-attack in the Brigade front area, or in the areas of Brigades on Right and Left.

(b) The formation of a defensive flank on the right of the Brigade, which would be roughly on the line K.27.Cent.- Q.3.Cent. or on the left flank roughly K.20.Cent. - K.25.Cen.

(iv) Seeing that the Brigade is situated in a pronounced salient, the principle of siting defences in depth is more important than ever.

S.O.S. Lines at present are K.11.Cent. and K.23.Cent.

(v) ACKNOWLEDGE.

Captain,
Brigade Major,
199th Infantry Brigade.

11.10.18.
HW.

6th Lan.Fus.
5th Innis.Fus.
6th R.Dublin Fus.
O.C., "A" Coy. M.G.Bn.
199th Inf.Bde.
No.3 Sig.Sec.

198th Inf.Bde.
No.B.M.231.

appendix (8)

1. The situation at 09.00, 11th October, appears to be as follows :-
199th Bde. on our right hold western bank of the LA SELLE River as far as K.29.a.0.0., 6th Lancs.Fus. hold from K.22.d.8.4. to the Church at K.22.d.0.6., and thence along the river to K.22.c.6.9. The bridges at MONTAY are broken, and the river is unfordable. LA FOUILLE Farm is not occupied by the enemy, and was held by our troops last night.
The 33rd Division on our left hold a line running from K.16.b.7.8. - K.16.a.8.7. - K.10.c.5.0. - K.9.a.6.0.

2. 6th Bn. R.Dublin Fus. will relieve 6th Bn. Lancs.Fus. in the outpost line tonight, taking over the dispositions of 6th Lancs.Fus.
On relief 6th Lancs.Fus. will be withdrawn into Bde. reserve in the positions at present occupied by 6th R.Dublin Fus. in K.26.c. Relief to be complete by 22.00 hours
All details of relief will be arranged direct between Commanding Officers concerned.

3. O.C., 5th Innis.Fus. will be responsible for the defence of the main line of resistance on the high ground in K.27.b. and d.

4. O.C., "A" Coy., 25th M.G.Bn. will detail two sections to report to O.C., 5th R.Innis.Fus. by 17.00 hours today, to assist in the defence of the main line of resistance.
Remaining two sections will be in Brigade Reserve in Q.1.a.

5. During the night 11/12th October, O.C., 6th Dublin XXXXXX Fus. will endeavour by means of small patrols to cross the river in K.29.b, K.22.d., and K.16, and penetrate as far as the Railway line, and endeavour to get into touch with troops of 98th Inf.Bde. in K.16.a.
The following localities will be patrolled by 6th R.Dublin Fus:-
(a) LA FOUILLE Farm, and to get into touch with 2nd Bn. Argyle and Sutherland Highlanders.
(b) West bank of the river in K.29.a. and K.28.d. to get into touch with troops of 199th Inf.Bde.

6. There will be a minimum of movement in the forward area.

Captain,
Brigade Major,
198th Infantry Brigade.

11.10.18.
RV.

"A" Form.
MESSAGES AND SIGNALS.

Army Form C. 2121.
(In pads of 100.)

TO: FEKE Appendix (8)

Sender's Number.	Day of Month.	In reply to Number.	AAA
BM 206	11		

Following message received from 82nd Brigade R.F.A aaa Am moving one 18 pdr and one section 4.5 how forward tonight to K.29.c possibly earlier visibility permits aaa Battery commander will get in touch with OC and engage M.G targets aaa Ends.

From: SUHU

198th Inf.Bde.
No.B.M.231.

6th Lancs.Fus.
5th Innis.Fus.
6th R.Dublin Fus.

Reference my B.M.231 of todays date.

The relief of 6th Lancs.Fus., by 6th R.Dublin Fus., is cancelled.

The whole Brigade is being relieved by the South African Brigade.

6th Lancs.Fus., and 5th Innis.Fus., will arrange to have one guide per Platoon, and 6th R.Dublin Fus. one guide per Company, to be at Eastern outskirts of REUMONT at 8.0 p.m. tonight.

6th Lancs Fus. will be relieved by 1 Coy. 1st South African Infantry; 5th Innis.Fus., by 1 Coy. 1st South African Infantry, and 6th R.Dublin Fus. by 4th Bn. South African Infantry.

Captain,
Brigade Major,
198th Infantry Brigade.

11 10.18.
RV.

```
66th Division "G"
6th Lancs. Fus.
5th Innis. Fus.
6th R. Dublin Fus.
"A" Coy. 25th M.G.Bn.
198th L.T.M.B.
Troop Northd. Yeomanry.
No.3 Sig. Sec
82nd Bde. R.F.A.
```

198th Inf. Bde.
No. B.M.234/1.

Appendix (8)

Reference this office No.B.M.234 of todays date, para.(v)

For "S.O.S. Lines at present are K.11.Cent to K.23 Cent", read, "S.O.S. Lines at present are K.11.Cent. to K.18.Cent."

Captain,
Brigade Major,
198th Infantry Brigade.

11.10.18.
RV.

...... Order No.117.

Serial No.	Date.	Unit.	To be relieved by.	Sector.	To proceed to after relief.
1.	11.10.18.	5th Innis.Fus.	4th Bn. South African Inf.	T.27.b.2.9. to T.27.d.9.9.	REUMONT.
2.	do.	6th Lancs.Fus.	2 Coys. 1st South Afn. Inf.	Outpost line in MONTAY.	REUMONT.
3.	do.	198th L.T.M.B.	-	Bde. Reserve.	REUMONT.
4.	do.	198th Bde.H.Q. & Sigs.	South African Bde H.Q. & Sigs.	Q.1.a.Cent.	REUMONT.

Appendix (8)

11.10.18.
RV.

SECRET.   Appendix (8)   Copy No...3....

198th INFANTRY BRIGADE ORDER No. 117.

11th October, 1918.

1.

1. The 198th Infantry Brigade will be relieved in the left sector of the 66th Divisional front by 4th South African Battalion, and 2 Coy, 1st South African Battalion, in accordance with attached relief table.

2. Troops of Northumberland Hussars will come under the South African Brigade.

3. Defence Scheme and any maps showing dispositions will be handed over. All other maps will be retained by units.

4. 6th R.Dublin Fus. will not be relieved and will proceed by march route to Camp in Q.7. Head of column will not pass cross roads K.33.a.8.5. until last Coy. of 2nd Coy. S.A. Infantry is clear of cross roads. *troops of*

5. Guides will be sent in accordance with this office No.B.M.231 of this afternoon. *issued*

7. 100 yards distance will be allowed between platoons.

8. On arrival in RUEMONT Area, Brigade will be at 2 hours notice.

9. Completion of relief will be/reported to this office by the code words "HORSE". *"EXPEDITE LOCATION RETURN"*   *immediately*

10. Brigade Headquarters will close at Q.1.a.Cent. on completion of relief, and open at RUEMONT on arrival.

11. ACKNOWLEDGE.

Captain,
Brigade Major,
198th Infantry Brigade.

11.10.18.
Time.........

DISTRIBUTION.

6th Lancs. Fus.	Copy	No.1.
5th Innis. Fus.	"	No.2.
6th R.Dublin Fus.	"	No.3.
South African Bde.	"	No.4.
198th L.T.M.B.	"	No.5.
O.C. "A" Coy M.G.Bn.	"	No.6.
Northd. Hussars.	"	No.7.
66th Division "G"	"	No.8.
Staff Captain.	"	No.9.
War Diary.	"	No.10, 11,12.
Office.	"	No.13,14.

Appendix Ⓘ

6th Lancs. Fus.
5th Innis. Fus.
6th R. Dublin Fus.
198th L.T.M.B.

198th Inf. Bde.
No. B.M. 239.

Following from Army Commander begins aaa Will you please convey to the 66th and 25th Divisions my warm thanks for their gallantry and determination in dirving back the enemy yesterday aaa I wish to congratulate the Corps and Divl. Staffs also on their success aaa All Staff arrangements particularly the Intelligence have worked most satisfactorily and the artillery have done some most excellent work in getting forward their guns aaa Ends aaa The Corps Commander adds his congratulations to the above.

A. Hunter B.
~~Captain~~,
~~Brigade Major~~,
198th Infantry Brigade.

11.10.18.
RHW

"A" Form.   Army Form C. 2121
MESSAGES AND SIGNALS.   No. of Message..........

| Prefix....Code....m. | Words | Charge | This message is on a/c of: | Recd. at........m. |
| Office of Origin and Service Instructions. | Sent At....m. To By | | *Approved* Service. (Signature of "Franking Officer.") | Date From By |

TO — ...

Sender's Number.   Day of Month.   In reply to Number.   A A A

[handwritten message, largely illegible, mentions "will move under B D ... platoon ... area ... 2 hours notice ... move to be reported ... move independently ... on receipt of this message"]

From ....
Place ....
Time ....

The above may be forwarded as now corrected.   (Z)
....
Censor.   Signature of Addressor or person authorised to telegraph in his name.
* This line should be erased if not required.

6th Lan.Fus.
5th Innis.Fus.
6th R.Dub.Fus.
"A" Coy. M.G.Bn.
199th Inf.Bde. (for information)

198th Inf.Bde.
No. B.M.229.

Appendix (8)

1. It appears from statements of prisoners, that the enemy does not intend to hold his present positions any length of time.

2. The situation at 00.30, 11th instant, appears to be as follows.
   Troops of 33rd Division are reported to have crossed River SELLE.
   6th Lancs.Fus. hold MONTAY and are not yet East of the River. They are in touch with troops of Kings Liverpool Regt. on their right.

3. It is the intention of the G.O.C. to exploit the success gained today, with the minimum of casualties, by "peaceful penetration", by small patrols.
   It is pointed out that good small patrols can obtain information more rapidly, and are less vulnerable than large patrols
   The Brigade will be disposed forthwith, as follows :-
   6th Lan.Fus., 1 Coy. MONTAY to Bridge, K.22.d.9.5.
   This Coy. will endeavour to get into touch with troops of 33rd Division. Remainder of 6th Lan.Fus., reorganizing in K.27.a. and c.
   5th Innis.Fus., 3 Coys. from Bridge, K.22.d.9.5., along W.bank of the stream to K.29.a.0.0., where they should be in touch with troops of 199th Inf.Bde. 1 Coy. on high ground in K.27.a. and c.
   6th R.Dub.Fus. and 1 section M.G.Bn. will be in Brigade reserve as at present located.
   The Divl.Commdr realizes the hard fighting carried out by the Brigade today, but he wishes it to be pointed out that it is only by "sticking it" a few degrees more than the enemy that we can hope to obtain a decisive result.

Acknowledge

02.15
11.10.18.

Captain,
Brigade Major,
198th Infantry Brigade.

"A" Form.
MESSAGES AND SIGNALS.

Army Form C. 2121.
(In pads of 100.)
No. of Message: 1

Prefix	Code	m	Words	Charge	This message is on a/c of:	Recd. at ___ m.
Office of Origin and Service Instructions.			Sent At ___ m. To ___ By ___		Service. (Signature of "Franking Officer.")	Date ___ From ___ By ___

TO — 5th R. Innis. Fus. / 6th R. Inniskilling Fus. / 6th R. Dublin Fus. / 196 L.T.M.B. / K.B. Bgde. / S.M.B. / 548 Bty R.F.A. / 66 Bgde.

Sender's Number.	Day of Month.	In reply to Number.	AAA
* G.E 21	12		

Regimental Band will precede Brigade March
as under Murphy will today

Unit		Time of passing Starting point
6th R. Dublin Fus		11.00
196 Oak M.G.		11.15
6th Innis Fus		11.30
5th Innis Fus		11.35
196 L.T.M.B.		12.00

Starting point: Road junction P.17.c.8.7.
250 yards distance between platoons.
Advance parties of 1 Officer and 5 O.R.
per battalion & 1 N.C.O. per L.T.M.B.
will report to the Staff Captain

From ___
Place ___
Time ___

The above may be forwarded as now corrected. (Z)

Censor ___ Signature of Addressor or person authorised to telegraph in his name.

* This line should be erased if not required.

"A" Form.
MESSAGES AND SIGNALS.

Army Form C. 2121.
(In pads of 100.)

Sender's Number.	Day of Month.	In reply to Number.	A A A
GE 21	12		

MOPQU C 27.6.7.5
at 10.15

ACKNOWLEDGE

From: 198 Bde
Place:
Time: 09.00

SECRET. Appendix (10) Copy No. 5

198TH INFANTRY BRIGADE ORDER NO. 117.

13th October, 1918.

Reference Sheet, 57b, 1/40/000.
----

1. 198th Infantry Brigade Group, constituted as under, will move by March Route to MARETZ today, the 13th inst:-

Unit.	Time of passing Starting Point.
5th R. Innis. Fus.	09.00.
6th Lancs. Fus.	09.15.
198th Inf. Bde. H.Q.	09.30.
6th R. Dublin Fus.	09.35.
198th L.T.M.B.	10.00.

Starting Point - Cross Roads P.26.d.8.2.

Transport will march in rear of their own units.
50 yards between platoons - 50 yards between every un vehicles

2. Advance parties of one officer and five O.R. will be at the Church, MARETZ, at 10.00 today to meet the Staff Captain.

3. Brigade H.Q. will close at MAUROIS at 09.00, and re-open at MARETZ on arrival.

4. ACKNOWLEDGE.

Captain,
Brigade Major,
198th Infantry Brigade.

Issued through Signals at ..05.00..

DISTRIBUTION.

Copy No.		
" "	1.	66th Division, "G".
" "	2.	66th Division, "Q".
" "	3.	6th Lancs. Fus.
" "	4.	5th R. Innis. Fus.
" "	5.	6th R. Dublin Fus.
" "	6.	198th L.T.M.B.
" "	7.	2/2nd Field Ambulance.
" "	8.	545 Coy., A.S.C.
" "	9.	B.T.O.
" "	10.	Staff Captain.
" "	11.	199th Infantry Brigade.
" "	12.	South African Brigade.
" "	13,14,15.	War Diary.
" "	16,17,18.	File.

SECRET.   Appendix (10)   Copy No. 3

109TH INFANTRY BRIGADE ORDER NO.121.

16th Oct.1918.

1. The following re-adjustments of the Brigade front will take place tonight in accordance with this office R.K.64. (Issued to Battalions only).

    109th Infantry Brigade will take over RED Line now held by 6th Lancs.Fus. from K.36.Cent. - L.36.a.0.9 This relief will be carried out by 9th Innsk.Regt., relief to commence as soon as possible after dusk and to be complete by 22.52, 16th October, 1918.
    Details of relief to be arranged direct between Commanding Officers concerned.

2. Immediately on completion of above relief, 6th Lancs.Fus. will take over RED Line in K.36.Cent. - K.6.b.6.0. from 2nd Bn.R.Dublin Fus. of 149th Inf Bde.   Details of relief to be arranged direct between Commanding Officers concerned.

3. Boundaries will be amended as follows :-
    Divisional
    Southern/Boundary, Q.6.b.6.0. - Q.6.a.0.0. - along Railway to Q.4.d.4.0. - Q.3.b.8.9. Railway exclusive to 66th Division.
    Dividing line between 109th Inf.Bde. and 149th Inf. Bde., will be , K.36.Cent. - K.36.c.5.3.- along CAMBRAI Road - through LE CATEAU, all inclusive to 109th Inf.Bde.

4. 6th Lancs.Fus. will report completion of relief by 9th Manchester Regt. by the Code word "PLUM". 6th Lancs.Fus. will report completion of relief as ordered in para.2., by the Code word "APPLE."

5. Headquarters, 2nd R.Dub.Fus. are at Q.2.c.9.6
   and Q.B.2. have been instructed to arrange officer OAS.2.F.8
   at K.35.d.44. to arrange details of relief.

6. 9th R.Innis.Fus. are moving to RAILWAY TRIANGLE, in accordance with orders already issued to them.

7. ACKNOWLEDGE.

                                            A.Eden
                                            Captain,
                                            Brigade Major,
                                            109th Infantry Brigade.

Issued through Signals at...22.10...

DISTRIBUTION.

    66th Division "G"   Copy No.1.
    6th Lancs.Fus.   "   No.2.
    2nd R.Dub.Fus.   "   No.3.
    9th R.Innis.Fus.   "   No.4.
    110th Inf.Bde.   "   No.5.
    149th Inf.Bde.   "   No.6.
    File.   "   No.7.
    197 T.M.B   "   No.8.

"A" Form.
MESSAGES AND SIGNALS.

Army Form C. 2121.
(In pads of 100.)

TO: 6 R Dublin Fus.

Sender's Number.	Day of Month.	In reply to Number.	AAA
Bm q.	15	—	

You will be prepared to move up at 1000 hours tomorrow 16th.

From 198 Inf Bde
Place HQ

"A" Form
MESSAGES AND SIGNALS.

Prefix...... Code........ m.	Words.	Charge.	This message is on a/c of:	Recd. at........ m.
Office of Origin and Service Instructions.	Sent			Date
	At........ m.		*Spencer* Service.	From (11)
	To........		(Signature of "Franking Officer.")	By
	By........			

TO { *[illegible addressees]* }

Sender's Number.	Day of Month.	In reply to Number.	AAA
BX151	15		

The Corps Commander is arriving about 10.30. He wishes to see COs & some of the men in billets. The BGC will meet him in front of the following H.Q's.
      Lancs Fus
      R Innis Fus
      R D.F.

Will COs please be
      Lancs Fus at Bde HQ.
      R Innis Fus
                    at W63central R F
      R D.F. at road jn U6d21.

The Corps Commander cannot stay long as he has other troops to visit.

From   SWHW
Place
Time   0907

The above may be forwarded as now corrected. (Z)

Censor.   Signature of Addressee or person authorised to telegraph in his name.

SECRET.   Copy No. 5

PRELIMINARY INSTRUCTIONS IN CONNECTION WITH

198th Infantry Brigade Order No. 120.

16th Oct., 1918.

Reference Sheet, 57b,1/40,000.

Appendix (12)

1. 198th Infantry Brigade will relieve the 9th Gloucester Regt., 2nd Bn,. South African Infantry and South African Brigade H.Q. immediately after dusk on 16.10.18 in accordance with attached Relief Table.

2. Units will carry out reconnaissances forthwith. Arrangements for guides will be made direct between units concerned.

3. Brigade H.Q. will open at Q.7.a.7.4 at 18.00 tonight.

4. ACKNOWLEDGE.

                                             Captain,
                                          Brigade Major,
                                      198th Infantry Brigade.

Issued through Signals at 16.40

DISTRIBUTION (Overleaf).

DISTRIBUTION.

Copy	No.	1.	66th Division, "G".
"	"	2.	66th Division, "Q".
"	"	3.	6th Lancs. Fus.
"	"	4.	5th R. Innis. Fus.
"	"	5.	6th R. Dublin Fus.
"	"	6.	198th L.T.M.B.
"	"	7.	South African Brigade.
"	"	8.	199th Infantry Brigade.
"	"	9.	Staff Captain.
"	"	10.	No. 3 Sig. Sec.

RELIEF TABLE.

Serial No.	Unit.	From.	To.	Relieving.	Remarks.
1.	~~H.Q. & 2 Coys.~~ 5th Innis. Fus. *less 2 coys*	REUMONT.	Line - Left Sub-sector.	9 Glouc. R.	Head of column to pass starting point at 17.00.
2.	1 Coy., 6th Innis. Fus.	do.	Front Line in Q.8.	1 Coy., 2nd S.A.Inf.	
3.	1 Coy., 5th Innis. Fus.	do.	Q.7.b.	-	-
4.	~~2 Coys.,~~ 6th RDF. *less 2 coys*	do.	Front Line in K.33.c. and d. & K.34.c	2 Coys., 2nd S.A.Inf.	Head of column to pass starting point at 17.30
5.	2 Coys., 6th R.DF.	do.	Q.2.	-	-
6.	6 Lancs. Fus.	do.	Q.7.a. & c.	-	Head of column to pass starting pt. at 18.00.
7.	198 Bde. H.Q. & Signals.	do.	Q.7~~.c.& d.~~ a.7.4	S.A.Brigade & Signals.	Head of column to pass starting point at 17.30.

Starting Point - P.12.c.5.2. 100 yards distance between platoons. 198th L.T.M.B. will be attached to 6th R.D.F. and will move in accordance with orders to be issued by 6th R.D.F.

"A" Form
MESSAGES AND SIGNALS.

Army Form C. 2121 (in pads of 100).

TO: 6 RDF
66 Bde G

Sender's Number: HX161
Day of Month: 16.

AAA

(1) 198 Inf Bde are given the task of mopping up LE CATEAU.

(2) This task will be undertaken by 6 RDF, who will employ two Companies for the purpose in the first instance.

(3) These Coys will cross the R SELLE by bridges to be thrown within night 16/17. They will cross at O+3 hrs. Should the battle proceed according to plan. O.C. 6 RDF will send a liaison officer to be at 3A Bde HQ in reserve in K 27 c from 22.00 hrs 16th. This officer will keep OC 6 RDF

"A" Form
MESSAGES AND SIGNALS.

Army Form C. 2121
(in pads of 100).

| TO | Sheet 2 | Appendix | 12 |

Sender's Number.	Day of Month.	In reply to Number.	AAA
HX 161	16		

informed as to the situation
& as to when the bridges are
sufficiently clear of SA Bde
for the 2 Coys to cross.

(4) 2nd Army to afford as much
protection as possible to SA
Bde. there two Coys 5 hmg
following close in rear will
turn off for their tasks.

(5) Mopping up will be
carried out methodically
by bounds, the pressure
being applied from the N &
NE.

(6) When the town is sufficiently

"A" Form
MESSAGES AND SIGNALS.

Army Form C. 2121 (in pads of 100).

TO { Sheet 3 Appendix (12)

Sender's Number.	Day of Month.	In reply to Number.	AAA
AX161	16		

cleared. The two Coys 6 R.D.F. in Q.34 will link up with the mopping up Coy, & the Eastern outskirts will be put in a state of defence.

(7) Speed in clearing prisoners is Essential

(8) No time will be lost in establishing the defences mentioned in para 6.

(9) 2 Stokes Mortars with A Company

"A" Form
MESSAGES AND SIGNALS.
Army Form C. 2121
(in pads of 100).

TO { Sheet 4 Offensive (12)

Sender's Number: HX161
Day of Month: 16
AAA

M. Company up Coz
10. Attention is drawn to
"Notes From plan of
le Plateau"

Acknowledge.

From: SUHD
Time: 17.00

Appendix 12

Amended MARCH TABLE, to accompany 198th Infantry Brigade Order No.119.

Serial No.	Unit	From	To	Route	Time of passing starting point
1.	6th R.Dub.Fus.	MARETZ	REUMONT	LAMROIS-REUMONT	10.00
2.	6th Lancs.Fus.	do.	do.	do.	10.10
3.	198th Inf.Bde. H.Q. & Sigs.	do.	do.	do.	10.20
4.	5th R.Innis.Fus.	do.	do.	do.	10.25
5.	198th L.T.M.B.	do.	do.	do.	10.35
6.	198th Inf.Bde. Transport.	do.	do.	do.	10.50

Distances.   50 yards between platoons.

1. Starting point, Fork Roads V.1.d.1.9.

2. Transport will not halt on the march, but will go straight through to its destination.

3. Units are reminded to send a runner who knows the exact location of their Headquarters, to Brigade H.Q. immediately on arrival in the REUMONT Area.

16.10.18.

Amended MARCH TABLE, to accompany 198th Infantry Brigade Order No.119.

Serial No.	Unit.	From.	To.	Route	Time of passing starting point
1	6th R.Dub.Fus.	MARETZ.	REUMONT.	MAUROIS-REUMONT.	10.00.
2.	6th Lancs.Fus.	do.	do.	do.	10.10.
3.	198th Inf.Bde. H.Q. & Sigs.	do.	do.	do.	10.20.
4.	5th R.innis.Fus.	do.	do.	do.	10.25.
5.	198th L.T.M.B.	do.	do.	do.	10.30.
6.	198th Inf.Bde. Transport.	do.	do.	do.	10.35.

Distances.   50 yards between platoons.

1. Starting point, Fork Roads V.1.6.1.9.

2. Transport will not halt on the march, but will go straight through to its destination.

3. Units are reminded to send a runner who knows the exact location of their Headquarters, to Brigade H.Q. immediately on arrival in the REUMONT Area.

16.10.18.

SECRET.   Appendix 12   Copy No...4.

198TH INFANTRY BRIGADE ORDER No.119.

October 16th, 1918

Reference Map 57b. 1/40,000.

1. The 198th Infantry Brigade Group will move to REUMONT to-day, in accordance with the attached March Table.

2. Transport will march separately, under orders of the Brigade Transport Officer.

3. Advance parties will meet the Staff Captain at the Fork Roads P.17.c.9.8. at 10.00.

4. ACKNOWLEDGE.

Captain,
Brigade Major,
198th Infantry Brigade.

Issued through Signals at............

DISTRIBUTION.

66th Division "G"	Copy No.1.
6th Lancs.Fus.	" No.2.
5th R.Innis.Fus.	" No.3.
6th R.Dublin Fus.	" No.4.
198th L.T.M.B.	" No.5.
No.3. Sig.Sec.	" No.6.
Staff Captain.	" No.7.
War Diary.	" No.8.9.10.
Files	" No.11.12.13.14.
B.T.O.	" No 13
199 Bde	" No 14
SA-15 de	" No 15

MARCH TABLE, to accompany 198th Infantry Brigade Order No.119.

Serial No.	Unit.	From.	To.	Route	Time of passing starting po...
1	6th R.Dub.Fus.	MARETZ.	REUMONT.	MAUROIS-REUMONT.	10.00.
2.	6th Lancs.Fus.	do.	do.	do.	10.15.
3.	198th Inf.Bde. H.Q. & Sigs.	do.	do.	do.	10.20.
4.	5th R.innis.Fus.	do.	do.	do.	10.25.
5.	198th L.T.M.B.	do.	do.	do.	10.30.
6.	198th Inf.Bde. Transport.	do.	do.	do.	10.35.

Distances. 50 yards between platoons.

1. Starting point, Fork Roads V.1.6.1.9.

2. Transport ill not halt on the march, but will go straight through to its destination.

3. Units are reminded to send a runner who knows the exact location of their Headquarters, to Brigade H.Q. immediately on arrival in the REUMONT Area.

16.10.18.

"A" Form
MESSAGES AND SIGNALS.

Army Form C. 2121
(In pads of 100)

No. of Message..........

Prefix......Code......m.	Words.	Charge.	This message is on a/c of:	Recd. at ....m.
Office of Origin and Service Instructions	Sent		*Offensive* Service.	Date (12)
....	At........m.			From........
....	To........			By........
	By........		(Signature of "Franking Officer.")	

TO { M A B E D H Q
     R MSN

Sender's Number.	Day of Month.	In reply to Number.	AAA
*	16		

6RDF will move to REYMONT at 0950 today in following order D A B C HQ aaa 50 yds interval between echelons aaa transport will march separately under orders of BSTO

7 Gladder Lyt

From	6RDF
Place	
Time	0830

The above may be forwarded as now corrected. (Z)
....
Censor. Signature of Addresser or person authorized to telegraph in his name.
* This line should be erased if not required.

16 Appendix (12)

Reference 199TH INFANTRY BRIGADE ORDER No.190.

In the event of move forward, Brigade Axis of liaison will be, Brigade - track running from Q.1.d.9.9 - Q.2.d.1.3. - Q.3.c. - Q.3.a. - Q.3.b. - Q.4.a.3.5.

Captain,
Brigade Major,
199th Infantry Brigade.

15.10.18.
RV.

Copies to all recipients of 199th Infantry Brigade Order No. 190.

6th R.Dublin Fus.
5th R.Innis.Fus.
5th Lancs.Fus.
198th L.T.M.B.
S.A.Brigade.
199th Inf.Bde.
O.C., 25th M.G.Coy.
66th Division "G".
No.3. Sig.Sec.

Appendix (12)

No.1.
ADDENDUM TO 198TH INFANTRY BRIGADE ORDER No.120

1. It has been decided that even if the Division on our right do not reach their first objective, that the South African Brigade will take the Railway Embankment in K.36.and 30.

2. The code word that this operation will take place in lieu of the bigger operation as at present planned, will be "REFUSAL".

3. In the event of "REFUSAL" being sent it is more important than ever that 6th R.Dublin Fus. should put their two mopping-up Coys in close behind S.A.Brigade. Close liaison will be maintained with this in view.

4. In the event of "REFUSAL" being sent 6th R.Dublin Fus.will establish a strong point at cross roads Q.4.b.4.0. in addition to those detailed para.13 of Order No.120.

5. In the event of the enemy withdrawing from LE CATEAU, before either of the operations referred to above, 6th R.Dublin Fus. will push patrols through the town and occupy the eastern edge.

6. ACKNOWLEDGE.

Captain,
Brigade Major,
198th Infantry Brigade.

16.10.18.
RV.

Secret   Copy No. 3

Administrative Instruction issued
in reference to 198 Infantry Brigade
Order No 120
                              Appendix 12

1. **Medical Arrangements**

Advanced Dressing Station and Walking Wounded Collecting Post is established at MAUROIS.

Bearer Relay Posts are established at every 1000 yards from MAUROIS to Cross Roads K.33.a.

Motor Ambulances now run as far as Road junction Q.1.b.10.4. As soon as the situation permits, they will run further forward.

2. **Prisoners of War.**

The DAPM will establish a P of W cage in the vicinity of the church at REUMONT, P.7.b.6.8. Battalions will be responsible for conducting prisoners of war to Brigade Headquarters.

Appendix 12

3. **Stragglers Posts**

Stragglers Posts are established as follows:

Road Junction	P	18	a. 4	2
Cross Roads	P	17	b. 8	5
Road Junction	J	35	c. 1	7
Cross Roads	J	30	b. 2	6

4. **Transport**

All transport will remain fully loaded and ready to move at short notice. Baggage wagons will remain with units.

5. **Acknowledge.**

16.10.18

MJ...
Captain,
Staff Captain
198 Infantry Bde.

Copies to:
(1) 6 Lancs. Fus.
(2) 5 R Inns. Fus.
(3) 6 R.D.b. Fus.
(4) 198 L.T.M.B.
(5) South African Bde.
(6) 199 Inf. Bde.
(7) FILE

A B C D H

① b R. D. T. will move forward at 17.20 in following order
b. B A D H Q

② 100 yds distance between platoons

③ Head of Coy to be at X road REUMONT P.17.B.8.5 at 17.20

④ Officer should report to adjutant now for B.O.2 time

S. Monaghan Capt
16/10/18 Adjt 6 N.F.

6 R.D.F.

ORDER OF BATTLE. Offended (12)

The presumed order of battle, and Divisional Sectors opposite the Corps front are as follows:-

30th Division - N. boundary K.9.d.
44th R. DIV. - K.9.d to K.29.c.0.0.
17th R. DIV. - K.29.c.00 to Q.16.a.0.0.
204th DIV - Q.16.a.00 to Southern Boundary.

There are still possibly elements of the 2nd Cyclist Brigade reinforcing opposite this front.

Thos. A. G. Prey
Capt.
B.I.O.
198. Inf. Bde.

14-10-18.

SECRET

Afterwards (12)

Copy No. 11

198TH INFANTRY BRIGADE ORDER No. 120.

16th October, 1918.

Reference Sheet, 57b., 1/40,000.
----

1. To maintain pressure on the enemy and to increase the difficulties of his withdrawal the 66th Division and Divisions on the right will attack on the 17th instant, at an hour to be notified later.

2. The attack on the 66th Divisional front will be carried out by the South African Brigade - having as objective :- Red Line K.29.a.1.8 - K.29.central - K.36.d.0.5.

3. At Zero the 198th Infantry Brigade will be disposed as follows in accordance with 198th Infantry Brigade Instruction No. 1.:-

    198th Infantry Brigade H.Q.   Q.7.a.7.4.
    5th R. Innis. Fus. H.Q.   K.28.d.0.0.
      2 Coys. Front Line.   K.22.c. and d.
      1 Coy. Front Line.   Q.8.
      1 Coy.   Q.7.b.
    6th R.Dub. Fus. H.Q.   K.36.b.5.5.
      2 Coys. Front Line.   K.34.c., K.36.c. & d.
      2 Coys.   Q.2.
    6th Lancs. Fus.
       (in Divl. Reserve).   Q.7.a. & c.

4. The 6th R. Dublin Fus. will be responsible for the mopping up of LE CATEAU, inside the area :-
Railway Crossing, Q.4.b.4.1 - Bridge Q.4.b.15.90. - River SELLE to Junction K.28.d.8.1. - Road K.28.d.9.1. - K.35.c.9.3. - Southern Boundary of Divisional front K.35.a.9.3. - Q.4.b.4.1.

Appendix (12)

5. O.C., 6th R. Dublin Fus. will effect this by passing two Companies of Infantry across the SELLE at Zero plus three hours, by bridges to be constructed between K.28.d.8.1 and K.29.a.1.3, and by entering the village from the Northeast East.

7. Detailed instructions for mopping up LE CATEAU will be issued to 6th R. Dublin Fus.

8. O.C., 6th R. Dublin Fus. will detail a liaison officer to report at H.Q., South African Brigade in K.27.c. immediately on receipt of this order.

9. This officer will keep O.C., 6th R. Dublin Fus. informed of the situation on South African Brigade front.

10. BOUNDARIES.

66th Divisional Boundaries are as follows :-

Northern Boundary - P.6.central - K.21.central - Road junction K.23.a.2.1 (exclusive to 66th Division).

Southern Boundary - Road P.18.b.5.5 - Q.9.c.8.4 - Q.4.b.4.0 (road exclusive to 66th Division, thence a straight line to road junction K.35.d.0.3 (inclusive to 66th Division) thence along road through K.35.d.6.0 to Cross Roads K.36.d.7.9.

11. When LE CATEAU has been cleared of the enemy 6th R. Dublin Fus. will establish posts on the Eastern edge of the town paying particular attention to in

    Railway in Q.5.a.
    Road Crossing, K.35.c.
    Suburbs, K.35.a.2.7.
    Factory, K.28.d.60.30.

12. Two Companies 6th R. Dublin Fus. holding the line of the river in K.34.c. will be available as Support to this line.

13. C.R.E. is arranging for the following strong points to be constructed.

/ (a)

-3-

(a) K.29.c.8.9 and about K.23.c.1.2 immediately after the capture of these places by the infantry.

(b) K.35.c.9.3 and K.35.d.0.0.

14. Two Companies 5th R. Inniskilling Fus. in Q.7.b. and Q.8 will be prepared to take over the line West of the River in K.34 on receipt of orders to be issued direct by Brigade.

15. 6th Lanc. Fus. will be in Divisional Reserve.

16. Eight Vickers Guns are being allotted to the Brigade for the defence of LE CATEAU and will be placed at the disposal of 6th R. Dublin Fus.

17. Units are reminded that they will not be the foremost infantry on the 17th inst. The flares will therefore NOT be lit by them.

18. Four guns No. 1 Special Co., R.E. under Lieut. C.F. HARRY will smoke the area round BAILLON FARM and xxx xxxx northwards from Zero plus 2 hour till Zero plus 129 minutes. From Zero plus one hour until the assaulting infantry is formed up East of the SELLE, a proportion of smoke will be mixed in the bombardment of the North Eastern and Eastern outskirts of LE CATEAU, in the area between the SELLE and the Railway North of BAILLON FARM, and on the slopes of the spur N.E. of MONTAY.

19. An officer representative from each Battalion will call at Brigade H.Q. as soon as possible after 19.30 hours 16th October with a watch, which will be synchronised.

20. Brigade H.Q. will open at Q.7.a.7.4 at 17.30 16th inst.

21. ACKNOWLEDGE.

Captain,
Brigade Major,
198th Infantry Brigade.

Issued through Signals at 13.30.

DISTRIBUTION.

66th Division, "G".	Copy No.	1.
66th Division, "Q".	" "	2.
6th Lancs. Fus.	" "	3.
6th R. Dublin Fus.	" "	4.
5th R. Innis. Fus.	" "	5.
198th L.T.M.B.	" "	6.
South African Brigade.	" "	7.
199 Infantry Brigade.	" "	8.
Staff Captain.	" "	9.
No. 3 Signal Section.	" "	10.

SECRET   Copy No. 5

198TH INFANTRY BRIGADE ORDER No. 120.

16th October, 1918.

Reference Sheet, 57b., 1/40,000.
----

1. To maintain pressure on the enemy and to increase the difficulties of his withdrawal the 66th Division and Divisions on the right will attack on the 17th instant, at an hour to be notified later.

2. The attack on the 66th Divisional front will be carried out by the South African Brigade - having as objective :- Red Line K.29.a.1.8 - K.29.central - K.36.d.0.5.

3. At Zero the 198th Infantry Brigade will be disposed as follows in accordance with 198th Infantry Brigade Instruction No. 1.:-

198th Infantry Brigade H.Q.	Q.7.a.7.4.
5th R. Innis. Fus. H.Q.	K.28.d.0.0.
2 Coys. Front Line.	K.29.c. and d.
1 Coy. Front Line.	Q.8.
1 Coy.	Q.7.b.
6th R.Dub. Fus. H.Q.	K.36.b.5.5.
2 Coys. Front Line.	K.34.c., K.36.c. & d.
2 Coys.	Q.2.
6th Lancs. Fus.	
(in Divl. Reserve).	Q.7.a. & c.

4. The 6th R. Dublin Fus. will be responsible for the mopping up of LE CATEAU, inside the area :-
Railway Crossing, Q.4.b.4.1 - Bridge Q.4.b.15.90. - River SELLE to Junction K.28.d.8.1. - Road K.28.d.9.1. - K.35.c.9.3. - Southern Boundary of Divisional front K.35.a.9.3. - Q.4.b.4.1.

6. O.C., 6th R. Dublin Fus. will effect this by passing two Companies of Infantry across the SELLE at Zero plus three hours, by bridges to be constructed between K.28.d.8.1 and K.29.a.4.5, and by entering the village from the Northeast.

7. Detailed instructions for mopping up LE CATEAU will be issued to 6th R. Dublin Fus.

8. O.C., 6th R. Dublin Fus. will detail a liaison officer to report at H.Q., South African Brigade in K.27.c. immediately on receipt of this order.

9. This officer will keep O.C., 6th R. Dublin Fus. informed of the situation on South African Brigade front.

10. BOUNDARIES.

  66th Divisional Boundaries are as follows :-

Northern Boundary - P.6.central - K.21.central - Road junction K.23.a.2.1 (exclusive to 66th Division).

Southern Boundary - Road P.18.b.5.5 - Q.9.c.8.4. Q.4.b.4.0 (road exclusive to 66th Division, thence a straight line to road junction K.35.d.0.3 (inclusive to 66th Division) thence along road through K.35.d.6.0 to Cross Roads K.36.d.7.8.

11. When LE CATEAU has been cleared of the enemy 6th R. Dublin Fus. will establish posts on the Eastern edge of the town paying particular attention to

  Railway in Q.5.a.
  Road Crossing, K.35.c.
  Suburbs, K.35.a.2.7.
  Factory, K.28.d.60.30.

12. Two Companies 6th R. Dublin Fus. holding the line of the river in K.34.c. will be available as Support to this line.

13. C.R.E. is arranging for the following strong points to be constructed.

-3-

 (a) K.29.c.8.9 and about K.33.c.1.2 immediately after the capture of these places by the infantry.

 (b) K.35.c.9.3 and K.35.d.0.8.

14. Two Companies 5th R. Inniskilling Fus. in Q.7.b. and Q.8 will be prepared to take over the line West of the River in K.34 on receipt of orders to be issued direct by Brigade.

15. 6th Lancs. Fus. will be in Divisional Reserve.

16. Eight Vickers Guns are being allotted to the Brigade for the defence of LE CATEAU and will be placed at the disposal of 6th R. Dublin Fus.

17. Units are reminded that they will not be the foremost infantry on the 17th inst. The flares will therefore NOT be lit by them.

18. Four guns No. 1 Special Co., R.E. under Lieut. C.F. HARRY will smoke the area round BAILLON FARM and northwards from Zero plus 1 hour till Zero plus 120 minutes. From Zero plus one hour until the assaulting infantry is formed up East of the SELLE, a proportion of smoke will be mixed in the bombardment of the North Eastern and Eastern outskirts of LE CATEAU, in the area between the SELLE and the Railway North of BAILLON FARM, and on the slopes of the spur N.E. of MONTAY.

19. An officer representative from each Battalion will call at Brigade H.Q. as soon as possible after 19.30 hours 16th October with a watch, which will be synchronised.

20. Brigade H.Q. will open at Q.7.a.7.4 at 17.30 16th inst.

21. <u>ACKNOWLEDGE</u>.

         Captain,
         Brigade Major,
         198th Infantry Brigade.

Issued through Signals at 13.30.

DISTRIBUTION.

66th Division, "G".	Copy No.	1.
66th Division, "Q".	" "	2.
6th Lancs. Fus.	" "	3.
6th R. Dublin Fus.	" "	4.
5th R. Innis. Fus.	" "	5.
198th L.T.M.B.	" "	6.
South African Brigade.	" "	7.
199 Infantry Brigade.	" "	8.
Staff Captain.	" "	9.
No. 3 Signal Section.	" "	10.

"A" Form
MESSAGES AND SIGNALS.

Prefix......Code......m.	Words.	Charge.	This message is on a/c of:	Recd. at......m.
Office of Origin and Service Instructions.	Sent			Date......
	At......m.		......Service.	From......
	To......		(Signature of "Franking Officer.")	By......
	By......			

TO

Sender's Number.	Day of Month.	In reply to Number.	AAA
HX 163	16		

C Co 23rd MG in trenches at
the disposal of O.C. 23rd Bn for
the defence of LE CATELET when
captured.

No less than 4 guns will
be kept to attain detail.
Provision for the Also to have
been supplied to C Co &
one platoon is attached ...
to D Co 23rd M.G. only)
OC C Co 23rd M.G ... at 6 Ruc
Jug at K33 b 5.5 before zero.

From   SOHP
Place   ...
Time   ...

This above may be forwarded as now corrected. (Z)

ADDENDUM No.2. to 108TH INFANTRY BRIGADE ORDER NO.120.

Para.4. line 6.   For "K.35.a.9.3." read "K.35.c.9.3."

Para.10.   line 2. amend Northern Boundary to read :-
"P.6.Cent.
K.26.Cent.
K.21.Cent. N.   Approved 12
                C.O."

Para.11. line 5. should be amended to read :-
"Road Crossing K.35.c.9.3."

Para.15. should read :-   "1 Coy is being allotted
to the Brigade for the defence of LE CATEAU,
and will be placed at the disposal of 6th R.
Dublin Fus."

ACKNOWLEDGE.

16.10.18.

Captain,
Brigade Major.
108th Infantry Brigade.

Copies to all recipients of Order No.120.

"A" Form
MESSAGES AND SIGNALS.

Army Form C. 2121 (in pads of 100).

Prefix....Code....m. Office of Origin and Service Instructions.	Words	Charge	This message is on a/c of: Sent At....m. To..... By..... Service. (Signature of "Franking Officer.")	Recd. at....m. Date 12 From..... By.....

TO { SA Bde, 6 Rifle Bns, 6 Kings Bns, 198 LTM B, S R [illegible] Bns, 60 Bde ? }

Sender's Number	Day of Month	In reply to Number	AAA
* AX 162	16		

A cable is being laid from Roman Road about Q7a2.6 (To 1 second rifle NE of REUMONT) to 198 Inf Bde HQ in Q7a 7.4.

There is not enough cable to make the line continuous.

The HQ are in an orchard of small trees.

From: [signature]
Place:
Time: 17-00

The above may be forwarded as now corrected. (Z)

Censor. Signature of Addresser or person authorised to telegraph in his name.

Appendix (13)

To OC D Coy 5th R. Innis. Fus
From OC 16 Platoon

Am at present in K.34.D.2.2.
Ref 20,000 sheet 57B NE.
Have got in touch with Sgt Hurlow
of Mr Boyd's Platoon C Coy DUBLINS
he is held up at this point
by enemy Snipers & M.G's firing
from a Southward & Eastward
direction. We have been fired
upon, on trying to get to our
position. Will stay here until
DUBLINS clear situation up, then
I will push out to my allotted
position.

Time 14.00
Place LE CATEAU
Date 17/10/18
By Runner

G. Brown 2/Lt
Comdg 16/Platoon

Message No 1

To OC D Coy
From OC 16 platoon

Appendix (13)

Am under command of Major Luke Dublins. Am mopping up village. Have you any orders?

Time 15 20
Place Le Cateau
Date 17/10/18

LY Brow 2/Lt

To C.O 6th R D F
from O.C D Coy

Herewith report of
2nd Lt Brown i/c of
platoon sent to get
touch with BLACKWATCH
I have repeated the
last message &
given it to the
Orderly

E A J Atkins OC
D Coy

C.O.
6th R.D.F.

To C.O. 6th R.DF
From O.C. D Coy Appendix (13)
5th R.INNIS.FUS

Herewith report of the platoon commander of this coy who went out to keep touch with 013th BLACK WATCH

E A J M Kinsela
O.C D Coy

15.50
by runner
17.10.18.

O.C. Oppsin ⑬
6th R.D.Fus.

We have crossed river and are pushing on to join "C" Coy.

I have a post on River to collect Prisoners.

From
O.C.
"A" Coy.

Appendix 13

To: C.O. 6th R.D.F.
From: O.C. D Coy
  5th R Innis. Fus

My outpost platoon is dug in at ~~Kingsley~~ K 34. c. 2. 3.

Reserve platoon is 100x W. of your H.Q. on main roads from LE CATEAU — INCHY.

Platoon to gain touch with 13th BLACK WATCH left at 12.10. No report yet received.

E A J Atkins Lt
OC D Coy

"A" Form
MESSAGES AND SIGNALS.

Army Form C. 2121
(in pads of 100).

TO: 6 Lancs Fus
6 R Dub Fus

Sender's Number: HX 1722
Day of Month: 17.

AAA

(1) 6 Lancs Fus will send forward on receipt of this message such officers + NCOs as they consider necessary to reconnoitre with a view

(a) To taking over line from R Dub Fus - Line now established K35 central - Road Rly crossing K35c 9.3 - Q4 6.3 - River — with advanced posts pushed forward to road jn K35d 6.0.

(b) To assemble on approximately front K35 central - K35 C 7.0 for an attack on the objective K36d 3.7 & K36a 00.95 (cross roads).

(2) In the event of (a) 198 L T.M.B. + the 2th M.G. Co now with 6 R Dub Fus will be to 6th LF aaa also a

"A" Form
MESSAGES AND SIGNALS.

Army Form C. 2121 (in pads of 100).

Appendix 13

TO: 2

Sender's Number: A× 1722

AAA

detachment of 1 off +10 OR of 431 Fd
Coy RE will report to OC b for leaving
present position for the purpose of
constructing strong point about
K35 c 9.3 – K35 d 6.0

(3) In the event of (b) 198 LTMB will
return into Bde Reserve – D Co 25th
Bn MG Corps will dispose 12 guns for
the defence of LE CATEAU and attach
4 guns to 6 LF for their use in
consolidation of objective. Orders
to this effect will be given direct
by OC 6 R[?] [?] detacht
RE will NOT go forward with
6 LF

(4) Whether (a) or (b) is the task of
6 LF depends on whether Rly△

"A" Form
MESSAGES AND SIGNALS.

Army Form C. 2121
(in pads of 100).

No. of Message..................

TO: Offrs AA (3)

Day of Month: 17.

in Q5 is taken tonight by
50th Div or not
(5) The orderly who takes this
message will be available
to guide reconn'tring party of
6 RF to HQ R Dub Fus &
will also take this message
to 6 R Dub Fus — After
delivering his message to
R Dub Fus he will return
to Bde HQ
(6) All arrangements for
guides etc will be made
direct by reconn'tring party
with 6 R Dub Fus direct
(7) ACKNOWLEDGE

From SJ HQ

"A" Form.
MESSAGES AND SIGNALS.

Army Form C. 2121.
(In pads of 100.)

TO: 6 Dublin... Offenkid (13)

Sender's Number.	Day of Month.	In reply to Number.	AAA
B.M 46	17		
Attack	by	Div	on
our	right	will	not
late	place	till	21.00
"	new	barrage	any point
and	same	objective	as
Their	consult	all	previous
time	fixed	for	for
attack	by	Division	an
our	right		

From: SWHU
Time: 18.15

MESSAGES AND SIG

Prefix	Code	m	Words	Charge	This message is on a/c of:	Recd. at	m
Office of Origin and Service Instructions.			Sent		Service.	Date	
			At	m.		From	
			To			By	
			By		(Signature of "Franking Officer.")		

TO — 7EKF — appendix (13)

Sender's Number.	Day of Month.	In reply to Number.	AAA
* B.M.48	17		

Heavy artillery are firing
barrage on line of
railway from K.35.C.9.3 to
K.35 central both inclusive
at 20.30 aaa ACKNOWLEDGE.

From SUHU
Place
Time 19.10

"A" Form
MESSAGES AND SIGNALS.

Army Form C. 2121 (in pads of 100).

Prefix....Code....m.	Words	Charge	This message is on a/c of:	Recd. at....m.
Office of Origin and Service Instructions.	Sent			Date..........
	At....m.		.......Service.	From..........
	To.......			
	By		(Signature of "Franking Officer.")	By..........

| TO | 6 Div Inf | Approved | (13) |

Sender's Number.	Day of Month.	In reply to Number.	AAA
HX 1713	17		

Div on right have taken Stn (Q.10)
from 5 to 5.30 there will be a
concentration of Heavy Artillery
on Rly △. At 5.30 Div on right
go for it.

Our leaders are bombarding Rly
embankment from Q.3 central
Southwards from 5.0 till 5.35
or 45 (not quite sure which) at which
time will lift.

Your chance to get S parts of the
town is therefore whilst △ is being
assaulted & our leaders still on
embankment. Forget crossing

From			
Place			
Time			

The above may be forwarded as now corrected. (Z)

Censor. Signature of Addresser or person authorised to telegraph in his name.

* This line should be erased if not required.

"A" Form
MESSAGES AND SIGNALS.

Army Form C. 2121
(in pads of 100).

No. of Message...........

Prefix......Code......m.	Words.	Charge.	This message is on a/c of:	Recd. at........m.
	Sent			
Office of Origin and Service Instructions.	At.......m.		..............Service.	Date..........
....	To.........			From...........
....	By.........		(Signature of "Franking Officer.")	By............

TO   2   Appendix (13)

| Sender's Number. | Day of Month. | In reply to Number. | AAA |

ing at Q35c8.3, directly on
heavies lift - aaa S.African
are going to work down Embankment
from the N - left thus it
should be easier to get the
line given in my HX1712.

rec 17.50 WM

From   SOJHO
Place
Time   1642

The above may be forwarded as now corrected. (X) A Hunter Bde
                                           Signature of Addressor

MESSAGES AND SIGNALS.

TO: 6th Dublin Fus Appendix (13)

Sender's Number	Day of Month	In reply to Number	AAA
B.M. 43	17		

Div on right are not rushing railway triangle at 17.30 but advancing under barrage which starts at 17.45 and finishes with its left just clear of road and railway crossing K.35.c.8.3. at 18.24 aaa Warn platoon pushed forward and seize opportunity to establish forward post on road to K.35.d.6.0. are the left of 5i Div Barrage should be just clear of line O.4.6.3.1 - K.35.c.8.3. South African Bde report that their right now at K.35. central

From: SUHU
Place:
Time: 17.40

H.P. Eden Capt

ACCOUNT OF OPERATIONS.

PART IV.

12th October, 1918 - 12.00 18th October, 1918.

THE CLEARING OF LE CATEAU.

-:-:-:-:-

PART V.

12.00 18th October - 18.00 18th October, 1918

THE ADVANCE TO THE RED LINE.

-:-:-:-:-

PART VI.

18.00 18th October, 1918 - 20th October, 1918.

PATROLS AND RELIEF.

-:-:-:-:-

PART IV.

12th October, 1918 - 12.00 18th October, 1918.

-:-:-:-:-:-

After the relief by South African Brigade, described in Part III, the 198th Infantry Brigade went into Divisional Reserve :- first at REUMONT at 2 hours notice, then at MAUROIS and finally at MARETZ where the Brigade was settled in Billets at 14.00 on 13th October.

The Brigade remained at MARETZ till the morning of the 16th when it moved to REUMONT. Later in the day it moved again and took up positions as follows :-

Unit.	Position.	In relief of.	Remarks.
Brigade H.Q.	Q.7.a.	S.A. Brigade H.Q.	
1 Coy., R. Innis. Fus.	Q.3 & Q.6.	S.A. Brigade.	Front Line posts.
R. Dub. Fus. less 2 Cos.	W. of LE CATEAU.	S.A. Brigade.	

/2 Cos., R. Dub. Fus.

from the road crossing K.35.c.9.3 northwards.
Messages were received from Division authorising the
employment of all the Dublins in this mopping up
(the force had been limited to two Companies at the
outset) and eventually all the Dublins and a platoon
or two of Inniskillings were employed.

At a telephone message from the Divisional
Commander placed 6th Lancs. Fus. at Brigade disposal
with instructions that as 50th Division had taken the
station and triangle, 6th Lancs. Fus. were to cross
the R. SELLE at ST. BENIN or north of it and attack
the objective - road crossing K.35.c.9.3. to
K.35.c.0.5 - with the idea of completing the clearing
of LE CATEAU promptly.

The Battalion was therefore sent off, and
succeeded in passing two companies across the river
at Mins. de Pont Chapelle in Q.9.b. The station
and railway triangle which dominate the valley
entirely were not in our hands. This was reported
by 6th Lancs. Fus. and eventually instructions were
received from Division to withdraw them again into
Divisional Reserve. This was done and completed at
 at the cost of some dozen casualties and a
certain amount of fatigue to the battalion.

The mopping up of LE CATEAU was going on slowly
in the mean-time and section after section of the
town was reported in our hands,- till the whole of
the main town was ours at 17.50 the Faubourg de
Landrecies being however still distinctly German,
and commanded from the Railway Triangle and the
embankment and crossing at K.35.c.9.3.

Throughout the night the situation on our right
at the Railway Triangle and the Station was obscure.
Notification was received of an attack being in
preparation to capture these two points by the
division on our right but this attack was postponed.
Under instructions from Division orders were therefore
issued at 23.45 to the 6th Lancs. Fus. (who were
placed at the disposal of G.O.C. at this time and
ceased to be in Divisional Reserve) to get into touch
with the 6th R. Dublin Fus. and reconnoitre with a

/view to

2 Cos., 6 R.Dub.Fus.	Q.2.central.	–	For clearing LE CATEAU from the N. & N.E. & E.
5 R.Innis.Fus. less 2 Cos.	Roman Road to N.W. end of MONTAY.	9 Glouc. Regt.	Front Line posts.
1 Co., 5 R.Innis.Fus.	Q.7.	–	Brigade Reserve.
Lancs. Fus.	Q.7.	–	Divl. Reserve.
198 L.T.M.B.	With R.Dub.Fus.		For clearing LE CATEAU.

On conclusion of relief, the S.A. Brigade concentrated in the ravines in K.26 and 27 preparatory to forcing the crossing of the SELLE and taking the Red Line K.36.d.o.5 to BAILLON FARM, with a defensive flank to the North.

The two Companies 6th R. Dublin Fus. were to follow close behind them and start mopping up LE CATEAU from the N.E. and E. - when they had made some progress the remainder of 6 R. Dublin Fus. were to press in from the West and finally the Eastern outskirts of the town were to be put in a state of defence.

The 50th Divn. on our right were to take the red dotted line which included the Railway Station and the triangle in Q.5 before the S.A. attack and the mopping up of LE CATEAU were to begin. On their reaching this line the Coy. of 5th R. Innis. Fus. in Q.3 and Q.6 would be unnecessary and the plan was for them and the Coy. in Brigade Reserve to move up and take the place of the Dublins W. of LE CATEAU.

In spite of the 50th Division not getting either the station or triangle, the S.A. attack was launched and the mopping-up Companies of the Dublins were put in. They had considerable difficulty in their task and first one and then the other Company of 5th R. Innis. Fus. were sent up to 6th R. Dublin Fus. so as to release more men of the Dublins for the mopping up of the town - which was urgent as S.A. Brigade were being much troubled by M.G. fire and small counter attacks along the railway

/from the road crossing

view to

(a) Taking over the line from the 6th R. Dublin Fus. and establishing their line from K.33. central - Road and railway crossing K.35.c.9.3 - C.4.b.3.1 - River with advanced posts pushed forward to road junction K.35.d.6.0.

(b) To assemble on approximate front K.35. central - K.35.c.7.0 for an attack on the objective K.36.d.3.7 - Cross Roads K.36.a.00 95.

The task (b) was only to be undertaken in the event of the capture of the railway triangle by the Division on our right.

At 06.50 on the 18th orders were issued for Task (a) to be carried out. During the night and previous to relief the 6th R. Dublin Fus. completed the mopping up of the FAUBOURG de LANDRECIES except that the railway crossing at K.35.c.9.3 could not be captured as long as the enemy held Railway Triangle.

Touch was obtained with the South African Brigade on the railway in K.35.central.

The relief of 6th R. Dublin Fus. by the 6th Lancs. Fus. in LE CATEAU proved very difficult to carry out. The enemy shelled the West end of the town throughout the night with a large proportion of gas shell of all kinds, and the difficulties of relieving posts and patrols scattered all over the town were very great. A mist added to the difficulties of relief. In spite of this the relief was complete shortly after 09.00.

Meanwhile the Division on our right attacked at dawn and captured the Railway Triangle about 06.30.

The 6th Lancs. Fus. immediately got into touch with the 13th Black Watch on their right who carried out this attack and pushed forward and seized the road and railway crossing at K.35.c.9.3.

This position was an extremely strong one and owing to the Railway Triangle not having been captured had resisted all our efforts to capture it throughout the 17th.

At 10.00 on the 18th the Brigade was therefore disposed as follows :-

6th Lancs. Fus.

Two Companies in depth along line of Railway from K.35.central where in touch with S.A. Brigade - K.35.c.9.0.

One Company in close Support in Eastern outskirts of LE CATEAU.

One Company in Reserve near Battalion H.Q. at K.33.b.5.4.

5th R. Inniskilling Fus.

In support in Q.2.

6th R. Dublin Fus.

In Brigade Reserve in Q.7.

198th L.T.M.B. was attached to the 6th R. Dublin Fus. to assist in the mopping up of LE CATEAU.
2 Guns were attached to the 2 Companies of 6th R.D.F. who worked round from the N. and N.E., and 2 Guns to the 2 Companies that worked into LE CATEAU from the West.
They were of considerable assistance in dealing with hostile M.G. posts in houses in LE CATEAU.
About 100 rounds were fired in all during the 17th, and 18th instant.

The total casualties sustained by the 6th R.Dub.Fus. during the mopping up of LE CATEAU, were :-
Killed - 13.
Wounded - 64 (including 3 at duty)
Missing - 9.

Captures during this action were :-

	Prisoners.	Lorries.	M.G's.
6 R. Dub.Fus.	95	3	? x
6 Lancs.Fus.	12	-	-
5 Innis. Fus.	-	-	2

x All material found in LE CATEAU is claimed and this includes many more M.G's, the number of which it is impossible to estimate.

PART V.

The Advance to the RED LINE.

12.00, 18th October to 18.00, 18th October, 1918.

-:-:-:-:-:-:-:-:-

After the capture of the line of the Railway, the 6th Lancs.Fus. pushed on towards the RED Line and at 16.30 held the following line with three Companies in depth:-
K.36.c.3.3. - K.35.b.5.5.
One Company and Battalion H.Q., at K.35.d.4.4.

On reaching this line the 6th Lancs.Fus. came under hostile machine gun fire. The Battalion accordingly halted for 45 minutes while arrangements were made for the co-operation of troops of the 25th Division on the Right for the final advance to the RED Line. This halt of 45 minutes also enabled the advance to be continued at dusk.

At 17.15 the advance was resumed and was very successful. The bad light hampered the enemy Machine Gunners, prisoners from whom afterwards stated that they were unable to see our men until they were right up to them.
The RED Line was reached from K.36.d.0.6. - K.36.a.0.9., 5 Machine Guns and 35 prisoners were captured, and severe casualties were inflicted on the enemy.

This engagement furnished an interesting instance of the vulnerability of hostile machine guns against infantry employing their own weapons skillfully and making the best use of ground.
More enemy could undoubtedly have been killed and captured had any Cavalry or fresh Infantry been available to exploit the success. Large numbers of enemy and some transport were seen retreating hurriedly eastwards.

The 6th Lancs.Fus. then consolidated the RED Line and pushed forward patrols towards RICHEMONT River. These patrols soon got into touch with more hostile Machine Guns

/ The 5th R.Innis.Fus

The 5th R.Innis.Fus. ~~pushed~~ moved up on to RAILWAY TRIANGLE (Q.5.) at 18.00 to be in Support to the 6th Lancs.Fus.

From the time of their relief of 6th R.Dublin Fus. until the capture of the RED Line, on the evening of the 18th, the 6th Lancs.Fus. captured 5 Machine Guns, and 47 prisoners (25 of whom were captured in the final advance to the RED Line).

In the same period they suffered the following casualties :-

    Killed   -   4 O.R.
    Wounded -   16 O.R.

PART VI.

18.00 18th October, 1918 - 20th October, 1918.

-:-:-:-:-:-

Under instructions received from Division, orders were issued to the 6th Lancs. Fus. at 18.15 on 18th October to re-adjust their front as follows :-

(a) To hand over the Red Line from K.36.central to K.36.a.0.0 to the 9th Manchester Regt. Relief to be complete as soon as possible after dusk.

(b) To take over the Red Line from K.36.central to Q.6.b.6.0 from 13th Black Watch (Scottish Horse) of 50th Division, as soon as the latter were definitely in possession of that portion of the Red Line.

The relief of 6th Lancs. Fus. by 9th Manchester Regt. was not complete until 02.00 on the 19th instant. In the meantime reports had been received from the 149th Infantry Brigade that the 13th Black Watch were not on the Red Line.

Orders were accordingly sent to the 6th Lancs. Fus. to side slip to their right on relief by 9th Manchester Regt. and establish themselves as far as possible on the Red Line from K.36.central to Q.6.b.6.0.

On reconnoitring to carry out this order 6th Lancs. Fus. found troops of the Gloucesters of the 25th Division on this portion of the Red Line.

As the Red Line was held throughout its length and relief by 9th Manchester Regt. could not be completed till very late at night O.C., 6th Lancs. Fus. decided to concentrate his Battalion about K.35.d.4.4. and carry out the relief of whoever was holding his portion of the Red Line as soon as possible after daylight. While 6th Lancs. Fus. were concentrating the Gloucesters of the 25th Division were withdrawn and the 13th Black Watch took over a portion only of the front establishing a post on the North side of the LE CATEAU - BAZUEL road about Q.3.b.8.8.

The 9th Manchester Regt. filled this gap by placing a post about Q.6.b.3.8.

Shortly after daylight 6th Lancs. Fus. took over their sector of the Red Line from the road at Q.6.b.5.0 where they were in touch with the 13th Black Watch to K.36.d.0.6. where they were in touch with 9th Manchester Regt.

The morning of the 19th instant was very quiet. There was practically no hostile artillery fire. Some hostile machine guns were active from about the line of road K.36.d.9.2 - K.36.d.8.9.

Arrangements were then made for 5th R. Inniskilling Fus. to push out strong patrols to the RICHEMONT River at dusk and to secure the line of the river as outpost line from the Mill at R.2.a.1.5 to GARDE MILL (L.31.a.90.85).

One Battery of 63rd Brigade, R.F.A. was detailed to assist 5th R. Innis. Fus. in their   to the outpost line, and a liaison officer for this purpose reported to this Battalion.

Verbal-orders were received from Division at 22.00 on 19th instant that the advance to the line of the RICHEMONT River would be carried out under an artillery barrage at 07.00 on 20th instant in conjunction with an advance by 1st Infantry Brigade. Orders were accordingly issued to 5th R. Innis. Fus. to report by 03.00 on the 20th the position of their patrols. If no report was received by that hour patrols would have to withdraw to the Red Line and advance under cover of the barrage at 07.00 in conjunction with 1st Infantry Brigade. There is

/little doubt

-3-

little doubt that patrols of 5th R. Inniskilling Fus. would have reached the line of the RICHEMONT river solely by the use of infantry weapons and without the assistance of an artillery barrage as the enemy had only a few machine gun posts along the line of the road K.36.d.7.2 - K.36.d.8.9. These were not dug in and could be enfiladed from the road at Q.6.b.6.0. Arrangements had already been made for enfilade fire to be brought to bear on them from a post at this point.

At 23.30 on the 19th instant verbal instructions were received from the Divisional Commander that the 18th Infantry Brigade would take over the front held by this Brigade at once from the Northern Brigade Boundary to K.36.d.6.0., and that the Southern portion of the Brigade front would be taken over at once by 25th Division.

The advance to the RICHEMONT River would be carried out by 18th Infantry Brigade on the whole Divisional front.

Patrols of 5th R. Inniskilling Fus. were accordingly withdrawn at once.

In order to enable the 6th Lancs. Fus. to be withdrawn without delay, the 5th R. Inniskilling Fus. (less two Companies) were instructed to take over the Southern portion of the Brigade front pending relief by the 25th Division.

6th Lancs. Fus. were relieved in the northern portion of the Brigade front by the 5th Manchester Regt, and the whole battalion was concentrated by 07.00 on 20th October in Q.7.

6th R. Dublin Fus. meanwhile moved from Q.2. to REUMONT and 2 Coys. 5th R. Innis. Fus. moved to Q.2.

The whole of the Brigade was thus relieved by 03.00 on 20th October except the 5th R. Innis. Fus. (less two Companies) who were awaiting relief by troops of the 25th Division.

The relief was considerably delayed and when finally arrangements were made for 20th Manchesters to carry out this relief the battalion reported that the relief could not be carried out until dusk owing to hostile machine gun fire.

/Relief accordingly took place

-4-

Relief accordingly took place at dusk on 20th October and the 5th R. Inniskilling Fus. (less two Companies) reached MAUROIS at 22.30 on 20th instant.

The remainder of the Brigade marched to MAUROIS on the afternoon of the 20th instant.

The following was the casualties sustained by this Brigade from the 13th October to 20th October, both dates inclusive :-

	Officers.			O.R.		
	K.	W.	M.	K.	W.	M.
8th Lancs. Fus.	--	1	--	4	38 x	2
5th Innis.Fus.	--	1	--	--	29 ø	8
8th R.D.F.	1	3	--	12	61 ø	9
	1	5	--	16	128	19.

ø Includes 3 at duty.
x   "   5 "   "

TOTAL CAPTURES (from 13th to 20th inst.)

Prisoners.	Lorries.	M.G's.
107.	3	9 x

x All material found in LE CATEAU is claimed and this includes many more M.G's, the numbers of which it is impossible to estimate.

"A" Form
MESSAGES AND SIGNALS.

Army Form C. 2121
(In pads of 100.)

Confirmation

TO: FEKE Appendix 13

Sender's Number: HX1714 Day of Month: 17

My HX1713 time on which uncertain now is 1700 hours to 1745 hours

From:
Place: SUH
Time: 1709

MESSAGES AND SIGNALS.

This message is on a/c of: appendix

From (13)

TO { 6' R Dublin Fus.
S.A. Bde. (for information)

Sender's Number	Day of Month	In reply to Number	AAA
B.m.24	17		

Prisoner captured last night reports large number of Germans in cellars in LE CATEAU aaa You many use a third company for mopping up town aaa A Coy 5" R Innis Fus is moving up into Q2 aaa You may use to replace Third company in support aaa Your third company should assist you to mop up LE CATEAU quickly aaa Capt. Luard RICHE-KELLY A Coy 5" R Innis Fus sent an officer to report with support to Coy

From SUHU

Place

Time 07.15

"A" Form.
MESSAGES AND SIGNALS.

Army Form C. 2121.
(In pads of 100.)

Prefix......Code.......... m	Words.	Charge.	This message is on a/c of:	Recd. at .... m
Office of Origin and Service Instructions.	Sent		*Approved* Service.	Date......
....	At........m.			From......
	To..........			
	By..........		(Signature of "Franking Officer.")	By......

TO { 6° Lancs Fus
      6° Dublin Fus (for information)

Sender's Number.	Day of Month.	In reply to Number.	AAA
* B.M. 37	17		

If	enemy	still	holds
station	in	Q 10	and
your	troops	are	under
heavy	fire	you	will
withdraw	to	original	position
in	Q 7	and	on
no	account	become	envolved
in	fighting	for	the
station	and	railway	triangle
in	Q 5	which	is
50°	Div	tank	and
If	these	points	have
been	cleared	by	50°
Div	and	you	are
not	under	heavy	fire
from	them	you	may
push	on	to	original

From ....
Place ....
Time ....

The above may be forwarded as now corrected.   (Z)   *[signature]*
....
                    Censor.   Signature of Addressor or person authorised to telegraph in his name.

* This line should be erased if not required.

(3796.) Wt. W492/M1647. 650,000 Pads. 5/17. H.W. & V., Ld. (E. 1187.)

"A" Form.
MESSAGES AND SIGNALS.

Army Form C. 2121.
(In pads of 100.)

| TO | | 2 | Appendix ⑬ |

Sender's Number.	Day of Month.	In reply to Number.	AAA
objective	aaa	Please	report
as	soon	as	possible
which	cause	you	are
taking			
ACKNOWLEDGE			
Adam	6th Seren	to	repeated
6th Dub Fus	(for information)		

From SUHU
Place
Time 13.00

"A" Form
MESSAGES AND SIGNALS.

Army Form C. 2121
(in pads of 100).

No. of Message..................

Prefix......Code......m.	Words.	Charge.	This message is on a/c of:	Recd. at......m.
Office of Origin and Service Instructions.	Sent At......m.		..................Service.	Date.......... From..........
	To.......... By..........		(Signature of "Franking Officer.")	By..........

TO Lancs Fus~~
    ~~Dub Fus~~   Appendix ⑬

| Sender's Number. | Day of Month. | In reply to Number. | AAA |
| HX 176 | 7 | | |

BM 35. Objective
for K 35 c 4.6 road
K 35 c 0.6

SuH u

11 27

From
Place
Time   A Hunter Bde

The above may be forwarded as now corrected   (Z)
Censor.   Signature of Addressor or person authorised to telegraph in his name.
*This line should be erased if not required.

A Form.
MESSAGES AND SIGNALS.

| TO | FEKE | Appendix 3 |

Sender's Number.	Day of Month.	In reply to Number.	AAA
Dm 23	17		

No acknowledgement received for
H.X.161 and H.X.162 aaa
Further copies are accordingly
enclosed aaa Please acknowledge.
receipt

From SUHU
Time 06.00

"A" Form.
MESSAGES AND SIGNALS.

Army Form C. 2121.
(In pads of 100.)

TO { 6" Leinster Regt
     6" Dublin Regt }   Appendix (13)

Sender's Number.	Day of Month.	In reply to Number.	AAA
B.17.35	17		

6" Leinster Regt will move at once crossing river at St BENIN if possible North of it and move N.E. between river and railway and attack with objective LE CATEAU — BASUEL road from K.35.C.4.6. — K.35.C.9.3. and will gain touch with 6" Dublin near bridge Q.4.b.1.9. and with 13" Black Watch in railway cutting Q.5. a.e.e. South African Brigade are on railway in K.35 and K.29 but actual position not known aaa 6" Dublin will continue mopping

From
Place
Time

"A" Form.
MESSAGES AND SIGNALS.

Army Form C. 2121.
(In pads of 100.)

TO: Appendix 13

up	LE CATEAU	and	securing
Eastern	outskirts	aaa	A
party	of	R.E.	is
being	Sent	forward	to
HQ "G"	Dublins	to	road
and	railway	consolidate	K.35.c.9.3
on	its	crossing	
ACKNOWLEDGE		capture	

From: SOHD
Time: 10.50

"A" Form.
MESSAGES AND SIGNALS.

Prefix......Code......m	Words.	Charge.	This message is on a/c of:	Recd. at......m
Office of Origin and Service Instructions.	Sent			Date......
	At......m.		......Service.	From......
	To......			
	By......	(Signature of "Franking Officer.")	By......	

TO { 6 R. Dublin ... / ... }   Appendix 13

Sender's Number.	Day of Month.	In reply to Number.	A A A
* R.M.28	17		

The whole of your
battalion is placed at
your disposal to move
up LE CATEAU. One "D"
Coy — ~~moving~~ is
mine Fun is moving
up to Q.2 as
well ~~soon~~ as "A" Coy of
that battalion aaa G.O.E.
is sending private note
aaa two Coys. ... from
Fun are NOT on
~~any~~ account to be
employed East of the
river.

From   SUHU
Place
Time   08.00

The above may be forwarded as now corrected.   (Z)   [signature] Capt

Censor.   Signature of Addresser or person authorised to telegraph in his name.

* This line should be erased if not required.

"A" Form.
MESSAGES AND SIGNALS.

TO 6' Dublin Fus Appendix ⑬

Sender's Number	Day of Month	In reply to Number	A A A
Bn 30	17		

One D Coy 25 Or
M G C has been placed
at your disposal for
defence of LE CATEAU
farm O.C. was instructed
to report to any
last night How
L done so

From: SUHV
Place:
Time: 08 15

"A" Form.
MESSAGES AND SIGNALS.

Army Form C. 2121.
(In pads of 100.)

Prefix....Code....m	Words.	Charge.	This message is on a/c of:	Recd. at ....m.
Office of Origin and Service Instructions.	Sent			Date........
....	At....m.		............Service.	From ......
....	To....		(Signature of "Franking Officer.")	By ....
....	By....			

TO { 6 Dublin Fus
     S A Bde (for info)   Appendix (+3)

Sender's Number.	Day of Month.	In reply to Number.	A A A
B.M 32	17		

Tanks are advancing on
O5 and should be
there by and are
South African Brigade held
up by are
in K 29 c and K 35 a
are for will [erased] found
on side be CATEAU
from the West cross
by patrols are South
African many have to
attack though can about
few all clear as
come as possible soon
Tanks should be of
another

From   SUHU
Place
Time   08.40

The above may be forwarded as now corrected.   (Z)
                                    [signature] Capt

"A" Form.
MESSAGES AND SIGNALS.

Army Form C. 2121.
(In pads of 100.)

Prefix	Code	m	Words	Charge	This message is on a/c of:	Recd. at ...... m.
Office of Origin and Service Instructions			Sent At ......m. To...... By......		...... Service. (Signature of "Franking Officer")	Date...... From...... By...... (13)

TO — 6 Dublin Fus
South African Bde (for information)

Sender's Number	Day of Month	In reply to Number	AAA
B.M. 36	17		
13	Black	Watch	one
at	Railway	Triangle	in
Q.5	and	South	African
both	in	position	do
railway	in	K.35	one
being	fired	on	from
Eastern	edge	of	LE
CATEAU	and	get	into
Fresh	will	13	Black
Watch	counter		right
and	attack	of	South
African	Royal	on	railway
on	left	as	soon
as	possible	and	get
on	with	clearing	two
as	Infantry	refuse	as
far	thereabouts	of	troops
From	SUHU	cannot	kill hill	we know
Place			
Time	10.25		

The above may be forwarded as now corrected. (Z)

Censor. Signature of Addresser or person authorised to telegraph in his name.

* This line should be erased if not required.

"A" Form
MESSAGES AND SIGNALS.
Army Form C. 2121 (in pads of 100).

TO: PEKE

Sender's Number: AX.1718
Day of Month: 17

Good clearing S of town aaa Posts K35a50 & K35a37 & should be pushed forward at once to make our line run K35 central — K35C8·3 — Q463 + so to RIVER aaa Report directly line is there by code word HOME aaa We continue the attack tomorrow. 6 DLF will do it & you will come into Reserve aaa. This attack will not take place unless 50 Dn take Rly △ tonight. It is still BOCHE — mind your right flank.

From: SWJL
Time: 21.45

"C" Form
MESSAGES AND SIGNALS.

Army Form C. 2123
(In books of 100.)

No. of Message..............

Prefix......Code......Words......	Received	Sent, or sent out	Office Stamp.
£ s. d.	From..............	At .... m	
Charges to Collect	By.................	To................	
Service Instructions		By................	

Handed in at .... Office ......m. Received ......m.

TO 6th R. DUB. FUS.
    afternoon ⑬

*Sender's Number	Day of Month	In reply to Number	AAA
	17/10/18	C.O. X 39 & 40	

I already have posts established at K.35.a.1.5., K.35.c.7.6 Q.5.a.9.1 and X roads S. of town (Q.4.6.4.2.) K.35.c.8.3 is still giving a lot of trouble but will manage it with the barrage & fresh platoon. L^t. O'HEA at K.5.a.1.9 is also up against against M.G. Lt WHYTE at X roads S of town reports all quiet. Lt HANNIN at K.35.a.1.5 is in position & in touch with Lt HARNEY "B" Coy

Q.5.6.a. Ruet.
K.36.c.

FROM
PLACE & TIME   *[signature]* Maj

* This line should be erased if not required.

"C" Form
MESSAGES AND SIGNALS.

Army Form C. 2123
(In books of 100.)

No. of Message ....

Prefix .... Code .... Words	Received	Sent, or sent out.	Office Stamp.
£ s. d.	From	At .... m	
Charges to Collect	By	To	
Service Instructions *Appended*		(13) By	

Handed in at .... Office .... m. Received .... m.

TO 6th R DUB FUS

*Sender's Number	Day of Month	In reply to Number	AAA
—	17/10/18	COX 43	

Have established posts as follows.

No 1 Post	Lt HANNIN	1 Platoon	K 35.0.2.5
" 2 "	Lt HARNEY	"	K 35.9 & 0
" 3 "	Lt BRUCE (SAM)	"	K 35 c.8.3
" 4 "	Lt O'HEA	"	Q 5.a.1.9
" 5 "	Lt WHYTE	"	Q 4.b.3.2

Have just received COX 43 & 44 will act accordingly.

Am going to place V Guns when they arrive somewhere in K 35 c. I was told they had been blown to bits hence delay in finding them. I have just returned from No 1 Post & things are fairly quiet there

FROM
PLACE & TIME 0029 hours O   "C" Coy

6TH R DUB FUS.

O. Lan. Fus.
5th Innis Fus
6th R.D.F
198 L.T.M.B.
Bde Q.M. Sgt.

P. 8

Appendix 12

I. Brigade Transport Lines are in P. 16.C + 15.d.

II. 192 No 27 Grenades per Bn or as many less as required will be drawn from Bde Quartermasters Stores at that point, any time after receipt of this message.

III. Instructions as to picks + shovels have already been issued.

IV. 198 L.T.M.B. will make their own arrangements for rations with Bde Quarter master Sgt. If possible their own limbers should be utilised for this service.

V. Battns will draw any pack mules they require up to the numbers specified by B.G.C. 198 I.B. at conference from Brigade Pack train.

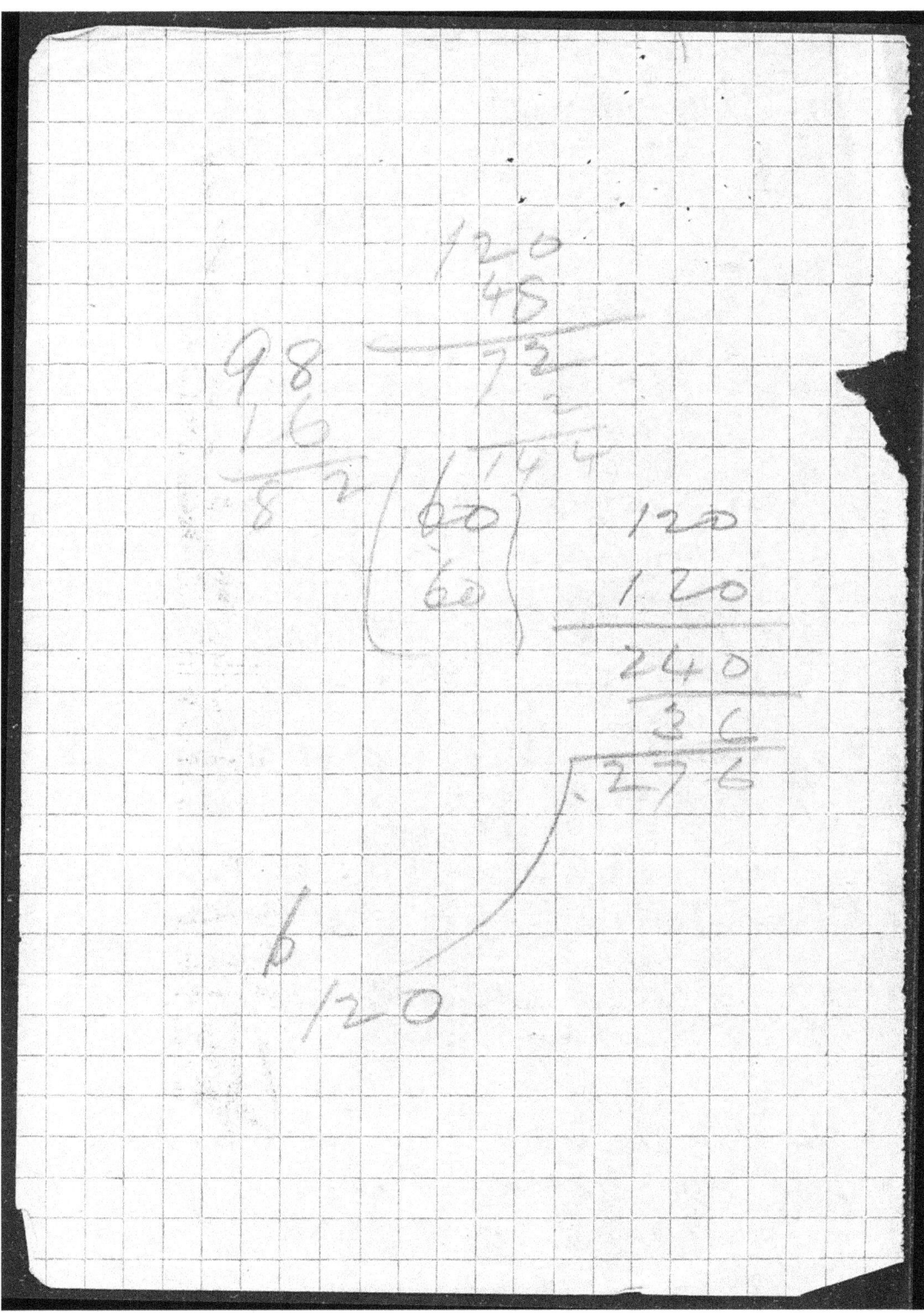

Appendix (2)

VI. Ammunition Officers will be detailed to report to Brigade HQ forthwith for orders

P. McGlenn
Capt
Staff Capt
198 I.B.

16-10-78

6th L. Fus
5th Innis Fus:
6th R.D. Fus:

P.10
Appendix (12)

I Reference P.8. para VI.
   Ammunition Officers will not be required

II Ref: para V.
   The Pack the BGC 195 I.B. stated he
   wished to retain at Bde HQ are
      5th Innis Fus   3
      6th R.D.F   3
      6th L. Fus   1

III Supply of ammunition will be
   as follows
   i Normal supply from Bde Transport
   ii 7 pack mules at Bde HQ with
      SAA & bombs
      Battns in urgent need of ammunition
   will send a demand together with guide
   to Bde HQ. Guide will take back pack
   mules with SAA.

                                P. Inghram
                                Staff Capt
16/10/18

"A" Form.
MESSAGES AND SIGNALS.

Army Form C. 2121.
(In pads of 100.)

TO	6" James Fuz		
	6" Dublin Fus		
	5" R. Innis Fus		

Sender's Number.	Day of Month.	In reply to Number.	AAA
* B.A. 13	16		

Ref	198"	Inf	Bde
Order	No	120	aaa
Zero	from	will	be
05.20	17"	instant	

From 198 Inf Bde
Place
Time 20.20

MESSAGES AND SIGNALS.

Prefix	Code	Words	Charge	This message is on a/c of:	Recd. at ...... m.
Office of Origin and Service Instructions		Sent At		Appenrist ...... Service	Date 12
		To			From
		By		(Signature of "Franking Officer.")	By

TO { 6" R Dublin Fus / 6 Leins Fus / 5 R Innis Fus / 198 L T.M.B

Sender's Number.	Day of Month.	In reply to Number.	AAA
B.M.15	16		

Advance of South African Brigade will not commence until until 08.05 on 17" instant, aaa Time mentioned in Para 5 198 Inf Bde order No 120 will not be changed aaa ACKNOWLEDGE

From 198 Inf Bde
Place
Time 2300

(Z) M? Edw Capt

MESSAGES AND SIGNA[LS]

Prefix	Code	Words	Charge	This message is on a/c of:	Recd. at
		20			

Office of Origin and Service Instructions: SUHU

Sent At ___ m. To 6 Dec 17
Service _____
Date ___ From ___
By ___ (Signature of "Franking Officer") By ___

TO: 7EKE

Sender's Number	Day of Month	In reply to Number	AAA
B.M. 18	16		
Have	you	received	R.M
No	120	and	ADDENDUM
No	1	and	ADDENDUM
No	2		

From: SUHU
Place:
Time: 23.20

The above may be forwarded as now corrected. (Z)

Censor. Signature of Addressor or person authorised to telegraph in his name.

* This line should be erased if not required.

(3796.) Wt. W 492/M1647. 650,000 Pads. 5/17. H.W.&V., Ld. (E. 1187.)

"A" Form
MESSAGES AND SIGNALS.   Army Form C. 2127
                                     (in pads of 100).
                                     No. of Message..............

Prefix.........Code..........m.   Words   Charge   This message is on a/c of: Recd. at..........m.
Office of Origin and Service Instructions.   Date...............
By runner   Sent   From...............
freely   At.............m.   ....Service.   By.................
                                  To.............
                                  By.............   (Signature of "Franking Officer.")

TO   C.R.D.W. M.P.   Apparent (?)

Sender's Number   Day of Month   In reply to Number   AAA
HX 174   17

Own outpost. One Bde on dotted
line (ie front line). Other Bde
all over river. Tanks also
over + moving N. 20th Gunner
Bn say very few enemy &
believe they have cleared already.

Absolutely essential Bn shd
get news of what is doing on
your front. Can you supply.

Some resistance by people in new
jtht apparently in Station +
Rly triangle (R5).

From   SU/H
Place
Time   0853

                         (2) Abmctr Bb
Censor   Signature of Addressor or person authorised to telegraph in his name.

6. DUB Fus Appendix (13)

South African troops on
left have reached the
railway in K.23.C and
K.29.a.
 Position of troops on right
rather obscure, but they are
believed to have reached
the railway in places.
 They are experiencing
a good deal of M.G. fire
 Your two companies are
thought to be following up
on right.
 Prisoners coming in are
17. Div. 76. Regt.
"Grey"

10-40 h.y
S.A.H.Q.
17.10.18

B.I.O.
SOHO

"A" Form
MESSAGES AND SIGNALS.

Army Form C. 2121
(in pads of 100).

TO: Officers

Dear Little,

From all accounts
of reinforcements it seems that
there are lots of Boche
in the Galleries. Your
whole battn is hereby
put at your disposal to
use at your discretion.
The thing to do is to get the
place mopped up quickly.
Two Coy R Irish Fus
are on their way up

"A" Form
MESSAGES AND SIGNALS.

Army Form C. 2121 (in pads of 100).

TO Appendix (13)

to O.R. are sending forward Dyer for instructions. The Second in Co. (D) Lt Atkins will not be up for some time. Hope your liaison with 51 Bde is all right. For Heavens Sake send us news early

"A" Form
MESSAGES AND SIGNALS.

TO: Officers (3)

as + may make the whole difference to the show. Heard people on right have got 3 battns over the canal. Le Cateau is full of civilians I believe. Good luck to A[?]

"A" Form.
MESSAGES AND SIGNALS.

Prefix........ Code........ m	Words.	Charge.	This message is on a/c of:	Recd. at
Office of Origin and Service Instructions.	Sent			Date
	At........m.		......Service.	From
	To			By
	By		(Signature of "Franking Officer.")	

TO — FEKE — Apprentist — (3)

Sender's Number.	Day of Month.	In reply to Number.	AAA
B.M.21	17		

Nothing received from you
since C.O.X 24 aaa Have
you completed relief and
are you in position
and Please give bearer
any news you have

From SUHU
Place
Time 05.30

"A" Form
MESSAGES AND SIGNALS.

Army Form C. 2121 (in pads of 100).

No. of Message..........

Prefix......Code......m.	Words.	Charge.	This message is on a/c of:	Recd. at......m.
Office of Origin and Service Instructions.	Sent			Date......
	At......m.		......Service.	From......
	To......			
	By......		(Signature of "Franking Officer.")	By......

TO 6 R.D.W. Fus. — Offer R/F (13)

Sender's Number.	Day of Month.	In reply to Number.	AAA
* HX1712	17		

Bde has orders take
& told following line &
to complete mopping of
LE CATEAU by dusk.
Line K35 central — along Rublet to
K35c 93 thence along Divl Boundary
to Q4b 30 — trial —
Forward posts to be established
on LE CATEAU - BAZUEL road as
far as road jn K35 d 6.0.
You will carry on with clearing
LE CATEAU up to line indicated,
using remainder of Divis Fusiliers
with you if necessary. Lancs
Fus will take over line from
you later. Let me have situation
on your left early (ie Rly Embankment)

From	S.H.W.	Enemy still hold Rly & Station but
Place		Div reports are attacking again
Time	1545	

The above may be forwarded as now corrected. (Z) — A. Hunter B/6

Censor. Signature of Addresser or person authorised to telegraph in his name.

*This line should be erased if not required.

6th Lancs.Fus.
6th R.Dublin Fus.
5th R.Innis.Fus.

198th Inf.Bde
No.B.M. 259

Appendix 14

      Places marked on the attached map are said to be mined. Mines are supposed to be connected to the station.
Care will be taken to avoid the neighbourhood of these mines as much as possible.

                                Captain,
                        Brigade Major,
18.10.18.   198th Infantry Brigade.
RV.

"C" Form.
MESSAGES AND SIGNALS.

Army Form C. 2123.
(In books of 100.)

Prefix	Code	Words	Received From	Sent, or sent out. At ... m. To ... By	Office Stamp. FEKE 18/9/17
Charges to Collect			By		
Service Instructions	Send priority warning order				

Handed in at .... Office ...... m. Received 17/0 ...... m.

TO FEKE.   Appendix (14)

*Sender's Number	Day of Month.	In reply to Number	A A A
BM 64	18		

Following adjustment of line
may take place tonight aaa
MQR1 to take over that portion
of red line between K.36 Central
and Q.36.C.0.9 provided that
line has been definitely
established by 1800 tonight
by division on right aaa
MQR1 to hand over red line
from K.36 Central to K.36.a.0.9
to unit of SOTA aaa FEHA
to be in support and
FEKE in reserve both east
of river SELLE ACKNOWLEDGE

FROM
PLACE & TIME   SOHO   1615.

* This line should be erased if not required.

"C" Form.
MESSAGES AND SIGNALS.

Prefix _AM_ Code _____ Words _13_
Charges to Collect
Service Instructions _SUHU_

Received. From _SUHU_ By _Rex a_
Sent, or sent out. At ___ m. To ___ By ___
Office Stamp. _FEKE_

Handed in at _SUHU_ Signal Office _7.14_ m. Received _23.15_ m.

TO _FEKE_ Affirmed (14)

*Sender's Number	Day of Month.	In reply to Number	AAA
HX1	15		
Send	early	tomorrow	morning
first	thing	to	collect
all	M.G.	equipment	lying
round	area	of	your
camp	aaa	dump	same
on	edge	of	road
informing	Staff	Passala	

FROM PLACE & TIME _SUHU_

*This line should be erased if not required.

"A" Form.
MESSAGES AND SIGNALS.

Army Form C.2121
(In pads of 100.)

No. of Message..........

Prefix......Code......m	Words.	Charge.	This message is on a/c of:	Recd. at ....m.
Office of Origin and Service Instructions.	Sent			Date 7 oc 4 18
	At......m.		Service.	From
	To......			TELEGRAPHS
	By......		(Signature of "Franking Officer.")	

TO ~~FEMA~~ FEKC ~~BEC~~   Appendix 14

Sender's Number.	Day of Month.	In reply to Number.	AAA
Rm B	18		
Ry Para 3 inclusive Amend	Ru aaa to order	Orders Railway 66 Jns accordingly	No 121 in aaa

From SUHV
Place
Time 22.15

TO: FEKE, MODY, FEHA

Appendix (14)

Sender's Number.	Day of Month.	In reply to Number.	A A A
*BM 56	18		

Ref	BM 58	and	BM 54
aaa	on	relief	FEKE
will	proceed	to	Q2
to	rear	of	FEHA
aaa	NOT	to	Q7
aaa	ACKNOWLEDGE		

From Place: SUHU
Time: 02.45

MESSAGES AND SIGNALS.

TO: 6 RDF Appendix 14

Sender's Number.	Day of Month.	In reply to Number.	AAA
S 10	18	COX 44	

Posts at present at K35 A 3.6 and about K35 A 4.8 with a small party in support in K34 B 9.9 aaa Have instructed posts to push forward to railway & will report when occupied aaa Had already sent up Platoon of D coy at Major LUKES request. aaa Bearer will guide ration party down

From: B coy
Place:
Time: 02.48

Hathaluith Capt

"A" Form.
MESSAGES AND SIGNALS.

Army Form C. 2121.
(In pads of 100.)

Prefix......Code....t......m	Words.	Charge.	This message is on a/c of:	Recd. at ......m.
Office of Origin and Service Instructions.	Sent At......m. To...... By......		......Service. (Signature of "Franking Officer.")	Date...... From...... By......

TO { 6" Lincs Fus
     /6" Dublin Fu
     5" R Innis Fus

Appendix (14)

Sender's Number.	Day of Month.	In reply to Number.	A A A
* B.m 51	18		

Ref	this	office	HX1722
of	17.10.18	our	of
the	railway	through	in
ase	as	not	captured
tonight	the	fast	will
be	act pub	by	the
code	word	RENWAL	then
action	will	be	taken
as	accordance	with	para 2 (a)
of	HX1722	as	of
6 th	cas	of	para
i (b)	ans	this	hour
will	be	05.30	to-day
aux	Barrage	will	com
down	Low	plan	33
minutes	on	low	200
East	of	railway	embankment

From ......
Place ......
Time ......

The above may be forwarded as now corrected. (Z)

Censor. Signature of Addresser or person authorised to telegraph in his name.

* This line should be erased if not required.

"A" Form.
MESSAGES AND SIGNALS.

Army Form C. 2121.
(In pads of 100.)

TO — 2 Appendix (14)

aaa will dwell three
for 5 minutes on
Copy of 66 pr orders
No 161 and addendum in
attached (6 Div xx only)

ACKNOWLEDGE

From SOHO
Time 00.45

Signature: M?Eden Capt.

"A" Form.
MESSAGES AND SIGNALS.

Army Form C. 2121.
(In pads of 100.)
No. of Message...........

Prefix......Code......m	Words.	Charge.	This message is on a/c of:	Recd. at ......m
Office of Origin and Service Instructions:—	Sent At ......m		..........Service.	Date...........
	To......			From...........
	By......		(Signature of "Franking Officer.")	By...........

TO { C Coy m
     C Dukes m
     ? Coy m }   Offenders ⑭

Sender's Number.	Day of Month.	In reply to Number.	AAA
BM 52	18		

Ref BM51 aaa REFUSAL

ACKNOWLEDGE.

From SOMU
Place
Time 00.50

The above may be forwarded as now corrected. (Z)

Signature of Addressor: M Rider Cap

"A" Form.
MESSAGES AND SIGNALS.

Army Form C. 2121.
(In pads of 100.)

Prefix.	Code.	m	Words.	Charge.	This message is on a/c of:	Recd. at .... m.
Office of Origin and Service Instructions.			Sent		.... Service.	Date ....
			At .... m.			From ....
			To			
			By		(Signature of "Franking Officer.")	By ....

TO { MOGI / FEKE }   Appendix (14)

Sender's Number.	Day of Month.	In reply to Number.	AAA
B.P. 53	18		

Take action in accordance with H.X.1722 para 1(a) aaa FEKE on relief will move to O.y aaa completion of relief to be notified by code word RATIONS aaa Detachment of 431 the Coy is reporting to MOGI forthwith

From **SUHU**
Place
Time **01.20**

The above may be forwarded as now corrected. (Z)
Censor.   A.P. den Cpt
Signature of Addressor or person authorised to telegraph in his name.
* This line should be erased if not required.

"C" Form.
MESSAGES AND SIGNALS.

Army Form C. 2123.
(In books of 100.)

No. of Message

Prefix	Code	Words	Received. From SUHU By Fletcher	Sent, or sent out. At m. To By	Office Stamp.
Charges to Collect					
Service Instructions					

Handed in at ____ Office 02·10 m. Received 2·25 m.

TO FEKE Appendix (14)

Sender's Number	Day of Month	In reply to Number	AAA
BM 55	18		

Ref BM 51 aaa Artillery programme will still be carried out

FROM SUHU
PLACE & TIME 02·15

"C" Form.
MESSAGES AND SIGNALS.

Army Form C. 2123.
(In books of 100.)

No. of Message _____

Prefix **CB** Code **21 37** Words **51**
Received. From **SUHU** By **Pilcher N**

Sent, or sent out. At ____ m. To ____ By ____

Office Stamp.

Charges to Collect _____
Service Instructions **3S11 Priority**

Handed in at _____ Office **21 37** m. Received **21 31** m.

TO **FEKE** Appendix 14

*Sender's Number	Day of Month	In reply to Number	AAA
BM 53	18		

Take action in accordance with LX 1722 para 1 (a) aaa Feke on relief will move to Q7 aaa Completion of relief to be notified by code word RATIONS aaa Detachment of 431 Fld Coy is reporting to you forthwith aaa Added MOP ~~Speak~~ FEKE and FEVR

FROM
PLACE & TIME **SUHU**

"C" Form.
MESSAGES AND SIGNALS.

Army Form C.2123.
(In books of 100.)

No. of Message ....

| Prefix | Code | Words | Received. From ...... By Polkey | Sent, or sent out. At ...... m. To ...... By | Office Stamp. |

Charges to Collect ......
Service Instructions ...... 7SH Priority

Handed in at ...... Office ...... m. Received 02·00 m.

TO FEKE Offensive (14)

*Sender's Number	Day of Month	In reply to Number	AAA
BM 56	18		

Ref BM 53 BM 54 aaa On relief FEKE will proceed to Q2 in rear of FEVA and NOT to Q7 aaa Acknowledge

FROM PLACE & TIME SUHU

02·45

*This line should be erased if not required.
(27802) Wt. W14832/M1523. [E 930]. 100,000 Pads—3/17. M.R.Co.,Ltd. Forms/C.2123.

"C" Form.   Army Form C. 2123.
MESSAGES AND SIGNALS.   (In books of 100.)
No. of Message..........

Prefix.... Code.... Words....	Received.	Sent, or sent out.	Office Stamp.
£ s. d.	From....	At.... m.	
Charges to Collect	By....	To....	
Service Instructions		By....	

Handed in at   SUHJ   Office 0918 m.   Received 0930 m.

TO   Hcke Appendix (14)

| *Sender's Number | Day of Month | In reply to Number | AAA |
| S1181 | 18 | — | |

Please report (A) time
you are handing over
(B) progress of relief
by 1700.

FROM   SU111
PLACE & TIME   0910

"C" Form.
MESSAGES AND SIGNALS.

Army Form C. 2123.
(In books of 100.)

No. of Message _____

Prefix ___ Code ___ Words ___	Received.	Sent, or sent out.	Office Stamp.
£ s. d.	From ___	At ___ m.	
Charges to Collect	By ___	To ___	
Service Instructions		By ___	

Handed in at __Sulva__ Office __9.50__ m. Received __11.16__ m.

TO — M001 FEKE Appendix (14)

*Sender's Number	Day of Month	In reply to Number	AAA
BM 29	18	—	
Div	on	our	right
holds	north	eastern	face
of	railway	triangle	on
95.	and	line	of
railway	on	96.	Our
M001	will	get	into
touch	with	troops	of
division	on	our	right
and	report	as	soon
as	they	have	done
so	as	information	is
also	urgently	required	as
to	~~situation~~	on	our
left	as	reports	from
both	our	left	are
conflicting	and	the	intention
is	as	soon	as

| FROM | touch has been obtained |
| PLACE & TIME | with division on right |

*This line should be erased if not required.
(27302) Wt. W14832/M1523. [E 930]. 100,000 Pads–3/17. M.R.Co.,Ltd. Forms/C.2123.

"C" Form.
MESSAGES AND SIGNALS.

Army Form C.2121.
(In books of 100.)

Prefix	Code	Words	Received From	Sent, or sent out At m.	Office Stamp
Charges to Collect			By	To	
Service Instructions				By	

Handed in at _____ Office _____ m. Received _____ m.

TO Offenders (14)

Sender's Number	Day of Month	In reply to Number	AAA
	18		

to	move	forward to
red	line	which moves
from	TSb.d.o.b	to Katising
and	MSQt	repeated FERE
and	SEFE	

FROM: SNHU
PLACE & TIME: 1045

*This line should be erased if not required.

SECRET.   Appendix (15)   Copy No. 3

198th INFANTRY BRIGADE ORDER NO. 123.

20th October, 1918.

Reference Sheet, 57b, 1/40,000.

1. 198th Infantry Brigade will move by march route to PREMONT tomorrow, 21st inst., as follows :-

Unit.	Time of passing Starting Point.
6th R. Dublin Fus.	10.00.
6th Lancs. Fus.	10.10.
198th L.T.M.B.	10.20.
198 Brigade H.Q.	10.25.
5th R. Innis. Fus.	10.30.
Transport (under Brigade Transport Offr.)	11.00.

Starting Point :- P.22.b.1.1.

Route :- MARETZ - U.18.c.0.2 - PREMONT.

2. Transport will not halt on the Roman Road.

3. Brigade H.Q. will close at MAUROIS at 10.00 and re-open at PREMONT on arrival.

4. ACKNOWLEDGE.

Captain,
Brigade Major,
198th Infantry Brigade.

Issued through Signals at 21.00

DISTRIBUTION.

6th Lancs. Fus.	Copy No.	1.
5th Innis. Fus.	" "	2.
6th R. Dublin Fus.	" "	3.
198th L.T.M.B.	" "	4.
66th Division, "G".	" "	5.
199 Inf. Bde.	" "	6.
B.T.O.	" "	7.
Staff Captain.	" "	8.
No. 3 Sig. Sec.	" "	9.
War Diary.	" "	10,1
File.	" "	13,1

Appendix 15

Reference 198th Infantry Brigade Order No. 193.

The following distances will be observed on the march :-

    500 yards between Units.
    100 yards between Coys.
    100 yards between platoons, with their transport
    50 yards between every 12 vehicles.

Units will clear the road at halts.

Captain,
Brigade Major,
198th Infantry Brigade.

"A" Form.
MESSAGES AND SIGNALS.

Army Form C. 2121.
(In pads of 100.)

No. of Message..............

Prefix......Code.......m	Words.	Charge.	This message is on a/c of:	Recd. at ....m
Office of Origin and Service Instructions.		Sent	*Official* Service.	Date.... ⑮
		At......m		From
		To......	(Signature of "Franking Officer.")	By
		By		

TO — FEHA / MGB / ~~FEHB~~ — Sec Sec H.Q.

Sender's Number.	Day of Month.	In reply to Number.	AAA
*V 17(m8)	20	—	

The Brigade will concentrate in MAUROIS today aaa Units will proceed independently on receipt of new orders aaa transport will proceed direct to Brigade transport lines aaa 2 Coys FEHA now in Q.2 will proceed independently to MAUROIS aaa FEHA less 2 Coys will proceed to MAUROIS on relief aaa Staff Captain will arrange billets aaa Bde HQ will close at Q.4.c.8.6 on completion of relief of 1st FEHA and reopen at MAUROIS aaa acknowledge

From: SOHO
Place:
Time: 12.30

The above may be forwarded as now corrected. (Z)

Censor. Signature of Addressee or person authorised to telegraph in his name.

* This line should be erased if not required.
(3796.) Wt. W492/M1617. 6,0,000 Pads. 5/17. H.W. & V., Ld. (E. 1187.)

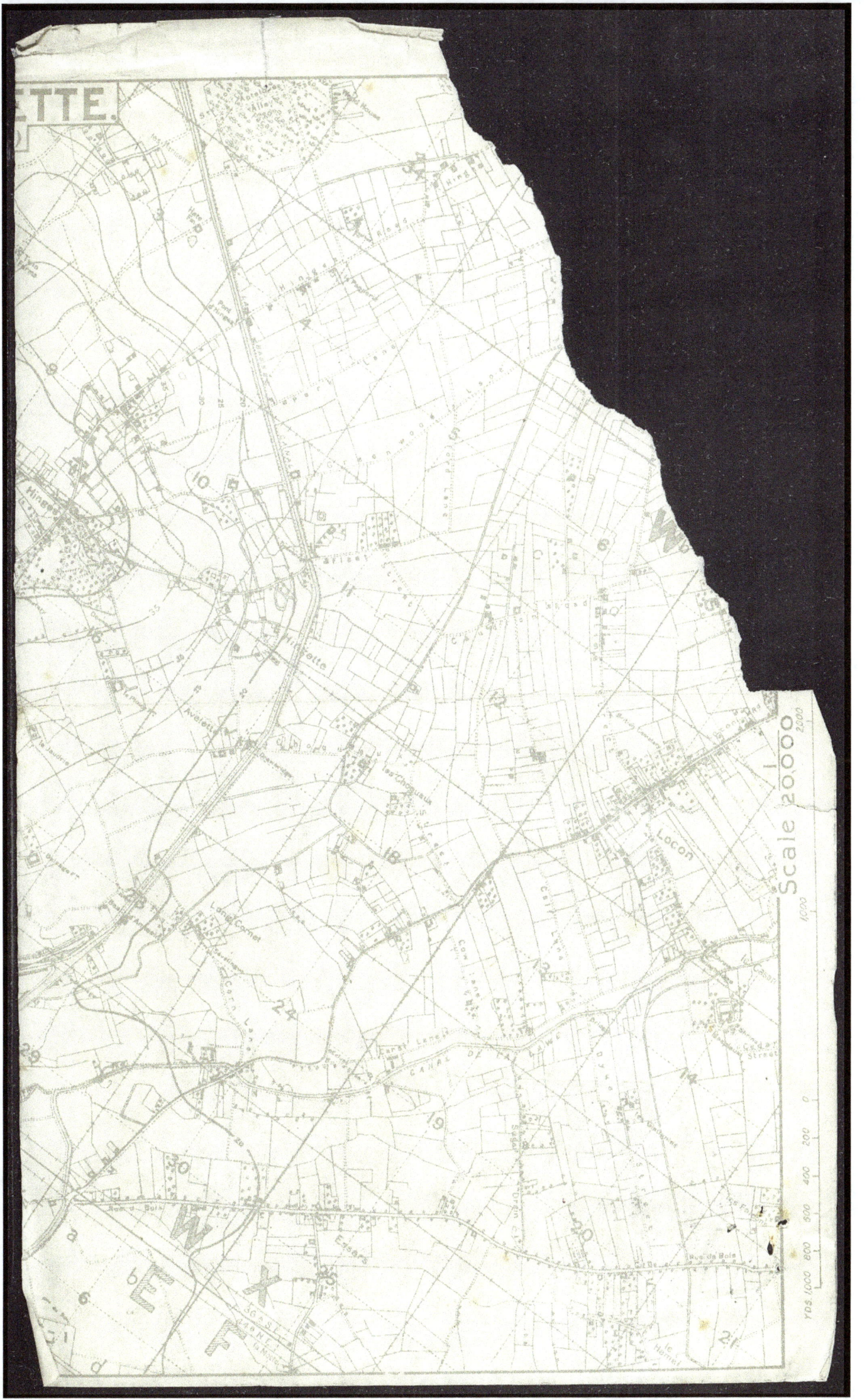

I AM AT _____

I AM AT _____

I AM TEMPORARY HELD UP AT
RIFLE; M.G FIRE FROM _____

I WANT MORE S.A.A. _____

MY CASUALTIES ARE _____

MY STRENGTH IS _____

INFORMATION ABOUT MY OWN FRONT IS AS FOLLOWS:-
_____
(MARK SITUATION IN ON MAP)

SITUATION ON MY FLANKS APPEARS TO BE:-
_____

I INTEND TO _____

TIME _____   SIGNED _____
DATE _____   REGIMENT _____

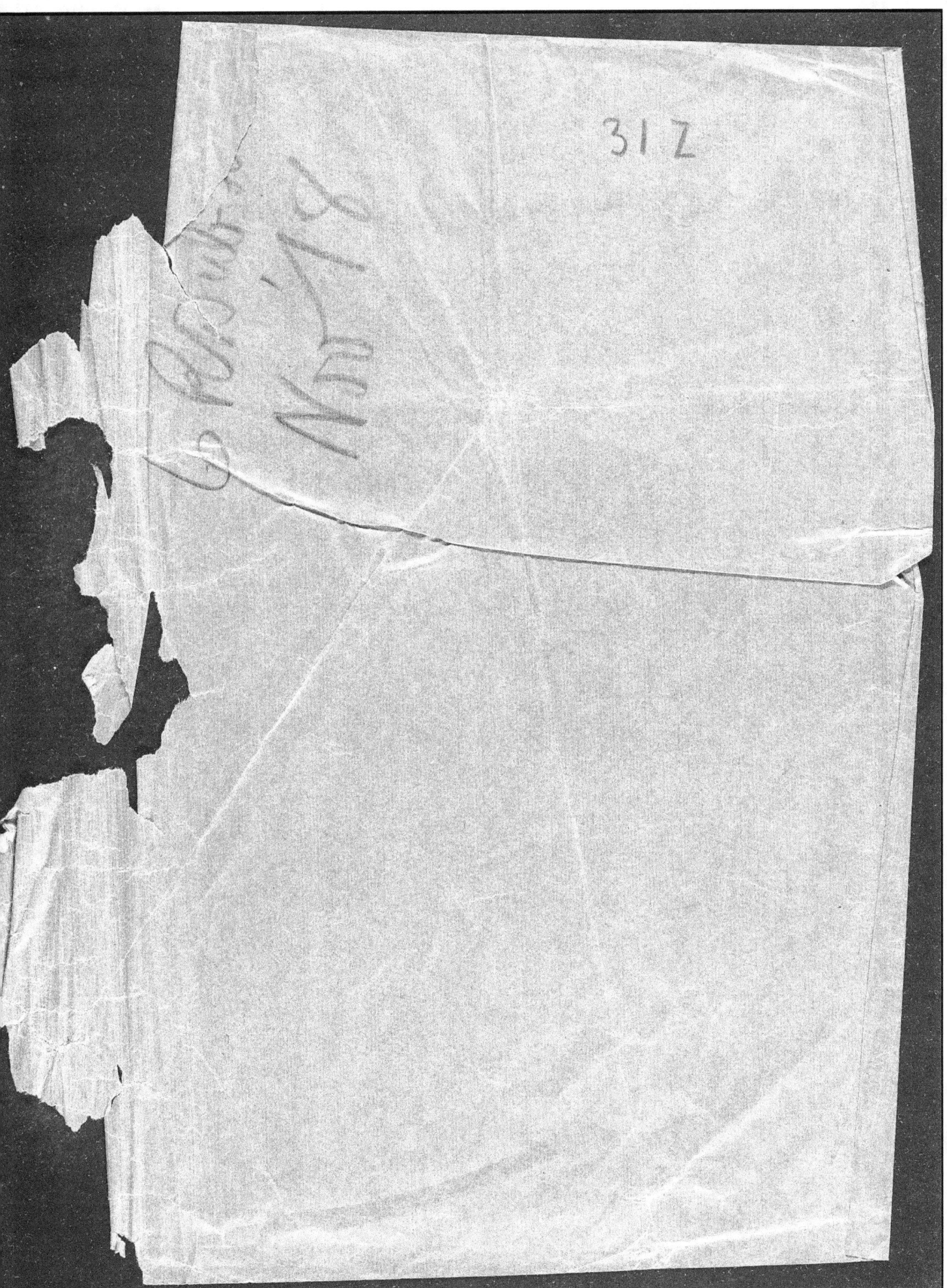

COPIES OF ORDERS AND MESSAGES

(Sept, Oct. & Nov. 1918)

Supplied by

Lieut.-Colonel W.B.Little DSO.MC.

(late Comdg 6/R.Dublin Fusiliers).

Operation Order No.

Ref: Map 57 b.
1/40:000.
----

1. Successful operations of yesterday will be continued this morning.

2. 198th Inf.Bde will be on our right and other troops on our left.

3. Boundaries - Northern. T.12.central - north corner Bois ? (undecipherable)

   Southern - 198th Bde ? ? ? (undecipherable)

4. Objective. 198 & 199th Bdes. Line adjoining O.30 central and U.1.b.1.8.

5. L.Fus: form up in U.14.b. and will advance so as to clear eastern outskirt of Ellincourt after which they continue to first objective - Bois de Pinon.

6. R.Inniskilling Fusiliers will follow close behind and attack and mop up Ellincourt from S & S.E.

7. 6/R.Dublin Fusiliers will form up in U.7 by first closing in.

- - - - - - - - - - -

C.O.X.21.

O.C. B.C.Coys.
             ? had
I have just (heard) a Hun prisoner (captured in north of Le Cateaux) examined at the S.A.H.Q's. He says that there are only one or two enemy patrols which visit the town and that it contains no permanent garrison. I think this statement can be taken as pretty accurate. He also said that there were several civilians in the cellars.
   The men should be warned accordingly so as to prevent casualties amongst them.

   Bn.H.Q. are in a cellar near Quarry previously named. A flag with blue diamond hangs outside. Any prisoners captured will be sent here.

16.10.18.

20.21.   (sgd) W.B.Little.

C.O.X.22.

O.C.   Coy.

A prisoner just captured by the S.A's says that there are only one or two enemy patrols which visit the town and that it contains no permanent garrison. There are many civilians in the cellars, and the men should be warned accordingly.

A & D.Coys will push across the river and endeavour to gain touch with C.Coy. on the first street running north and south just east of the river, after mopping up has commenced.

A South African officer says an enemy M.G. was in position last night in the house just east of the bridge at K.34.a.9.a. This bridge is passable for troops and runners to H.Q. should come this way.

(sgd) W.B.Little.

20.21.

C.O.X.24.

S.A.H.A.

Posts were established by the 2nd Bn.S.A.I. last night as follows: (1) East of river at K.34.d.1.5. (2) west of river at K.34.a.9.d.2.

Ref: (1) It is reported that the officer and party who established this post have not been heard of since early this morning. I accordingly endeavoured to get a patrol across the river to investigate, but failed owing to heavy M.G.fire at close range from eastern side.   I have, however, established a post on the west of river at this point.

(2) This was reported to have been driven in early this evening.   I have now re-established it by occupying houses on both sides of the street. Considerable opposition was met with in the form of M.G.fire from Eastern side of river.

Addressed S.A.M.A.
Repeated S.A.Bde.   (sgd) W.B.Little.
                                          1/R.Dub.Fus.
23.45
16.10.18.

C.O.X.25.

O.C. Coy.

A & D.Coys met with considerable M.G.fire while establishing posts at K.34.a.9.2. and K.34.c.9.5. respectively. The M.G. appear to be in houses just east of the river at these points. The S.A. post which was established east of the river at the latter point last night appears to have been captured.

(sgd) W.B.Little.

C.O.X.26.

O.C. Coy.

1. Zero hour will be 05.20 17th inst. B. & C. Coys. will cross bridges in rear of 2nd and 4th Battns S.A.I. at Zero plus 3 hours.
   Advance of S.A's commences at 08.05.

2. Vickers guns will not now report to companies as their tasks are being allotted direct.

3. Even if division on right do not reach their objective it has been decided that the S.A's will take railway embankment in K.36 and 29.

4. Code word that this operation will take place in lieu of bigger operation will be REFUSAL.

5. Should this happen it is more important than ever that B & C. Coys should follow...................(line indecipherable). Close liaison will therefore be maintained by companies.

6. In event of lesser operations only C.Coy. will also establish a strong point at cross roads Q.4.b.4.0.

7. In the event of enemy withdrawing from Le Cateau before either of the operations referred to, A & D.Coys. will push patrols through the town and occupy eastern edge until relieved by B & C.Coys, when they will become support companies.

12.10.18.

01.17.   (sgd) W.B.Little.

C.O.X. 27.

S.A.H.A.

Ref. B.N.21.

Relief was reported complete and companies in position by code under D.F.3. viz: O.O. No.120 complied with.

A good number of gas shells have fallen round Bn.H.Q. area, also in O.2. There was only slight shelling in reply to Zero barrage. A very thick mist is prevalent at present time. Nothing further to report yet.

07.25.
17.10.18.

(sgd) W.B.Little. Lt.-Col.
PEKE.

S.A.H.A.   C.O.X.28.

Ref: H.X.174.

Have just received a message from my liaison officer with S.A.Bde that there is nothing yet to report.

Capt.Grey has just come in and he is sending you some information.

Fog was very thick here and I could not get touch with my two companies moving from O.2 to mop up Le Cateau. South Africans have just brought 12 prisoners to their Bn.H.Q., but the escort is not clear as to where they were captured.

09.30
17.10.18.   (sgd) W.B.Little. Lt.-Col.

C.O.X.29.

To.198th Inf.Bde.
Ref: 57b S.E. and N.E.

The situation at 10.15 hrs. was as follows: 1st Bn.S.A.I. and 4th Bn.S.A.I. were being counter-attacked and had been driven back to the railway embankment in K.23.c.2.3. - K.29.a. The right flank of 4th Bn.S.A.I. was reported to be surrounded. Two M.G's and a sniper were giving considerable trouble. The gun on left flank in Red House on W.side of Rly.Embankment and K.22.c.3.2. approx, and the gun on the right flank in the station of Le Cateau. At 10.10 hrs. two companies of 6/R.D.F. under Major Luke were preparing to cross the River at K.22.d.9.6. by means of bridges for the purpose of mopping up and clearing the hostile M.G's. Major Luke is in touch with S.A's and No.I.Bn called on him for K.8 to assist.

I have sent a third company to follow up the two coys. entering Le Cateau from the north. With another platoon I

have effected a crossing of the river about K.34.c.4.2. with
a view to working northwards, and I have sent another
platoon to reinforce it. I shall get in touch with
Black Watch as ordered.

11.05.
17.10.18.

        (sgd) W.B.Little. Lt.-Col.

P.S. My adjutant has just returned and reports Major
Luke's and Capt Shadforth's companies are mopping up now.
  The situation regarding the right battalion S.A's
is still obscure, so the C.O. of this battalion
informed my adjutant.

        (Init) W.B.L.

S.A.H.A.   C.O.X.30.

  Reference my C.O.X.29. The platoon which crossed the
river about K.34.c.4.a. have captured a M.G.post on east
side of river, and have sent back 9 prisoners of 265th
Regiment. They are working north to gain touch with
companies working in opposite direction.

11.30.
17.10.18.   (sgd) W.B.Little.
         FEKE.

S.A.Bde.   C.O.X.31.

  I have 3 companies now mopping up Le Cateau from
north easterly direction. Other two platoons have
effected a crossing of the river about K.34.c.9.2. and
have captured a M.G.post. They are now working in a
northerly direction to gain touch with companies coming
in from north.
  Another platoon has been ordered to establish a post
at K.35.c.8.3.

11.45.
17.10.18.

        (sgd) W.B.Little.
         6/R.Dub.Fusiliers.

C.O.X.32.

Major Luke and Capt. Shadforth.

    C & B.Coys. should be engaged solely in mopping up. This work must be pushed on with. A.Coy. has crossed the river about K.34.c.9.3. and is working north to meet you after having sent back prisoners. The 50th Division hold the railway triangle in Q.5 and tanks are in this square. I have sent a platoon of Innisk's to establish a strong point at K.35.c.8.3. The L.F's have been ordered to attack from south-east of town and make good road running from Le Cateau to K.35.c.8.3. The whole success of the operation depends on B.C. & D.Coys. getting on with the mopping up. Pass this message on to Capt. Shadforth.

12.10.

17.10.18.   (sgd) W.B.Little.

- - - - - - - - -

6th R.Dublin Fusiliers

Order No.15.

Ref: Map. 57B. N.E.
       57B. S.E.

1. The 66th Division will attack at an hour to be notified later. The 50th Division will attack on the right flank.

2. The 66th Division attack will be carried out by the S.A.Bde - objective RED LINE K.29.a.1.8 - K.29.central - K.36.d.0.5.

3. At Zero the 6/R.D.F. will be disposed as follows:- A & D.Coys - front line with posts at K.34.d.1.5 (east of river), K.34.a.9.2. (west of river) with remainder in support.

4. The 6/R.D.F. will mop up Le Cateau inside the area - railway crossing Q.4.b.4.1.- Bridge Q.4.b.15.90 - River Selle to junction K.28.d.8.1.- Road K.28.d.9.1.- K.35.c.9.3.- southern boundary of division front K.35.a.9.3.- Q.4.b.4.1.

5. B & C.Coys will undertake this task as arranged at C.O's conference.

6. The bridges over which these companies will pass are being constructed tonight between K.28.d.8.1. and K.29.a.1.3. The village will be entered from the north or north-east.

7. A & D.Coys will push patrols across the river and gain

touch with C.Coy when mopping up has commenced.

8. When Le Cateau has been cleared of the enemy B & C.Coys will establish posts on the eastern edge of the town as already arranged, paying particular attention to Railway in Q.5.a - Road crossing K.35.c. - Suburbs K.35.a.2.7. - Factory K.28.d.60.30.

9. A & D.Coys. will act as support to this line e.g. A to B and D to C.

10. C.R.E. after the capture of the following points, will assist in constructing strong points at K.35.c.9.3. and K.35.d.0.8.

11. Two companies 5/Innis.Fus: in Q.7.b. will be prepared to take over the line west of the river in K.34 on receipt of orders from the brigade.

12. Eight Vickers guns are being allotted to the battalion for the defence of the town. Four will be detailed to report to B & C.Coy. respectively after capture of the town.

13. Four guns No.1 Special Coy.R.E. under Lieut. Harry will smoke the area of the North-eastern and eastern outskirts from zero plus 1 hour until the assaulting infantry is formed up east of the Selle.

14. Lieut.Drury will keep liaison with the S.A.Bde so as to obtain the latest information.

15. O.C.Coys will each send an officer or N.C.O. to Battn. H.Q's before Zero to obtain this information. They should know the route (B & C Coys) which the companies will take in order to intercept them, if necessary, on their way to the bridges.

16. B & C.Coys will follow close in rear of the S.A's across the bridges.

17. Speed in clearing prisoners and the establishment of posts mentioned in para.8 is essential.

22.55.

16.10.18. (sgd)W.B.Little.

Action of C.Coy. 6/R.Dublin Fusiliers, from 16th - 18th October 1918.

Ref: 1/20:000 FRANCE; Sheets 57B.N.E & S.E.

16.10.18.

15.30. Went out to reconnoitre pt. of assembly Q.2.cent. and up to road junction K.28.c.75.25.

17.20. Bn. moved forward from billets in Ruesmont, met Coy at Q.2.cent. waiting hour of Zero. Coy. ordered to cross River Selle between K.29.a.20.25 and K.28.d.85.30. known as the bridges, 3 hours after Zero, to mop up the town of Le Cateau.

Zero Hour 0520. 17.10.18.

0720. B & C.Coys marched up to The Bridges, encountered gas at K.33.b.6.1. and pretty heavy shell fire in K.34.a. where company suffered 5 casualties and lost H.Q. platoon in thick mist.

0745. Halted for quarter hour in sunken road at Q.28.c.75.00. heavy shelling and T.M.barrage in this area.

0815. Moved into Chateau Demesne to about K.28.d.2.3. where we appeared to come under rifle and M.G.fire. This, on investigation and touch being gained with the S.A.Bde, was found to be coming from the high ground E. of R.Selle; moved to K.28.d.45.20. Here we learnt from B.A. casualties that they had not made all their objectives.

0930. Sent Coy. under Lt.A.R.Whyte with orders to get into the town and commence mopping. Waited myself at K.28.d.45.20 for D.Coy and one platoon of B.Coy. which I had been informed were coming to join me.

1030. Crossed river with 1 platoon of B.Coy and 1 platoon D.Coy. under 2/Lt.Sutherland and 2/Lt.Miller respectively. Encountered no opposition in the town.

1300. Joined up with coy at K.34.d.70.35. where it was held up by M.G.fire. Also at this point with Capt.M.J.Hayes A.Coy.

1100. Met C.S.M.Synnott of B.Coy. who told me Capt. Shadforth was almost cut off and he wanted some men to try to relieve him, so sent 2/Lt.Sutherland and his platoon to try to get to K.35.d.8.3. and establish strong post there.

1500. This was not done. I again sent him out to K.35.d.8.3. with some extra men to establish two posts one as mentioned & the other at K.35.a.3.1.

1730. My position was:
    Lt.Whyte   1 platoon at Q.4.b.3.2.
    Lt.O'Hea   "   "   Q.5.a.2.8.
    H.Q. with 2 platoons R.Innis Fus. and 2 platoons
        A.Coy at K.34.d.70.35.
    Sgt.Stanton, 1L.G. 8 men at K.34.d.7.8. (x roads)
        in touch with B.Coy. on my left.

1830. Sent Lt.Hannin to K.35.a.20.55.

1920. Heard K.35.c.8.3. was not good, so barricaded streets round H. Q. Sent Lt.Armstrong to road parallel to and just E. of river with N.C.O's to reconnoitre positions firing up all roads running east and west.

2300. Went out to Lt.Hannin's post. Sent Lt.Harney and his platoon, by this time very weak, to K.35.a.3.1.

18.10.18.

0200. Sent Lt.Miller to Q.4.a.7.4.

0325. Sent Lt.Bruce.R.Innis Fus: under cover of barrage to K.35.c.8.3. He established himself on this side of the cutting and went across himself and ran into the German M. Gunners, some already dug in, others in. He shot two and threw a bomb in another pit and got back into the cutting where he was bombed for about ½hour till he found what turned out to be the outlet of a big underground drain by which he got back to the centre of the town. After a considerable time (he was entirely ignorant of the lie of the town, having been guided to me and on to jumping off point for his attack on K.35.c.8.3) he rejoined his platoon then at K.34.d.90.65. They had been trench mortared and machine gunned out of their position by the Germans who had been reinforced at the cessation of the barrage at 0335, just before Lt.Bruce crossed the cutting.

0400. L.Fus. officers turned up to relieve us. Lieut.Bruce arrived and reported as just related.

0100. Relief completed.

NOTES: The town of Le Cateau was very hard to mop up, owing to the big sewers throughout the town, one of which has already been mentioned; these are connected with many of the larger cellars in town. They allowed determined machine gunners with a good knowledge of them, to move from place to place causing trouble and finally to retire to their own lines.

    I would specially like to mention Lieut.Miller for the cool, determined and cheerful way he undertook all his duties.

(sgd) J.L--- Major

O.C. "C" Coy.

Operations 16th, 17th & 18th October.
"B" Coy. 6/R.Dublin Fusiliers

Ref: Sheets 57B.N.E. and S.E. 1/20:000 and Town Plan LE CATEAU.

16th.

1530. Reconnoitred route from Reumont to bridges in K.29.c. Rejoined company in Q.2. where we remained till 07.15 on 17th.

17th.

07.15. Left sunken road Q.2. proceeded via K.33.b.5.2., K.28.c.7.2, Chateau, to road in K.28.d. Thick fog. Enemy barrage heavy after crossing main Le Cateau road. Gas and M.G.fire in grounds of Chateau. No.5 Platoon lost coming through barrage and did not rejoin Coy till following morning.

0830. Got in touch with S.A.Scottish, reconnoitred bridges which were under shell fire and M.G.fire from just N, of Baillon Fm.

0930. Took B.Coy followed by C. across bridge at Dahomey Factory. Sent No.6.Platoon to K.35.c.9.3., No.8 to K.35.c.4.9. No.7 to start mopping up down main road K.35.a, K.34.d in touch with C.Coy. One L.G.section No.7 remained and consolidated at K.35.a.5.8. Coy.H.Q. at K.35.a.2.6.
   Owing to S.A.Bde not reaching objectives, Nos.6 & 8 became involved in front line in K.35.a and did not get to their positions.

1100. Having failed to get touch with 6 & 8 Platoons, I proceeded with my Coy.H.Q. in search of them as far as K.35.c.6.8., where we found the enemy still occupying the railway. Myself and 5 men got cut off in house just N.E. of figure (54) by M.G's and bombers.

1300. Got away with my party and returned to cross roads K.35.a.2.5. Being unable to get in touch with anyone, returned to Dahomey Factory at 1400.

1400. Collected about 60 men of B.C.D.Coys and reorganised them into 3 platoons for defence of bridges, as S.A's were being counter-attacked and their left flank seriously threatened.

1930. Established posts at K.35.a.4.8. and K.35.a.3.6. with 2 platoons B.Coy. and sent remaining platoon (D.Coy) to Major Luke at his request.

18th.

0300. K.35 central occupied by B.Coy.

11.10. Relieved by Lanc.Fus. and returned to Q.2 central.

Strength going in - 4 officers 99 O.R's.
Casualties - 1 officer killed - 2/Lt.Bell
            1   "   wounded - Sutherland.
            8 O.R's killed.
            2   "   missing, 21 wounded, 2 gassed.

19.10.18.   (sgd) H.Shadforth. Capt.

"D" Coy. 6/R.Dublin Fusiliers.

Ref: Map 1/40:000 Sheet 57B.

TO: The Adjutant, 6/R.Dub.Fusiliers.

On the night of the 16th inst D.Coy. was ordered to relieve C.Coy of the 2nd S.A.Regt at K.33.c.3.3. and establish posts in the following manner.

One platoon at K.33.d.5.1. and another at K.33.d.3.7. and 3 sections at Coy.H.Q. at K.33.c.3.3. The remaining platoon and one rifle section was detailed to relieve a S.A.post at K.34.d.0.2. on the E.side of the river. Owing to no report having been received from this post for nearly 12 hours the situation was rather obscure. We proceeded to K.34.d.0.2.W.side of the river and were there fired on by enemy machine guns, showing that the S.A.post had either been wiped out or taken prisoners, so we established a post on W. side of river. This post was to remain here until relieved. All posts having been established we awaited further orders.

At 0200 hours on the 17th inst we received orders to move at 08.20 and mop up the town of Le Cateau on W. side of river. At 08.20 three platoons, minus one rifle section proceeded to K.33.b.4.3. and there received orders to proceed to K.28.d.5.2. and reinforce B & C.Coys (who had orders to mop up the town of Le Cateau from the N.E.) At K.28.d.5.2. the Coy. was split up, one platoon was attached to C.Coy and the remaining platoons and H.Q's to B.Coy. On the morning of the 19th inst we were relieved by Lanc.Fusiliers and companies were ordered to proceed to Q.2.central.

        (sgd) W.B.English. Capt. (D.Coy).
           / 6/R.D.Fus;

19.10.18.

To. O.C. 6/R.D.Fus:.   Ref: Sheet 27 B.N.E. 1/20:000.

16th October 1918.

On the night of 16th Oct. at 1930 hours we took over the line occupied by 2/S.A. at K.33.c.central, and relieved their posts at K.33.d.4.8. (1 platoon) K.34.a.9.2. (1 platoon) and K.34.a.9.1. (2 sections).

17th October 1918.

On the morning of the 17th at 1830 hours, remainder of company (2 platoons less 2 sections) marched up to K.33.b.5.1. At 1000 hours A.Coy less 1 L.G.section (left to guard bridges and receive prisoners) marched across the river at K.34.a.10.1 and commenced mopping up from the main road to the church area. K.34.d.2.5., K.34.d.2.9., K.34.d.6.4. K.34.d.6.8. The company experienced considerable opposition from snipers and M.G's, and it was until about 1500 hours that we got int touch with C.Coy, which was held up E. of church. In course of mopping up we captured 17 prisoners, 2 of which number we subsequently shot for breaching. At 1530 hours Major Luke took command of all troops in Le Cateau and made his own dispositions.

18th October 1918. At about 1030 hours the company was relieved by the Lancashire Fusiliers and marched to present position. Position of Mr.Hannin's platoon on relief was from about K.35.central to south of ∅ C. in CATEAU.

(sgd) H.Hayes Capt.
O.C."A" Coy. 6/R.Dub.Fus: .

In the Field.
19.10.18.

The following incidents occurred during operations.

on 17th & 18th October.

17th Oct. We had just captured two prisoners about 1100 hours when a runner from C.Coy reported that one of their platoons was held up by enemy M.G.post and the Platoon Officer (Lt.Bell) and one O.R killed. Mr.Hannin and a L.G. section screened by the two prisoners advanced on the enemy position and called upon them to surrender, about 10 Germans came forward as though to surrender but instead opened fire with a M.G. killing one of our men. Whereupon our men killed the two prisoners and fell back to a sheltered position where we created a barricade and got two L.G's in position.

About 30 minutes later C.S.M.Cooke reported to me that there were more Germans in a wine cellar that he was mopping up. We captured them (4 in number) Lieut.Whyte who speaks German fluently instructed one of them to call upon the enemy gunners to surrender (about 20 in numbers) telling them that they would get safe conduct through our lines, they refused. We gave the prisoner to understand that should they fail to return, we would kill his three comrades.

19.10.18.   (sgd) H.Hayes Capt. O.C."A"Coy.

S.A.H.A.   C.O.X.33.

  Enclosed see message and sketch from C.Coy. Major Luke.
It appears that most of B.Coy. have been taken by the
S.A's to reinforce their left flank, and this has inter-
fered with the mopping up. I have given orders for this
work to be pushed on with. From observation the platoons
which crossed river west of village appear to be going well
and are unofficially reported to have reached the church.
  I have sent 4 Vickers guns to follow up Innis.platoon
which have gone to make good area round K.35.c.8.3. The
bridge at K.34.a.9.2. has been cleared of enemy and troops
can pass over planks. Packs can ford the river.

12.27.
11.10.18.   (sgd) W.B.Little.

C.O.X.34.

  Reference C.O.X.29 regarding 2 enemy machine guns and
sniper. Map reference should read K.23.c.3.2. and not
K.32.c.3.2..

  Reference crossing point of river of two platoons which
crossed west of town. This should read K.34.a.9.2. and not
K.34.c.9.2. Enemy are still holding the latter crossing.

13.10.
17.10.18.   (sgd) W.B.Little.

C.O.X.35.

  An officer who has been mopping up reports
(reference town plan Le Cateau) Coys from north have cleared
up to points 68 & 69 and 61 and are in touch with platoons
who crossed from west side. Many guards have had to be left
at cross streets, and this has absorbed most of my men.
Considerable opposition has been met with from houses 98 to
78, and I have ordered 1 platoon Innis. to outflank this
positions from the south or south-east. The enemy are
fighting vert stoutly and the party referred to have refused
to surrender (tried through an interpreter) One party who
apparently offered to surrender turned and shot some of my
men. Naturally the prisoners in possession at that time were
disposed of. I have not yet heard from the platoon sent
to 35.c.9.3. My reserves now consist of 1½ coys. Innis.
Only 13 live prisoners have been taken. That portion of
town already reported clear will have to be gone over again.

14.32.
                                    (sgd) W.B.Little.

O.C. "D" Coy. Inniskillings.   C.O.X.36.

If your platoon commander who has gone into the town is held up give him orders to return to bridge K.34.a.9.2. and proceed east along main street to objective. He can then get into touch with Black Watch along railway. Town has been cleared beyond church and also all the northern portion of town. He should report directly he is in position when R.E's will go up to consolidate. Another platoon of D.Coy Inniskillings has been ordered to envelope southern part of town and clear out M.G's.

15.00.
17.10.18.   (sgd) W.B.Little.

- - - -

C.O.X.37.

Report received from Platoon Commander Inniskillings, who was sent to establish strong point at K.35.c.8.3., that he is held up at K.34.d.2.2. and is in touch with some Dublin Fusiliers. I have ordered him to return to Bridge K.34.a.9.3. and proceed south-east along main street to his objective.

15.10.
17.10.18.   (sgd(W.B.Little.

- - - -

C.O.X.38.

Reference Town Plan.

Situation at present as follows:- Am holding houses about 61-68-69-51-93. Am endeavouring to establish post about K.35.d.9.3. although this point at present strongly held by enemy. Severe fighting has been taking place and m.g!s are commanding most streets.

Reference situation on left - See reports from Capt. Shadforth and message from O.C. S.A.Scottish. Capt. Shadforth has seen the letter message and is taking necessary steps. I am sending one platoon of the Innis. to support him in this task. Have only 2 Vickers guns across the river, and they have gone with one of my sergeants to point 51. Am sending 2 more to protect bridges under Capt.Shadforth. Very heavy enemy shelling of western outskirts of Le Cateau.

17.5
17.10.18.   (sgd)W.B.Little.

Capt. Shadforth.   C.O.X.38.

Am sending you 1 platoon of 'Skins' and 2 vickers guns.
Situation at present: Our men are holding points
61-68-69 - with you I presume about 2 (reference Town
plan) Major Luke with 1 platoon of Skins is endeavouring
to clear street from church to 35.d.9.3. Your Sergt
Morley has been to see me and he with Sutherland are at
point 51.
(Following just received from Brigade:- Brigade has orders
to take and hold line as follows and to complete mopping
up of Le Cateau by dusk. Line K.35.Central along embankment to K.35.c.9.3. thence along divisional boundary.
Forward posts to be established on Le Cateau - Basofi road
as far as road junction K.35.d.6.0.)
You will immediately establish posts about K.35.a.3.7.
and K.35.a.5.0. and endeavour to get into touch with your
platoon at Point 51.

17.30.
17.10.18.   (sgd) W.B.Little.

Major Luke.   C.O.X.39.

Ref: Town Plan and 57B.Map.

I have a report that you are about Point 51. We also
appear to hold Points 68-69 and 61. Capt.Shadforth at
present is back at 28.d.6.4. but I have sent him another
platoon and orders to establish posts at K.35.a.5.0. and
35.a.3.7. Am sending you another platoon of Skins. You
must then establish posts at Q.4.b.6.4 - Q.5.a.2.3. and
K.35.c.9.3. With remainder of troops you have, continue
the mopping up and report early results.
The latter point has been heavily bombarded, which
should have cleared out many of the enemy. If you are
in touch with A.Coy. you can give them orders to establish
the southern post.

17.45.
17.10.18.   (sgd) W.B.Little.

Major Luke.   C.O.X.40.

Hope you have by now received my previous orders and
report on situation. I have ordered Capt.Shadforth to
establish posts and consolidate at K.35.a.4.8 and 35.a.5.0.
You push out and seize points K.35.c.9.3. establish strong
points also at Q.5.a.3.8. and about cross roads south of
town. Div. on right are attacking at 21.00 under a barrage
to clear railway embankment up to near K.35.c.9.3. barrage
lasts 35 minutes. This will be your chance to rush up
and capture this point, and if no or little opposition met
with, establish a post also at road junction K.35.d.6.0.
Get these posts established as soon as possible and you will
have done damned well. Ref.your message. It is not clear
as to part of town cleared of enemy. Do you mean railway
crossing W or E. of town. Please repeat whole situation
again. Did you mean up to triangle in Q.5.a. Bde message

just received says - Heavy artillery firing barrage on
line of railway from K.35.c.9.3. to K.35.central both
inclusive at 20.30. Move up soon as possible after this.

Report results early.

20.5.   (sgd) W.B.Little.

C.O.X.40.

Capt.Shadforth,

Your S.8.received. Give Harney instructions to
patrol to K.35.c.9.3. I expect Major Luke's party to
get there about 20.30. I think you should send an officer
of D.Coy. with a patrol round the posts you are
establishing and to get in touch with Luke's party in
the first instance about (51) (Town plan) and later to
K.35.c.9.3. Report when they have had touch. Luke reports
the town now clear of enemy. Am sending you 2 more V.G's
which you can put in the posts.

20.20.   (sgd) W.B.Little.

C.O.X.41.

Herewith situation report from Major Luke. Garrisons
for posts about K.35.a.5.0. and 35.a.3.7. are on their
way out from Shadforth's Coy. Luke is establishing
posts south of these.

20.30.

                                  (sgd) W.B.Little.

17.10.18.

C.O.X.42.

Situation is now as follows: Le Cateau as far as can
be ascertained is clear of the enemy. I have posts
established at:-
1. Q.4.b.4.2.
2. Q.5.a.1.8.
3. K.35.c.7.6.
4. K.35.a.5.0.
5. K.35.a.1.5.
6. Another north of this (location not yet known)
    K.35.c.8.3. is giving a lot of trouble, but am
tackling it with a fresh platoon. Heavy M.G.fire comes from
approximately railway embankment Q.5.b.6.0. and K.36.c.
    All these posts are in touch with one another.
    Shall now take action in accordance with your H.X.1718.

22.30.
17.10.18.   (sgd) W.B.Little.

C.O.X.43.

Major Luke,

Message received. Very good work done.
Hope you get K.35.a.8.3. established then push K.35.a.7.6.
forward to railway embankment and instruct Lt.Harney to do
the same so as to make our line run K.35.c.8.3.-K.35.central.

Railway Triangle in Q.5.a. is still Bosch, so your
right flank wants watching.

6/L.F's continue the attack tomorrow and we come into
reserve.

Report directly this new line is established, as it
is very important. If you want any more V.Guns or another
18 men say so.

22.50.

(sgd) W.B.Little.

17.10.18.

Am sending you T.Mortar ammunition.

C.O.X.44.

Capt.Shadforth.

Major Luke has posts established Q.4.b.4.2.- Q.5.a.1.9.-
K.35.c.7.6. - K.35.a.1.5. He is now tackling Q.35.a.9.3. I
want you to push your posts forward to railway embankment
Q.35 central as this is most urgent for tomorrow's
operations, which will be continued by 6/L.F's while we
come into reserve. You can use some of D.Coy for this
purpose, if you wish.

Report directly you have gained railway embankment.
Send a runner to H.Q. to guide up ration party.

22.50.
17.10.18.   (sgd) W.B.Little.

C.O.X.45.

Major Luke.

Herewith 2 officers of L.Fus. to reconnoitre all the
posts including B.Coy. Make necessary arrangements as they
are to carry on the attack later in the morning. Do everything
possible to push posts out to K.35.d.6.0. and along line
K.35.c.central then this will crown our success. Can
you report by bearer position of B.Coy.posts.

02.15.
18.10.15.   (sgd) W.B.Little.

Major Luke: C.O.X.46.
Capt. Shadforth.
----

1. The 6/L.F's will relieve the 6/R.D.Fus. before dawn.

2. On relief the battalion will move into Q.7.b. (near Brigade H.Q.) and be in Brigade reserve.

3. Machine Gun and L.T.M.B. personnel will remain in position and come under orders of 6/L.Fus.

4. Major Luke and Capt. Shadforth will give necessary orders to all troops of other companies under their command.

5. On moving out these officers will report personally at Bn.H.Q. that all companies have been relieved.

6. The utmost endeavour will be made to hand over posts at K.35.d.6.0. and K.35.central in touch with S.A's.

                                           (sgd) W.B.Little.

                                            C.O.X.47.

Major Luke.

             Reference yours. We have not seen anything of your H.Q.platoon. Endeavour to find them will have to be made in daylight.

                                       (sgd) W.B.Little.

6th Bn. Royal Dublin Fusiliers.

OPERATIONS 16th-17th Oct.1918.

Ref: Map: Sheets 57B. S.E. & N.E.

10.00. Battalion moved by route march from Maretz to Ruemont.

13.00. Attended G.O.C.Conference at Ruemont and received instructions for the battalion to mop up Le Cateau in combination with larger operations on the morning of the 17th inst.

15.00. Went forward with company commanders to reconnoitre point of assembly for 2 coys and Q.2., and to arrange details for the relief of the 2nd Bn.S.A.I. with remaining 2 coys. in outpost line west of Le Cateau.

    Arrangements for mopping up Le Cateau were as follows:-
B & C.Coys were detailed to cross bridges between R.Selle between K.29.a.20.25 and K.28.d.85.20 in rear of the assaulting troops and S.A.Bde, enter the town from the north-east and clear the town in bounds, which were

7.

definitely arranged. A & D.Coys were to cross the river, if circumstances permitted, with patrols and gain touch with the 2 companies working from the north-east. If this crossing could not be effected easily the forward posts were to keep the enemy on the east bank engaged while they were taken in rear by the other companies. B & C.Coys. under the commands of Capt.Shadforth and Major Luke respectively had orders to cross the bridges at ZERO plus 3 hours.

17.20. Bn.H.Q. moved to house at K.33.d.5.2. and companies to respective positions.

19.00. Capt.W.D.English O.C. "D" Coy. reported that on the night of the 15th inst the 2nd Bn.S.A.I. had affected a crossing of the Selle about K.34.d.1.5. and had established a post on the eastern bank with 1 officer and 14 O.R's, but that nothing had been heard from it since the early hours of the 16th inst. I gave him orders to try and cross the river and investigate matters. This he endeavoured to do, but failed owing to M.G.fire at close range from the eastern bank. A.post was then established on the W.bank. O.C."A" Coy. reported that the post which the S.A's had peviously held on the west bank of the river about K.34.a.8.2. had been driven in earlier in the evening. I gave orders for 1 platoon to re-establish this post at all costs. The night was very light and on the patrol proceeding down the street, heavy M.G.fire was brought to bear on it by the enemy. A Lewis gun was quickly got into action and after some skirmishing our men got into the houses on both sides of the street near the demolished bridge with two casualties.

07.00 (17th inst) B & C.Coys left position of assembly and proceeded via K.33.b.5.2. - K.28.c.7.2. -Chateau - Road in K.28.d. to bridges. A very thick fog prevailed and at the time a heavy gas and H.E.barrage was being put down by the enemy. Box respirators had to be worn and this made the question of keeping direction and touch a very difficult problem. B.Coy lost No.5 platoon and C.Coy. its H.Q. platoon, the former owing to the connecting files having become casualties.

08.15. Both companies got touch with the S.A. Bde about Chateau Demesne and at this pperiod came under heavy M.G. rifle and T.M.fire. Several casualties resulted. Information was received that the S.A's were held up on the east side of the river.

07.15. Companies crossed the bridges near Dahoney Factory. No.6 Platoon was ordered direct to railway crossing at K.35.c.9.3.to make good this point and intercept enemy retreating from Le Cateau. No.8 platoon was ordered to establish a strong point about K.35.c.4.9. to further assist in cutting off the enemy. No.7 Platoon and C.Coy commenced mopping up the town. Later it was ascertained that Nos.6 & 8 Platoons had become involved in the fighting with the S.A's, as they were held up on the right. One Lewis gun section had been ordered to consolidate in K.35.a.5.8. On this information reaching me I withdrew D.Coy (less 1 platoon holding river crossing K.34.d.1.5) and ordered it to reinforce B.Coy. In the meantime No.5 platoon which had lost direction had been located near Bn.H.Q. and I sent it under the adjutant to rejoin its company . Capt.Shadforth had not learned that 2 of his platoons had been involved in the fighting with the S.A's and proceeded to get in touch with them at 11.00. He went direct to K.35.c.6.8. with 5 men and was promptly cut off by the enemy who commenced to machine gun and bomb this party. They got into a house just N.E. of (54), reference Town Plan, and managed to keep the enemy at bay until 13.00, when by piling furniture against a wall they got out, though a shell hole in the wall at the back of the house and escaped back to K.35.a.7.8. In the meantime C.S.M.Sinnott B.Coy. who had escaped in the first instance located Major Luke informing him of what had happened. A party was sent to rescue Capt.Shadforth and his 4 men, but failed to get near the house owing to M.G.fire on the railway. Major Luke then took command of all the mopping up parties and set to work systematically.

At 10.00 I realised that the mopping up from the north-east was not proceeding sufficiently fast, and I decided to affect a crossing of the Selle from the west bank and work ~~and work~~ up the street from bridge to 34.6.0.1. to church to join forces with those working from the N.E. One platoon of A.Coy. was ordered to effect this crossing; this they did by avoiding the bridge at   and fording the stream lower down. A machine gun post consisting of 9 men was quickly captured. This being successful I ordered a second platoon of A. to follow up the first and work from bridge to K.34.d.2.5 - K.34.d.6.4. and K.34.d.6.8. The remaining two platoons less 1 M.G.section left to guard bridge at K.34.6.0.1. were despatched soon afterwards to clear in a north-easterly direction (This was made possible by orders being received from Brigade that I could use all my battalion for mopping up purposes and that 2 companies 5/R.Innis.Fus: were being sent to my support). A.Coy. met with considerable opposition from all quarters by M.G's and snipers. The enemy were a very brave and stout lot of fellows, and I regret to say treacherous. About 11.00 one platoon had just taken two snipers when a runner reported that another platoon was held up and the platoon officer and others killed. Lieut.Hannin and a L.G.Section immediately put a screen of prisoners in front of them and proceeded direct along the street and called on them to surrender. Ten came out with their hands up apparently for this purpose, but instead of surrendering opened fire with a machine gun killing some of our men and taking cover. Needless to say the prisoners in possession were promptly despatched to another world. Our party then quickly fell back to cover and erected a barricade in front of 2 Lewis guns which were turned on to the house and good street fighting began. Half an hour later C.S.M.Cooke reported to his company commander, Capt.Hayes, that there was another strong party of about 20 in a house with machine guns in another street, and that he had captured 4. Lieut.Whyte, who speaks German fluently, instructed one of them to go down the street and tell his comrades that if they would surrender they would get a safe conduct through our lines, and that if he himself, who was covered with rifles, did not return, his other 3 comrades would also be shot. This prisoner did as he was instructed, but the reply he got was "No surrender". Curiously enough this man was allowed by the party referred to to return safely to us. On hearing of this obstinacy I despatched a platoon of 5/R.Innis Fus., who had come up, round to the south of the town for the purpose of enveloping these parties. This was successfully done.

15.00. A.Coy got touch with B & C.Coys coming from the north-east. These companies had also had several M.G's and snipers to deal with.

14.00. Capt.Shadforth on urgent messages from S.A.Scottish collected 60 men of B.C & D.Coys and reorganised into 3 platoons to defend bridge over river.

12.10 On learning that 2 platoons of B.Coy had become involved with the S.A's, and fearing other platoons would be called upon to help I sent an order to Major Luke and Capt.Shadforth that all 6/R.Dublin Fusiliers from this time would be employed on mopping up and defending Le Cateau. Capt.Shadforth did not receive this message, being at the time imprisoned.

12.27. Reported to Brigade that mopping up from west going well and the Church had been reached.

12.00. Hearing that Railway crossing K.35.c.9.3. had not been made good I despatched one platoon 5/R.I.Fus to this point.

15.00. Report received from this Platoon Commander that he was held up at K.34.d.2.2.

17.30. Southern portion of town was cleared of the enemy and posts definitely established at Q.4.a.3.2. Q.5.a.2.8. and K.34.d.9.7.
One platoon 5/R.I.Fus. and 2 Vickers guns were sent to support Capt.Shadforth at north of town, but only 3 men reached him as remainder had become casualties by shell fire.

17.00. Sent 2 Vickers guns with Capt.Morley,B.Coy., to about Point (51.Town Plan) to command eastern exits of town.

18.30. Post established at K.35.a.2.5. This area of the town was under constant fire from the railway embankment.

19.00. Streets being entirely patrolled in case of lurkers coming out.

19.30. Posts established at K.35.a.4.8. and K.35.a.3.6.

20.30. Two Vickers guns despatched to these posts.

03.00 (18th inst). Post established at K.35.central.

03.25. Lieut.Bruce 5/R.I.Fus. sent under cover of barrage to capture and hold K.35.c.9.3. Later he reported that he reached the west side of the cutting and crossed the railway line, himself meeting many of the enemy some established with M.G's and others digging in. He shot two with his revolver and threw a bomb amongst the remainder. He got back into the cutting and found what appeared to be an outlet of a big underground drain. Entering this he travelled along until he found an opening which brought him out into the centre of the town. His platoon had meantime returned to K.34.d.9.6.

04.30. Post at Q.5.a.2.8. moved forward to Q.5.a.3.5. and touch gained with 50th Division in The Triangle.

The 4 Trench Mortars did useful work, 2 with B.Coy and 2 with A.Coy. The former was employed in clearing out

M.G's for the South Africans, and the latter on M.G.nests in the town.

Hand grenades No.26 and smoke grenades No.27 were freely used in the mopping up.

Many prisoners were sent back out of the town without escort, for which receipts were not obtained. Receipts for five only are in possession. It was impossible to make an inventory of the captured material. At least 3 motor lorries were seen.

Casualties - Officers 4
            O.R's. 81.

19.10.18.   (sgd) W.B.Little. Lt.-Col.
                                        6/R.Dub.Fusiliers.

Total casualties todate:

	K.	W.	M.	TOTAL
Officers	2	15	0	17
O.R's.	53	318	16	387

- - - - - - - - - - - - -

6th Bn. Royal Dublin Fusiliers

OPERATIONS - 7th - 11th October 1918.

7th.

07.00. Went forward from St.Emelie with Coy.Commanders to reconnoitre battle sector.

10.45. Battalion moved by march route from St.Emelie to Le Catlet, under the Adjutant, arriving 14.30.

22.00. Battalion moved to tape line via Canal bridge - A.12 central - fork road B.1.d.2.1. Night very dark and slight hostile shelling.

8th.

24.45. C.Coy reached assembly tape and commenced taking up positions.

01.00. Intensive gas, shell and M.G.barrage opened by enemy. B.Coy were only a short distance from the tape and laid down in groups. A & D.Coys were in the valley and scattered inkm out. Considerable confusion was caused and about 100 casualties including 4 officers resulted.

03.30. Barrage still intense. Parties who had scattered were collected together and sent forward to the tape.

04.00. Barrage slackened somewhat but m.g's kept up heavy fire.

04.45. Coys. now in positions on the tape with 5/R.Innis. Fus. on right, considerable gap between battalions.

05.10 . ZERO. Our guns put down a splendid barrage and companies went forward to the attack. A & C. leading, D & B. in support. Bn.frontage 600 yards - each Coy. on a two platoon front. As right coys were now very weak I ordered Capt.Shadforth, B.Coy., to send one of his platoons from left support to the right. This was done in the first stage of the barrage.

05.20. Unnamed Farm was captured under the barrage without difficulty and yielded 40 prisoners to No.5 Platoon.
Advance to Petit Varger Farm continued, troops keeping well under barrage. At this stage heavy M.G. fire was brought to bear from T.6a c & d. T.21.b and T.15.d. No.6 platoon from support deployed to the left and destroyed the nearest guns which were in another battalion area. By so doing they enabled the leading line which had halted to catch up the barrage before reaching Petit Vergar Farm. This farm and the rifle pits in the vicinity were captured with little difficulty and about 50 prisoners collected. Time 06.00. The attack was continued, but was held up on the line T.23.a.8.7. - T.22.b.4.6, primarily by 2 M.G's firing from 200 yards west of Marliches Farm and snipers. An endeavour was made to get a Stokes Motar into action, but it was found impossible as the team had become casualties. Our artillery at this time was firing smoke shell and 18-pdrs. short. A good smoke screen was afforded however, and taking advantage of it B.Coy, under Capt.Shadforth, leap-frogged and pushed on for Marliches Farm. One platoon 4/60th Rifles at this

point got in touch with our left flank. The sunken road
T.23.b.3.8. - T.17.c & d. was assaulted and yielded about
40 prisoners. The Farm was then captured but was untenable
owing to M.G.fire from the front, left flank and left rear.
Field guns were also firing over open sights, but these 3
guns were silenced by a Lewis gun section which enfiladed
their flank.

The front line now fell back gradually to the
sunken road and the right company got in touch with the
5/R.I.Fus on the flank by shutter.

Capt.Shadforth now took over command of all companies,
they having been considerably reduced in strength and
reorganised. The sunken road became very unhealthy as
enemy machine gunners had worked out on the left flank
and were enfilading it. The shooting, however, was
bad and in the meantime the troops on the left had
advanced and had commenced clearing Villers Outreaux.
Just at this time a Whippet tank came up, but got stuck
in the sunken road and was machine gunned until all the
crew became casualties. An officer, Lieut.Mannion, 4/60th
Rifles, was also wounded in trying to rescue them. By
now resistance on the left flank had slackened, and the
advance again commenced.

13.00. Little or no opposition was met with and Coys.
proceeded to establish posts near Lampe Farme where touch
with the 8/Manchester was gained, T.12.c and T.11.central.

Casualties:-

    Officers   9
    Other Ranks 262

Captured - prisoners 120
    Field Guns   14
    M.G's.   41
    Anti-tank rifles 3
    L.T.M's.   2

9th.

02.30. Orders received from brigade for advance to continue. The battalion was told off as support with
orders to mop up Elincourt from the west with the
5/R.I.Fus. on the right flank.

04.30. Coys. assembled in Sunken Road T.12.a & b.

05.20. Advance commenced and as touch with rigt flank could
not be obtained, 2 companies were sent in to mop up the
whole of Elincourt. Later touch with 1 coy. R.I.Fus: was
made.

Only 11 prisoners were taken in Elincourt. The
enemy had apparently made a hurred departure as food was
found on the tables in some houses.

10.00. Reorganised, having come into reserve and marched in
column of route with advanced guard out for Iris Copse.C.35.
central.

12.00. Reached Iris Copse.

10th.

0001. Orders received to continue the advance to Le Cateau.

Advance Guard 6/L.Fus.
Main Guard 5/R.Inns. Fus.
            6/R.Dub.Fus.

03.30. Battalion marched via L'Eppinette and Maretz along Roman Road to Ruemont.

06.50. Passed through Ruemont under artillery fire and received orders to be in Bde.Reserve following up the 5/R.Innis.Fus. who were in support with the 6/L.F's leading. Right flank boundary - Roman Road exclusive.

07.30. Advance continued in artillery formation, considerable hostile shelling. Leading three companies - A.C. & D. crossed Le Cateau - Cambrai road and dug in.
    Bn.H.Q. established in A.26.d.0.0.

Casualties: Officers   2
             O.R's.   48.

11th.

0400. Orders received for battalion to relieve 6/L.F. in outpost position.

18.00. Reconnaissance of outpost line completed.

18.50. Orders to relieve 6/L.F. cancelled, and orders to withdraw into Divisional Reserve received.

21.00 Moved back to billets in Maurois (3 casualties on way)

Total casualties to date:

	K.	R.	M.	TOTAL
Officers	1	12	-	13
O.R's.	41	255	9	305.

(sgd) W.B.Little.
O.C. 6/R.Dub.Fus:

Ref: Town Map and Map 57 B.   C.O.X.39.

Major Luke.

I have a report that you are about Point (51). We also appear to hold points (61)(68)(69). Capt. Shadforth is at present back at 2.8.d.6.4., but I have sent him another platoon with orders to establish posts at K.35.a.5.0. and K.35.a.3.7. Am sending you another platoon of the "SKINS" You will then establish posts Q.4.b.6.4., Q.5.a.2.9. and K.35.c.9.3. With the remainder of troops you have continue the mopping up of the town and report early the results.

K.35.c.9.3. has been heavily bombarded which should have cleared out many of the enemy. If you are in touch with A.Coy. give orders for them to establish the southern post.

17.45.
17.10.18.   (sgd) W.B.Little.

O.C."B" Coy.   C.O.2.

1. At zero minus two hours all covering troops now out
in front will be withdrawn. Troops will be warned that
these men are to come in and covering parties as already
arranged will be put out by C & D Coys. These will be
withdrawn 10 minutes before zero.

50

2. 50th Division report enemy is gas shelling Gouzincourt
Fme. On approaching the line signs of gas will be looked
for and box respirators put on if necessary.

3. Visual signalling and runners only will be used
between companies and battalion H.Q's as no wire is
available.

20.00.

                                 (sgd) W.B.Little.

----

198 Inf.Bde.   C.O.3.

Ref: R.T.2.

Zero. B.2.b.70.20.

Unnamed Farm - T.27.d. about Z plus 45 min.

Petit Verger Fme. T.22.d. about Z plus 1 hour 15 min.

Fork Road T.23.b.2.9. about Z plus 1 hour 50 min.

19.20.

                                 (sgd) W.B.Little.
                                 6/R.Dub.Fus.

                                 C.O.4.

O.C.Coys.

1. Coys will get into position soon as possible after
reaching tape and report on doing so.

2. Brigade   every assistance must be given to
troops at present in front to withdraw by ZERO minus two
hours.

3. Zero hour will be 05.10. This must not to told to
the troops until just before the time.

C.O.X.60.

198th Inf.Bde.

      Reference your G/65/12 dated 29.10.18. The battalion will move off from fork roads near Bn. H.Q. at 0800, and will move in artillery formation as soon as clear of Premont.

      A scheme will start at 10.30 in V.25.b.

29.10.18.   (sgd) W.B.Little.Lt.-Col.
                                          6/R.Dublin Fus.

6th Royal Dublin Fusiliers

O.Order No. -

Secret.

Ref:MAP:Sheet 57A.

1. Situation. General line appears to run as follows: Copse K.20.a.5.9 - K.13.b-K.8.central - K.2.central - E.26.c. - thence along track through E.26.a - E.20.c. - E.20.central.
      An attempt is being made to capture Semousies tonight.

2.   The attack will be continued this morning, 9th inst, with a view to gaining objectives as given for the 6/Lanc.Fus. in Operation Order No - and will be carried out by the 6/R.Dub.Fus.
      The 5/R.Innis.Fus. will be in support and the 6/Lanc.Fus. in reserve. The 5/R.Innis.Fus. will give special attention to the flanks.

3.   The battalion will attack on a 3 Coy.frontage with one company in reserve. Coys. will attack on a two platoon frontage. Right Coy.D - Centre Coy.A. Left Coy.B. Reserve Coy. with Bn.H.Q's C.

4.   Objective and boundaries as in previous order.

5.   Zero 0900 hours.

6.   Assembly position in rear of pesent front line.

7.   Artillery. Programme of arrangements are attached (care must be taken to having these thoroughly understood and every advantage will be taken of them).

8.   Battalion H.Q. Farm K.1.b.5.2 for first bound and Farm K.2.b.9.2. for second bound.

9.   One battery of field guns and 4.5" Hows. 1 sect. M.G. Coy. 1 sect cyclists. 198 L.T.M.B. will be attached to the battalion. Troop 12th Lancers will be used for reconnaissance purposes.

0100.   9.11.18.   (sgd) W.B.Little. Lt.-Col.
                                                 6/R.D.Fus.

WARNING ORDER

1. The battalion will move to Dompierre tomorrow 10th Nov.

2. Starting point will be track near Battn.H.Q. and time about 07.45 hours.

3. Coys. will act on these instructions and make arrangements accordingly.

4. Order of march H.Q. A.B.C.D.Coys.

5. It is probable Lewis guns will be loaded on to limbers on passing transport lines in J.6.

6. Two representatives per Coy. will report at Bn.H.Q. at 07.00 for billeting purposes.

23.35.
9.11.18.
(sgd) W.B.LITTLE.
6/R.Dub.Fus.

C.O.X.61.

6th Royal Dublin Fusiliers.

Operation Order No.19.   Instruction No.1.

Ref: MAP:57A.
    1:40,000.
----

1. The attack up to the Blue Line (Grande Helpe Rail) from I.3.d.0.0. - I.2.b.9.9. - C.26.d.2.2., will be carried out by the 5/R.I.Fus. who in addition to capturing tactical points up to this line will establish at least two bridgeheads over the Grande Helpe Rail between I.3.d.0.0. and I.3.a.0.5.

2. The following tactical features will be seized in this area :-
   (i) Rue des Haies spur H.6.c and d. where touch will be gained with 9/Manc.Reg. in H.12.
   (ii) Villages of Basse Noyelles and Rue du Grand Marais.

   (III) Village of Taisnieres and crossings over the Grand Helpe Rail, getting into touch with 9/Manc.Reg. on their Blue Line which is the road from I.15.c.0.0. - I.3.c.8.0.

3. Attack on the Brown Line. O.C. 6/Lanc.Fus. will keep in close touch with 5/R.I.Fus. and as soon as the latter have seized the crossings over the Grand Helpe Rail he will continue the attack to the Brown Line - J.2.c.9.0.- J.2.a. central - D.26.c.3.3.

4. 5/R.I.Fus. will reform as soon as the 6/R.Dub.Fus. have passed through them on the Blue Line and will move to I.4.central, where they will remain in Brigade reserve.

5. 6/R.Dublin Fusiliers will move forward in close support to 6/L.F's.

6. The following tactical features will be seized by xax the 6/L.F's in their advance to the Brown Line.

   (i)   Villages of Les Cattiaux and Les Ecreutes.

   (ii)   High Ground in I.4.b & d.

   (iii) Spur in I.5. where touch will be gained with the 5/Connaught Rangers at the Chateau (I.11.a.8.8) and assistance given in its capture from the high ground to the north if necessary. Touch will also be gained with troops on our left in C.29.d. In the event of no touch being gained 6/R.Dub.Fus. will detach a party to hold the high ground in C.29.d. as a defensive flank against attack from the north.

   (iv)   Spur in I.6.d. and village of Dompierre, touch will be gained in the latter with 5/Conn. Rangers.

   (v)   High ground in J.I.

7. **Exploitation.**

The South AF.Bde will be prepared to exploit the hight ground in J.2.b & d., J.3.b and J.3.a & c. passing through the 198 and 199 Inf.Bdes, or they may be ordered to cover the right flank of the division.

N.B. For the first phase the 66th Division will be in Corps Reserve.

For the second phase the 66th Division will pass through the 25th Division on the Green Line and operate with the IX.Corps on the right and 50th Division on the left. The 199th Inf.Bde will operate on the right of the 198th Inf.Bde.

4.11.18.
10.20.
                                          (sgd) W.B.Little.
                                                  6/Dub.Fus.

SECRET.   C.D.X.62.

Notes issued with O.O.No.19.

Instructions No.1.

1. The country in which the battalion will be fighting is very enclosed and keeping direction will be difficult. Officers will check their variation of compasses and make sure that compasses are set to grid bearing EAST.

All officers and as many O.R's as possible will carry compasses even if they are not prismatic. The Q.M. may have a few of the latter in store.

2. Hedges are thick and strong and bill hooks will be issued for making gaps. These will be carried in the entrenching tool case. Shovels will be rendered unserviceable if they are used for breaking down fences.

3. Communications will be difficult. Lamps and flags will be used if possible, but runners and signals to aeroplanes will be the mainstay of communications. All ranks must be warned to look out for the latter and signal to them by any available means, viz: flares, pocket torches, waving tin helmets or anything that can be got hold of. These signals <u>must be repeated</u> to every contact aeroplane.

4. Machine Guns may be well concealed in this thick country. Field glasses will be most useful.

5. The battle will be chiefly a platoon commanders and section leader's battle. Clever leading and enterprise coupled with constant reports will go far to ensure great success.

Don't forget to keep pushing the Lewis guns sections through any gap found or using them to create gaps. Warn the L.G.section leaders to work their teams in pairs within platoons as far as possible. Any M.Gun or other strong position can be done in by a Lewis guns worked well forward on the flank.

Be quick in all decisions and don't give the enemy time to settle down or organise.

4.11.18.

(sgd) W.B.Little. Lt.-Col.
O.C.6/R.Dublin Fusiliers.

C.O.X.63.

Battalion Headquarters will be situated as follows:-

1st bound.   Cross roads H.4.c.9.4.

2nd   "   H.6.c.7.5.

3rd   "   Cross roads I.2.d.8.4.

4th   "   Cross roads I.4.d.9.8.

5th   "   Fork roads I.6.d.7.7.

20.00.
4.11.18.   (sgd) W.B.Little.

- - - - - - -

6th Royal Dublin Fusiliers Order No.20.

Ref: MAP.
Sheet 57A.

1. According to latest reports our line now runs from cross roads on southern corps boundary J.21.b.5.5. - J.16.central - J.10 central - J.5.central - D.29.d.0.0.
   The enemy is occupying the east bank of the stream in advance of this line.
   At 16.00 on 7.11.18 enemy were holding spur in J.11 central and probably Lacroisett Farm with a few M.G's.

2. The 198th Inf.Bde with the 199th Inf.Bde on the right and the 150th Bde on the left will continue the pursuit at 07.30 today, 8th inst.

3. Boundaries - Northern Brigade Boundary D.29.d.0.3.- E.26.c.0.3. along Les Trois Paves - Sars Poteries road (inclusive to 198 Bde) E.28.a.9.5. - E.23.c.0.1.

   Southern Boundary: Grid Lane J.3.c.0.0. - K.5.c.0.0.

4. Objectives. General line K.4.d.9.0 - E.28.d.5.0. - E.28.b.1.5. where a liaison post will be established with 150th Inf.Bde.
   On securing this line infantry patrols will clear the ground 500 yards east of the objective, whilst cavalry patrols will ascertain whether Felleries and Beugnies are held by the enemy or not.

5. 5/R.Innis Fus: will carry out the attack as far as the Avesnes - Maubeuge road, between K.1.d.1.0. and road junction E.25.d.9.2 (inclusive)
   6/Lanc.Fus: will pass through 5/R.Innis.Fus: when the latter have reached their objective.

6/R.Dublin Fusiliers will be in Brigade Reserve and will keep in close touch with 6/L.Fus, 6/R.Dub.Fus. will follow the 6/Lanc.Fus. through the 5/R.Innis Fus. in close support and pay particular attention to the flanks.

When the 6/L.Fus. have captured final objective 6/R.Dub.Fusiliers will concentrate in support if situation permits, in valley in K.3..

6. <u>Success signals.</u> 5/R.Innis.Fus. will fire two RED Very Lights in quick succession after capture of their objective, and 6/Lanc.Fus. three ditto after capture of final objective.

<u>Instructions.</u>

7. The battalion will form up at the Church ready to move at 06.00 hours in following order B.D.A.C.H.Q's.

<u>Route:</u> via cross roads J.2.a.

8. <u>Formations.</u> B.Coy.left leading company - D.Coy, right leading company - A.Coy. support - C. right support

If any artillery fire is experienced companies will open out into platoon artillery formation on leaving Dompierre.

A distance of 500 yards will be maintained in rear of 6/L.Fus. until reaching the valley in K.3. where companies will halt unless otherwise engaged.

Companies will send connecting files forward to ensure touch being kept.

Centre line of advance Grid Line D.2.central - K.3 central.

9. <u>Battn.H.Q's.</u> will advance along this line. Bounds for Bn.H.Q. 1st bound J.2.b.60.05: 2nd bound J.4.a.10.00 - 3rd bound J.6.a.3.0. 4th bound K.1.6.5.1. 5th bound K.2.b.8.1.

10. <u>Assembly position.</u> In rear of trees from J.2.d.0.5. to J.2.b.0.5. Two right companies south of the road and two left companies north of road.

This position may be altered by the C.O. according to the positions the 6/L.Fus.occupy.

04.30
8.11.18.   (sgd) W.B.Little.

198th Inf.Bde.   C.O.X.63

Ref: Order No.135.

    Battn.H.Q's will be established in bounds along centre line of advance as under :-

1st bound Point 189.

2nd   "   J.2.b.60.05.

3rd   "   J.4.a.1.0.

4th   "   J.6.a.3.0.

5th   "   K.1.b.5.1.

6th   "   K.2.b.9.1.

8.11.18.   (sgd) W.B.Little.
                                 6/R.Dub.Fus.

                                C.O.X.64.

Major Vance,

    Leave Oliphant and a few signallers where you are to keep in touch with Brigade. Bring all the remainder up here with guide including Sergt.Fay to keep in touch with L.Fus. Then when we move from here Oliphant will come up and join us.

07.55.
8.11.18.   (sgd) W.B.Little.

- - - - -

6/Lanc.Fus: C.O.66.

    I have moved my H.Q. to house about J.4.d.2.4. so as to be in close touch with you. Please let me know where you intend to move forward so that I can move in close support.
    My Battn. is on high ground in J.4.b.

10.35.
8.11.18.

                             (sgd) W.B.Little.

C.O.X.67.

O.C.Coys.

1. From present position the advance will be continued on a 3 company frontage. Each coy. will move on a 2 platoon frontage with 1 platoon in reserve.

(Right Coy - D) (Centre - A) (Left - B).

2. D.Coy's right platoon will advance along southern boundary as near as possible. B.Coy's left platoon along northern boundary keeping just south of the road from E.26.c to E.27.d.

3. Coys. will not advance beyond road K.4.c. - E.27.d. unless the 6/L.F. require support.

4. C.Coy. will move with Bn.H.Q.

5. A.Coy. will immediately get into position in rear of Battn. H.Q's.

6. Leading companies will get into touch on main road J.6.c & a before advancing, on the order being given.

7. A distance of 400 yards will be kept in rear of 6/L.F's reserve coy. A.Coy.centre will direct.

(sgd(W.B.Little.

- - - - - - - -

O.C.   Coy.   C.O.X.68.

Advance from road referred to in para 6 C.O.X.68 will commence at 14.00. Coys. will immediately get into position.

13.35.

(sgd) W.B.Little.

To Lt.-Colonel W.B.Little DSO.MC.

B.M.4. Day of month 18th.

1. You will command the Advanced Guard tomorrow. 198 Inf.Group is responsible for protection of Division front from 11.00 on 19th. For Div.Front see 198 Inf. Bde. Order No.140.

2. You will perform the duties laid down in above orders para 7 (ii) & (III)

3. The French are on our right and the 1st British Division on our left. You will gain touch with right and left.

4. The Advanced guard will consist of :-

    6/R.Dublin Fus. less 2 coys. and unnecessary transport.
    A/330 Battery R.F.A.
    1 Sec, 1st Aus.Tun.Co.R.E.
    1 Coy. 9/Gloucester R. (P)
    1 Sect. 431 Fd.Co.R.E.

Tunnellers and Pioneers all in Cerfontaine. Battery at Froidcapelle. Head of main body passes Rance Stn at 0800.

There will be an hours halt from 1200 to 1300. No halt at 11.50.

From:

    198th Inf.Bde.

                      (sgd) A.HUNTER. B.G.

TO: O.C.Adv.Guard   No.3 Sig.Sect.
    431 Fd.Co.R.E.   1st Aust. Tunn.Co.R.E.
    9/Gloucesters.   Staff Capt. B.I.O.

Senders No. B.M.10.   Day of month 18th.

1. In addition to previous orders the following will be
attached to 198th Bde Advanced Guard and will report at
Rance Stn at 07.30 19th.   2 M.M.P. 2 Bde observers.
Detachment No.3 Sig.Sect for D.R. and visual communication.

2.   When O.C.Advanced Guard is satisfied that necessary
R.E. and Pioneer work is complete up to line Vodecee -
St.Aubin he will return sec. 431 Fd.Co.R.E., sec. Tunn.Co.
and Co.Pioneers to their units in Philippeville where
they will billet. Battery RFA and remainder 6/Dub.Fus.
will be at disposal of O.C. Adv.Guard for outposts on
divisional front.

From 198 Inf.BDE.

21.50.   (sgd) H.EDEN. Capt.

- - - - - - - -

            Captured by 6/R.Dub.Fusiliers   8.10.18.

No.1 numbered 221   at T.22.c.8.7
   2.   "   22846   T.22.b.5.5.
   3.   "   7897   T.22.b.8.7.
   4.   "   52)
   5.   "   2101) T.17.c.8.2.
   6.   "   1152.)
   7.   )
   8.   )
   9.   )   NOTE: These guns were removed before
  10.   )   the number could be obtained.
  11.   )   )
  12.   )   )   T.28.a.50.15.
  13.   )   )   T.17.a.20.15.
  14.   )   )

        All 77 m.m guns.

C.O.5.

S.A.H.A.

MARLICHES

Have reorganised and am pushing forward to occupy strong points as shown on map including Lampe Farm. K.R.R's hold Marliches. I anticipate no opposition as enemy has withdrawn. Malincourt appears free from enemy.
Am pepared to exploit further on receipt of orders.
Bn.H.Q. established in sunken road T.23.b.50.95.

12.51.   (sgd) W.B.Little.

My strength is:

	Officers	O.R's.
Battn. H.Q's.	3	35
A.Coy.	2	58
B.Coy.	1	52
C.Coy.	1	43
D.Coy.	2	55
	9	223

C.O.6.

O.C. "B", "D" & "A" Coys.

After securing present positions push patrols forward and get in touch with 21st Division in Malincourt and east of village by patrols.
Report when this done.

13.35

                (sgd) W.B.Little.

C.O.7.

S.A.H.A.

13.20. Enemy seen retiring in large numbers into Mill Wood and Gard Wood, also over spur in T.33. Artillery informed.

13.45. Have secured all objectives in Green Line and have sent out patrols to get in touch with 21st Division, reference your H.X.87.

Three field guns captured in T.17.c. In addition to the Anti-tank gun in T.22.c. M.G's not counted.

13.46.   (sgd) W.B.Little. Lieut.-Colonel.

- - - - - -

C.O.8.

1. Am halted on general line north-west of Elincourt and am mopping up the village as the 5/Innis. do not yet appear to have reached it. Am in touch with 6/L.Fus: in front. Elincourt seems to have been evacuated as there is no apparent opposition. L.F's are going well. Other troops are advancing on our left flank.

07.5.

(sgd) W.B.Little.

- - - - - - -

C.O.9.

O.C."B" Coy.

If you are not likely to meet with any opposition I shall take remainder of battalion on to Iris Copse.D.35.

- - - - - - -

C.O.11.

Not attached in Message Book

My C.O.10 should have been timed 0742 and not 0712. Since this 3 prisoners (already sent down) came out of hiding and gave themselves up and two more found in the cellar are sent ~~herewithx~~ herewith. There were signs of a hasty retreat as hot *food* was on tables in some houses.

Reference my C.O.8 one platoon reports having got in touch with the 5/Innis.Fus. in the village. Am now moving up to O.35.

08.25   (sgd) W.B.LITTLE.

S.A.H.A.

C.O.12.   10.

Have reached 26 d. Battn. H.Q. at 26.d.0.0. Leading troops are working up to high ground in 27.

09.10.   (sgd) W.B.Little. Lt.-Col.

- - - - - - -

C.O.13.

S.A.H.A.

Culvert under main road about K.26.d.0.0. apparently prepared for demolition. Have had about 30 casualties from shell fire. Leading troops appear held up in K.21.c. and K.21.b.

11.02.
10.9.18.   (sgd) W.B.Little.

Dear Colonel,

Your message received. My H.Q. are in same place as you saw me this morning. I have Bde orders to remain in present position until receipt of orders from them. Hope you are not feeling very ill effects from your wound today. My fighting strength is now under 200, having had about 45 casualties today. Trust show this evening was a success.

20.00.
15.9.18.   (sgd) W.B.Little.

- - - - - - -

Secret.

198th Inf.Bde.   A.G.1.

B.M.12 received. R.E.Section rejoined its coy. at Philippeville. Battery R.F.A. billetted in north-west corner of Hemptinne. Guns are in readiness in transport lines there.
My dispositions are as follows:-
(1) No.1 outpost Coy. in Hemptinne with a picquet of 2 platoons in Farm at   200 yards east of last E in B5 -Tilfore. They have orders to   double sentry group on road at this point and patrol to Vouecee.
(2) No.2 Outpost Coy. in Hemptinne (north corner) with double sentry group posted 500 yards on Hemptinne - St Aubin road. They have orders to patrol to St.Aubin.
(3) Nos.3 & 4 Coys. in reserve in Hemptinne.
(4) Bn.H.Q's near Church.

14.45. 19.11.18.   (sgd) W.B.LITTLE. Comdg.Outposts.

198th Inf.Bde.   A.G.1.

(1) Heavy Advanced Guard reached Hemptinne 15.00.

(2) Two companies from main body arrived 16.00.

(3) Picquets have been sent out.

14.35.
19.11.18.   (sgd) W.B.Little.

- - - -

                           A.G.6.
198th Inf.Bde.

    At 19.15 hours No.2 Outpost Coy. reported having got touch with 12th Lancers in St.Aubin. The Regiment, less 1 squadron, is reported there. No report yet from No.1 Outpost Coy.

                           (sgd) W.B.Little.

- - - -

                           A.G.6.
198th Inf.Bde.

(1) At 19.15 hours No.2 Outpost Coy reported having got in touch with 12th Lancers in St.Aubin. The Regiment, less 1 squadron is reported in that village. No.2 Outpost Coy. reports (20.00 hours) sentry group posted on road referred to in A.G.1, and patrol out.

21.45.
19.11.18   (sgd) W.B.Little.

Appendix (I)

SECRET.   Copy No. 4

198TH INFANTRY BRIGADE ORDER No.125.

1st November, 1918.

1. The 198th Infantry Brigade will move by march route to HONNECHY to-morrow, the 2nd November, as follows :-

Unit.	Time of Passing Starting point.
5th R.Innis.Fus.	09.00
6th Lancs.Fus.	09.15
198th Inf.Bde. H.Q. & Sigs.	09.30
6th R.Dublin Fus.	09.35
198th L.T.M.B.	10.00

   Starting point :- Cross roads, U.29.b.4.8.

   Route :- Cross roads V.27.b.70.95 - BUSIGNY.

2. All transport will march in rear of their own Units.

3. Brigade Headquarters will close at PREMONT at 06.30, and open at HONNECHY on arrival.

4. ACKNOWLEDGE.

                                        R.P.Aden
                                        Captain,
                                        Brigade Major,
                                        198th Infantry Brigade.

Issued through Signals at 17.45

DISTRIBUTION.

66th Division	Copy No.1.
6th Lancs.Fus.	" No.2.
5th R.Innis.Fus.	" No.3.
6th R.Dublin Fus.	" No.4.
198th L.T.M.B.	" No.5.
No.3 Sig.Sec.	" No.6.
Staff Captain	" No.7.
B.I.O.	" No.8.
B.T.O.	" No.9.
War Diary	" No.10,11,12.
File.	" No.13, 14, 15.

Bn Out Inn movement order no 16

1. Bn Out Inn will move by march route to Herrecy tomorrow: moving off at 09.20. Following in order A B C D + a

2. Route:-
   X roads v 27. 6. 70. 05 - BUSIGNY

3. Dress
   Battle order Great coats will be carried on Packs

4. Bn Transport will march in rear of Bn

5. Following intervals on March:-
   100 yds between coys

6. One representative from each coy will proceed under Lt A R Whyte at 08.00 to take over billets

7. 1 Motor Lorry is allotted to Bn for carriage of Blankets
   Coys will detail guard to report at Bn HQ at 07.00 tomorrow. This lorry will be used for one journey only.

8. All Blankets to be placed at Bn Stores by 07.30

9. On arrival in new area coys will at once send runner to Bn HQ who will allot position of his Coy HQ and conduct runner from Bn HQ. This will always be done on arriving in new areas.

10. Leather Jerkins will be worn tomorrow

11. Lts & tools will be carried on transport for march tomorrow

12. B[attalion] [?] & [?] will be [?] tomorrow [?]

Copy 1 Maj. Vance   [signature]
     2 OC A   ADJT C R R
     3 " B
     4 " C
     5 " D
     6 " HQ to warn all concerned and 2 bind
     7 " [?]

SECRET.

6th Bn. Lancs. Fusrs.
5th Bn. R.Innis.Fus.
6th Bn. R.Dublin Fus.

No. 1853/6/A

ADMINISTRATIVE INSTRUCTIONS ISSUED IN REFERENCE TO 198th INFANTRY BRIGADE ORDER NO. 125.
-o-o-o-o-o-

1. Extra transport for carriage of blankets is allotted as follows :-

   1 lorry per battalion for one journey only.

   Battalions will send a guide for lorries to Brigade Headquarters at 7.00 hours.
   Commanding officers will ensure that lorries do one journey only, as they are 66th Divisional supply lorries and must be at Railhead at 12.00 hours.

2. Greatcoats will be taken at the discretion of Commanding Officers. If dumped, they must be taken to the Brigade Dump at MARETZ.
   Baggage wagons may do a second journey for this service.
   Battalions will notify Brigade Headquarters as to what they propose to do in this matter by 8.00 hours to-morrow.

   Jerkins will be worn on the man or carried in the pack at the discretion of Commanding Officers.

3. Billetting parties will be sent on ahead by battalions to billet in the area allotted to them, to-day. If any difficulty is experienced, they will apply to the Staff Captain or his representative, who will be either at the Area Commandant's, HONNECHY, or at Brigade Headquarters, No.17 billet. Battalions will make their own arrangements for guides to meet them from their billetting parties on arrival at HONNECHY.

   Brigade transport will be located on the right-hand side of the MARETZ - HONNECHY Road, just before entering the village, P.23.d.3.1.

                                              Captain,
                                              Staff Captain,
                                              198th Infantry Brigade.

1.11.18.
HBC

8th Bn. Lancs. Fusrs.
5th Bn. R. Innis. Fus.
6th Bn. R. Dublin Fus.
198th. L.T.M.B.

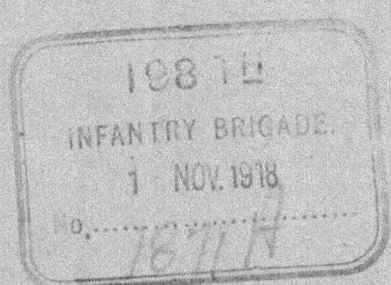

    In view of the more wooded nature of the country further East, it is probable that a large number of billhooks will be carried on the man.

    It has been found from experience that these go well in the entrenching tool carrier.

    Units will be prepared for this.

                                          Captain,
                                    Staff Captain,
                            198th Infantry Brigade.

1.11.18.
HBC

ADMINISTRATIVE

ADMINISTRATION OF THE TOWN of LE CATEAU.

The Area Commandant of LE CATEAU will be responsible for the administration of the Town. As it lies within several Divisional areas it is essential that Divisions should allow him as free a hand as possible, so that the orders which he issues may be equally applicable to all parts of the Town.

BILLETING and ACCOMMODATION. will be allotted solely by the Area Commandant.

SANITATION. The O.C. Sanitary Section (No.16) under the orders of the D.D.M.S. Corps, will advise the Area Commandant on all sanitary matters, and will keep A.Ds.M.S. of Divisions in touch with the situation.

Town cleaning will be carried out by troops billeted in the town. The Area Commandant may demand parties of these daily up to 1%, except from technical Units. Civilian labour may be hired by the Area Commandant for the same purposes.

Public latrines and urinals, incinorators, refuse pits, etc., will be provided under a scheme prepared by the O.C. Sanitary Section in consultation with the Area Commandant.

FIRE PRECAUTIONS. A Fire Piquet of 2 Officers and 60 O.R. is furnished by the Pioneer Battalion of the Reserve Division. One of the officers will perform the duties of Firemaster as detailed in para 3 of G.H.Q. letter No.14005 (QD2) of 13th. May 1918.

The Area Commandant will be in charge of all British fire appliances, and will arrange with the Maire for the maintenance and use of the local Fire appliances.

A scheme will be drawn up for the dealing with outbreaks in the various parts of the Town, and practices will be arranged by the Area Commandant in communication with Divisions.

WATER SUPPLY. The O.C. Sanitary Section will mark all water supplies. The Town supply is being repaired under the orders of the C.E. Corps.

SALVAGE. The Area Commandant will arrange to collect all salvage in the Town and for its evacuation, in communication with the Left Division "Q".

LIGHTS. Strict orders are to be issued, and must be enforced by the police, in regard to the screening of all lights after dark. Lights are not to be lit until windows and doors are effectively screened.

POLICE. The police arrangements and Traffic control of the Town will be organised under the orders of the A.P.M. Corps.

CIVILIANS. The Area Commandant is responsible, under Corps H.Q., for all arrangements which have to be made by the British Military Authorities on behalf of the civilian population. He will keep in close touch with the French Mission attached to Corps Headquarters, and with the Maire. Everything possible will be done to help the inhabitants.

Administration of civilians should be carried out in accordance with Fourth Army Standing Orders paras 502-535.

(sd) S.W. ROBINSON?
Brig-General,
D.A.& Q.M.G. XIII Corps.

31.10.1918.

6th.Lancs.Fus.
5th.R.Innis.Fus.
6th.R.Dublin Fus.
198th.L.T.M.B.

        Forwarded for information.

                                                Captain,
                                          Staff Captain.
1.11.1918.   198th.Infantry Brigade.

SECRET. *appx II* Copy No. 4

198TH INFANTRY BRIGADE ORDER No.136.

2nd November, 1918.

1. The 198th Infantry Brigade will move to LE CATEAU to-morrow, 3rd November, in accordance with the attached March Table.

2. Transport will be brigaded and will march under the orders of Brigade Transport Officer.

3. Transport will march straight through to LE CATEAU, without halting.

4. Advance parties will meet their units at the Cross roads, Q.4.b.5.0.

5. Brigade Headquarters will close at HONNECHY at 15.15 and open at LE CATEAU on arrival.

6. ACKNOWLEDGE.

                                        Captain,
                              Brigade Major,
                      198th Infantry Brigade.

Issued through Signals at 19.30

DISTRIBUTION.

66th Division "G"	Copy No.1.
6th Lancs.Fus.	" No.2.
5th R.Innis.Fus.	" No.3.
6th R.Dublin Fus.	" No.4.
198th L.T.M.B.	" No.5.
No.3.Sig.Sec.	" No.6.
Staff Captain.	" No.7.
B.I.O.	" No.8.
B.T.O.	" No.9.
War Diary.	" No.10,11,12.
File.	" No.13,14,15.

MARCH TABLE to accompany
198TH INFANTRY BRIGADE ORDER No.128.

Serial No.	Unit.	From.	To.	Route.	Time of passing Starting Pt.	Remarks.
1.	6th Lan.Fus.	HONNECHY	LE CATEAU Station	Station (P.29.d)-Q.4.	15.30	Road to be cleared at halts.
2.	5th R.Innis.Fs.	do.	do.	do.	15.40	
3.	198th L.T.M.B.	do.	do.	do.	15.45	
4.	198th Bde.H.Q. & Signals.	do.	do.	do.	16.00	
5.	6th R.Dub.Fus.	do.	do.	do.	16.05	
6.	Brigade Transport.	do.	do.	do.	16.35	

Starting Point - Fork roads P.29.a.4.8.

2.11.18.
RV.

Reference 198th Infantry Brigade Order No. 128.

Starting Point will be amended to read as follows :-

Fork Roads, P.29.d.2.4.

Acknowledge

Captain,
Brigade Major,
198th Infantry Brigade.

Distribution as for 198th Inf. Bde. Order No. 128.

SECRET.

1853/7/A.

6th Bn. Lancs. Fus.
5th Bn. R.Innis.Fus.
6th Bn. R.Dublin Fus.
198th L.T.M.B.

Reference 198th Infantry Brigade Order No. 128.

1. Extra transport is allotted for the move to-morrow as follows :-

2 G.S. Wagons per battalion. (These wagons may do two journeys if required, in which case Commanding officers will make arrangements direct with billetting officers for guides for these wagons.) Guides for these wagons will report at Brigade Headquarters at 8.00 hours.

2. Billetting parties will commence billetting in their respective areas in LE CATEAU at 9.00 to-morrow.

As it will be necessary to guide troops to their billets in the dark, larger parties that in customary should be sent.

Transport will be located in battalion areas, or failing that, on the open ground West of LE CATEAU.

The Billetting officers will report to the Staff Captain or his representative at the Area Commandant's Office, LE CATEAU immediately he has completed the billetting of his unit, or if in any difficulty. He will detail guides to meet his unit at the cross-roads, Q.4.b.5.0. He will also detail a guide to meet transport at this point. Care must be taken that the guide for the transport is there in readiness, as transport is not allowed to halt in the town.

P. Ingham

Captain,
Staff Captain,
198th Infantry Brigade.

2.11.18.
HDC

SECRET.   Copy No. 4

199TH INFANTRY BRIGADE INSTRUCTION No.5.

ISSUED UNDER

198TH INFANTRY BRIGADE ORDER No.127.

                                                      4th November, 1918.

COMMUNICATIONS.

1. The Brigade Axial line of Communication will be along the following roads :-

   H.14.a.2.6. - H.4.c.9.2. - H.5.Central -
   H.5.c.8.3. - H.11.b.3.3. - I.1.a.4.7. -
   I.1.d.3.9. - I.2.c.9.2. - I.3.b.5.1. -
   I.5.d.0.3. - I.6.a.9.0.   (Tracing Enclosed)

2. Brigade Headquarters and Advanced Report Centres, will be located as follows :-

	Brigade H.Q.	Advance Report Centre
	FERME OF CATILLON. (H.14.a).	H.4.c.8.3.
1st Bound.	H.4.c.6.3.	H.6.c.Central.
2nd "	H.6.c.Central.	I.2.c.8.3.
3rd "	I.2.c.8.3.	I.4.d.2.7.
4th "	I.4.d.2.7.	I.6.a.9.3.

   If accommodation permits, Brigade H.Q. may move to the CHATEAU at I.11.a.9.9.
   In the event of this, O.C., No.3.Sig.Section, will arrange to place a Notice Board at the Cross Roads I.5.d.0.4.

3. A line will be laid from Brigade H.Q., to the Advanced Report Centre at each bound.

4. All messages forward of Brigade Headquarters, will be sent by the Advanced Report Centre, except those sent by mounted orderly.

                                                    /5. Visual will be

-2-

5. Visual will be established when possible from Brigade H.Q. to the Advanced Report Centre and from the Advanced Report Centre to the leading and Support Battalions.

6. Wireless will be established at Brigade H.Q. and at the Advanced Report Centre.

7. Battalion H.Q. will move by bounds.

As far as possible units will choose their H.Q. on the Axis of Liaison, the Support Battalion near the Advanced Report Centre and the reserve Battalion near Brigade H.Q.

Battalions will report H.Q. selected by them as soon as possible.

7. ACKNOWLEDGE.

(signature)

Captain,
Brigade Major,
198th Infantry Brigade.

Issued through Signals at 1345

DISTRIBUTION.

Copies to all recipients of Instruction No. 1, and 450th Field Co., R.E.

SECRET.

6th Lancs. Fus.
5th R. Innis. Fus.
6th R. Dublin Fus.
198th L.T.M.B.
No. 3 Signal Section.

198th Inf. Bde.
No. G. 32/10

WARNING ORDER.

The Brigade will be prepared to move to POMMEREUIL tomorrow, the 4th inst.

Head of Column will not leave LE CATEAU before 10.00.

"B" teams will remain in LE CATEAU.

Acknowledge

Captain,
Brigade Major,
198th Infantry Brigade.

3.11.18.
RHW

SECRET.   Copy No.

Reference 198th Infantry Brigade Order No. 129.

Units will march to POMMEREUIL today as instructed in that order except that times will be altered as follows :-

Unit.	Time of Passing Starting Point.
5th R. Innis. Fus.	16.00.
198 Bde. H.Q.	16.10.
6th Lancs. Fus.	16.15.
8th R. Dublin Fus. —	16.25.
198 L.T.M.B.	16.30.
Brigade Transport.	16.50.

Brigade H.Q. will close at LE CATEAU at 16.45 and open at POMMEREUIL on arrival.

ACKNOWLEDGE.

Captain,
Brigade Major,
198th Infantry Brigade.

Issued through Signals at .....

DISTRIBUTION.

As to recipients of 198th Inf. Bde. Order No. 129.

SECRET.   Copy No...5...

198TH INFANTRY BRIGADE ORDER NO. 129.

                                                4th October, 1918.

Reference Sheet, 57B, 1/40,000.

1. 198th Infantry Brigade will move by march route to POMMEREUIL today, the 4th instant, as follows :-

Unit.	Time of Passing Starting Point.
5th R. Innis. Fus.	11.00
198 Inf. Brigade H.Q.	11.10
6th Lancs. Fus.	11.15
8th R. Dublin Fus.	11.25
198th L.T.M.B.	11.35

   Starting Point - Cross Roads K.35.c.0.6.

   Route :-   Q.5.b.60.95.   L.31.

2. Transport will be Brigaded and will march under the orders of the Brigade Transport Officer.

   Time of passing Starting Point - 11.50.

   Transport will march straight through to POMMEREUIL without halting.

3. ACKNOWLEDGE.

                                                Captain,
                                            Brigade Major,
                                         198th Infantry Brigade.

Issued through Signals at 06.00.

DISTRIBUTION.

Copy No.	1.	66th Division, "G".
" "	2.	66th Division, "Q".
" "	3.	6th Lancs. Fus.
" "	4.	5th R. Innis. Fus.
" "	5.	6th R. Dublin Fus.
" "	6.	198th L.T.M.B.
" "	7.	No. 3 Signal Section.
" "	8.	Staff Captain.
" "	9.	B.I.O.
" "	10.	B.T.O.
" "	11,12,13.	War Diary.
" "	14,15,16.	File.

SECRET.   Copy No. 7

198th Infantry Brigade Order No. 130.

                                                4th October, 1918.

1.   198th Infantry Brigade will move by march route to the
valley in G.9.a and c to-morrow, as follows:-

    Unit.   Time of passing Starting Point.

    5th R.Innis.Fus.   08.00
    198th Inf.Bde.H.Q. & 1 Sec. 100   08.15
    6th Lancs.Fusrs.   M.G.Bn.   08.20
    198th L.T.M.B.   08.35
    6th R.Dublin Fus.   08.40

    Starting Point: Cross-roads, L.20.b.2.0.

    Route: Road fork, L.16.b. - Cross-roads, L.11.c. -
Road Junction, G.7.b. - G.8.d.7.5.

2.   Lewis gun limbers will march with their companies.
Remaining transport except G.S. wagons will march in rear of
battalions.
        G.S. wagons and Quartermasters' Stores will remain in
POMMEREUIL.

3.   Blankets will be dumped at units' present transport lines
and will be moved by Quartermasters to a dump at the present
Brigade Headquarters.

4.   Troops will be given a good breakfast before starting
the march.

5.   Brigade Headquarters will close at POMMEREUIL at 08.00 hours
and open at the road and railway junction, G.8.d.7.5. at 08.30.

6.   ACKNOWLEDGE.

                                                (signed)
                                                Captain,
                                                Brigade Major,
                                                198th Infantry Brigade.

Issued through Signals at 23.55

                        DISTRIBUTION.

    66th Divn. "G"   Copy No.1.   5th Bn. R.Innis.Fus. Copy No.6
    66th Divn. "Q".   "   2.   6th R.Dublin Fus.   7.
    199th Inf.Bde.   "   3.   198th L.T.M.B.   8.
    S.A. Brigade   "   4.   War Diary,   9,10,11
    6th Bn. Lancs.Fus.   "   5.   File.   12.13.14

    Sec.100 M.G.Bn.   "   15   No.3 Signal Section   16.
    12th Lancers.   "   17   A Bty, 331 Art.Bde.   18.
    430 Fld.Coy. R.E.   "   19   Staff Captain   20
    Brigade Transport Off." 21   Bde.Intelligence Officer, 22.

SECRET.

6th Lancs. Fus.
5th R. Innis. Fus.
6th R. Dublin Fus.
198th L.T.M.B.
430th Field Co. R.E. (for information)

198th Inf. Bde.
No. G.38/12.

The Brigade will be prepared to move forward from POMMEREUIL, from 06.30 hours to-morrow, 5th inst.

Captain,
Brigade Major,
198th Infantry Brigade.

4.11.18.
RV

SECRET.      Copy No...5..

198TH INFANTRY BRIGADE ORDER No.131.

5th November, 1918.

1. 198TH Infantry Brigade Group will move to the portion of LANDRECIES West of the Canal as follows :-

Unit.	Time of Passing Starting Point.
...	14.45.
198th M.G.C. & Signals.	15.00.
9th Lancs.Fus.,	15.05.
198th L.T.M.B.	15.30.
9th R.Dublin Fus.	15.35.
Troop 19th Lancers.	15.40.
Section M.G.C.	15.40.
"A"Bty.331 Bde R.F.A.	15.30.
450th Field Co. R.E.	16.05.

2. Starting Point. G.9.d.7.5. (ARRET).

3. Route. G.9.,10., G.15., G.16.

4. Billeting parties will be sent at once to the ARRET at G.15.D.5.9., where guides will also meet Units on arrival.

5. Troops will not halt on the march. It is at the discretion of Commanding Officers, whether Units march in 4s, or file.

6. All Transport, including baggage wagons, will accompany Units.
   B.T.O. will instruct baggage wagons to report to Units at once.
   Baggage wagons can be sent back for blankets, if Commanding Officers wish to do so.

7. Brigade Headquarters will close at G.8.d.Central., at 15.00, and open in G.16 on arrival.

8. ACKNOWLEDGE.

                                               Captain,
                                          Brigade Major,
                                     198th Infantry Brigade.

Issued through Signals at......

DISTRIBUTION.

25th Division "G"	Copy	No.1.
66th Division "Q"	"	No.2.
9th Lancs.Fus.	"	No.3.
5th R.Innis.Fus.	"	No.4.
9th R.Dublin Fus.	"	No.5.
198th L.T.M.B.	"	No.6.
No.4.Sig.Secn	"	No.7.
Troop 19th Lancers	"	No.8.
Sect.198Bn.M.G.C.	"	No.9.
"A"Bty.331 BdeRFA.	"	No.10.
450th Field Co.R.E.	"	No.11.
Staff Capt.	"	No.12.
B.I.O.	"	No.13.
B.T.O.	"	No.14.
War Diary.	"	No.15, 16, 17.
...	"	No.18, 19, 20.

SECRET.   Copy No. 4

198TH INFANTRY BRIGADE ORDER No. 132.

5th November, 1918.

1. On November 6th, 32nd Division, 25th Division and 66th Division are continuing their advance with present boundaries continued Eastwards and objective main MAUBEUGE - AVESNES Road.

2. If the advance continues successfully 66th Division will move as under with a view to concentrating in area MAROILLES - TAISNIERES - MARBAIX.

    198th Brigade Group to TAISNIERES.
    To be prepared to move from 12.00.

3. The Brigade Group includes attached Artillery.

4. The Squadron of 12th Lancers at present attached to 66th Division will concentrate at 08.00 at Fme. du CATAILLON (H.14.a.). O.C. Troop, 12th Lancers, attached to 198th Brigade, will get into touch forthwith with O.C., Squadron, 12th Lancers, with a view to joining his Squadron.

5. Units will pay attention to the following points:-

    (a) Feet Inspection.
    (b) Boot Inspection.
    (c) Regular daily issue of 5 grains quinine to all ranks.
    (d) Every man to be in possession of two complete days' hard rations in addition to whole or unexpended portion of current day's rations.

6. ACKNOWLEDGE.

                                            Captain,
                                        Brigade Major,
                                    198th Infantry Brigade.

Issued through Signals at 0430

DISTRIBUTION.

         Copy No. 1.   66th Division.
          "   " 2.   6th Lancs. Fus.
          "   " 3.   5th R. Innis. Fus.
          "   " 4.   9th R. Dublin Fus.
          "   " 5.   198th L.T.M.B.
          "   " 6.   No. 3 Signal Section.
          "   " 7.   Troop, 12th Lancers.
          "   " 8.   Section, 198 M.G.C.
          "   " 9.   "A" Battery, 331 Bde., R.F.A.
          "   " 10.   430 Field Co., R.E.
          "   " 11,12,13. War Diary.
          "   " 14,15,16. File.

"A" Form
MESSAGES AND SIGNALS.

Army Form C.2121 (in pads of 100).

TO: 6th R.D.F

Sender's Number: S.C.2 **Day of Month:** 5

QM Stores of all units are now moving up to G4 & 6.4 where they will remain until further orders a.a.a unless otherwise instructed transport at present with units will continue to move with them a.a.a Blankets will be left dumped at POMMEREUIL

From: 198 I.B
Time: 10.45

P. Inglison Capt

"A" Form
MESSAGES AND SIGNALS.

Army Form C. 2121 (in pads of 100).

TO	Sheet 2		

probably be underneath to 198 Bde. Otherwise Bde boundaries continue as Grid E from Brown Line

(3) There are at present no cavalry or cyclists available

(4) Reconnaissance parties & advances of up to few ORs will join SR trains this — tonight Bridging material with infantry and RE will be made use of in case the GRAND OE HELPE is not properly bridged

(5) The above details are purely tentative.

Sheet 3

MESSAGES AND SIGNALS.

| TO | C. R. Div Sig |

Sender's Number.	Day of Month.	In reply to Number.	AAA
G47	5		

Rd	Order	127	para
8	are	for	map ref
G.13.a.55	read	H.13.a.55	

From 198 Bde
Place
Time

"A" Form.
MESSAGES AND SIGNALS.

Army Form C. 2121.
(In pads of 100.)
No. of Message..............

Prefix......Code......m.	Words.	Charge.	This message is on a/c of:	Recd. at......m.
Office of Origin and Service Instructions.	Sent		..................Service.	Date............
....	At............m.			From............
....	To............			
....	By............		(Signature of "Franking Officer.")	By............

TO: 6. RD Dublin Fus

Sender's Number.	Day of Month.	In reply to Number.	AAA
G53	5	—	
Ref	Order	134	Dara
3	aaa	delete	10
aaa	Route	in	G.9
G15	G16		

From: 198 Inf Bde
Place:
Time:

9th Lancs.Fus.
5th R.Innis.Fus.
6th R.Dublin Fus.   *appro J*   198th Inf.Bde.
Sect.100th Bn. M.G.C.   No.B.M.114.
198th L.T.M.B.
No.3.Sig.Sec.
A/331st Bde R.F.A.
66th Division "G"
7th Infantry Brigade.

    198th Infantry Brigade will take over the front held by the 7th Infantry Brigade, to-night.

    Northern Brigade Boundary, K.26.d.0.5. - K.27.d.0.5. - K.28.d.0.5. - K.29.c.0.5.
    Southern Brigade Boundary, J.8.Central - J.12.Cent.

    5th R.Innis.Fus will take over the front line; 9th Lancs.Fus., will be in support, and 6th R."Dublin Fus in Reserve.
    9th Lancs Fus, will be in houses along the main road from J.2.Central - J.3.d.0.0.
    6th R.Dublin Fus., Sect.100th Bn. M.G.C., and 198th L.T.M.B. will remain at DOMPIERRE.

    Headquarters, Front Line and Support Battalion and Brigade Advanced Report Centre, will be at J.3.c.9.9.

    Brigade Headquarters are now at J.7.a.5.9.

    Details of relief will be arranged direct between Commanding Officers concerned.

    Units will pass Starting Point as follows :-

        5th R.Innis.Fus.   18.45
        9th Lancs.Fus,   20.00.

    Starting Point. J.7.a.5.9.

    ACKNOWLEDGE!

                                    Captain,
                                  Brigade Major,
7.11.18.   198th Infantry Brigade.
RV.

SECRET.   Appendix 6   Copy No. 4

198TH INFANTRY BRIGADE ORDER No.135.

7th Novr.1918.

1. According to last reports, received 19.15, our line now runs from cross roads on Southern Corps Boundary J.21.b.5.5. - J.13.Central - J.10.Central -J.5.Central - D.29.d.0.0. with an advanced post established East of the River in J.16.d..

The enemy is occupying the East bank of the stream in advance of that line.

At 16.00 hours on 7.11.18 the enemy were holding the spur in J.11.Central and probably LA CROISETTE Farm with a few Machine Guns.

2. The 198th Infantry Brigade (with the 199th Infantry Brigade on the right and 150th Infantry Brigade on the left) will continue the pursuit at 07.30 to-morrow.

The attack will be carried out on a one battalion front.

3. Boundaries. Northern Brigade Boundary, D.29.d.0.3. - K.26.c.0.3. along LES TROIS PAVES - SARS POTERIES road (inclusive to 198th Inf.Bde) - E.20.a.9.5. - E.23.c.0.1.

Southern Brigade Boundary, GRID Line J.3.c.0.0 - K.5.c.0.0.

4. OBJECTIVES. The Brigade objective will be the general line K.4.d.9.0 - E.28.d.5.0. - E.22.b.1.5. where a liaison post will be established with troops of 150th Infantry Brigade.

On securing this line infantry patrols will clear the ground 500 yards East of the objective whilst Cavalry will ascertain whether FELLERIES and BEUGNIES are held by the enemy or not.

5. Brigade Plan of Attack.

5th R.Innis.Fus. will carry out the attack, as far as AVESNES - MAUBEUGE Road, between K.1.d.1.0. and road junction E.35.d.9.2 (inclusive)

6th Lancs.Fus. will pass through 5th R.Innis.Fus. when the latter have reached their objective, as detailed in para.4.

6th R.Dublin Fus. will be in Brigade Reserve and and will keep in close touch with 5th Lancs.Fus.

When 6th Lancs.Fus. have passed through the 5th R.Innis.Fus., the 6th R.Dublin Fus. will follow 6th Lancs.Fus. in close support to them, paying particular attention to the flanks.

When 6th R.Dublin Fus. have passed through 5th R. Innis.Fus., the latter will concentrate in K.1.a.and c. in Brigade Reserve.

When 6th Lancs.Fus. have captured the final objective the 6th R.Dublin Fus. will, if the situation permits, concentrate in Support in the valley in K.5.

6. **Cavalry.** A Troop 12th.Lancers will be in Brigade Reserve.

7. **Artillery.** 1 Section, A/331st Brigade R.F.A., (18 pdrs)
   1 " B/331st Brigade R.F.A. (4.5" Hows)
will be attached to 5th R.Innis.Fus., till 1st objective is gained, after which both sections will come into Brigade Reserve.

One Section A/331st Brigade R.F.A., will be attached to 6th Lancs.Fus.

ABtty., 331st Brigade R.F.A., (less 2 sections) will be in Brigade Reserve.

In addition to the above, 150th Brigade R.F.A., with one Battery 60 Pdrs., and one battery 6" Hows. will co-operate with fire as follows :-

Time.	Targets.
07.30 - 07.45	E.of road through J.6.a and c.
07.55 - 08.00	Wood in J.b. and d.
08.00 - 08.10	Spur in K.1. and K.7.
08.55 - 09.10	Spur in K.5.

The Targets given are the most westerly points on which 150th Brigade R.F.A. will put their fire.

8. **Machine Guns.** 1 Coy. 25th Bn. M.G.C., and One Section, 100th Bn. M.G.C., will be in Brigade Reserve.

/9. R.E.

9. **R.E.** 1 Section 430th Field Co. R.E. is allotted to 198th Infantry Brigade. They will be attached to the 5th R.Innis.Fus., and will, if required, bridge the stream in K.1.

They will report to O.C., 5th R.Innis.Fus. (H.Q. J.3.c.9.2.) at 06.00 on 8th October, 1918.

10. **Cyclists.** 1 Section XIII Corps Cyclists will be attached to Brigade Headquarters.

11. Positions of Brigade Headquarters and Advanced Report Centres, and Axis of Liaison, are attached.

12. **Success Signals.** 5th R.Innis.Fus. will fire two Red Very Lights in quick succession after capture of 1st objective.

6th Lancs.Fus. will fire three Red Very Lights after capture of Final objective.

13. **Contact Planes.** Advanced troops will be ready to light and make signals in the event of a call flare being received from contact aeroplane.

14. Brigade Signal Officer, will arrange to synchronise watches.

15. ACKNOWLEDGE.

Captain,
Brigade Major,
198th Infantry Brigade.

Issued through Signals at......

DISTRIBUTION.

66th Division "G"	Copy	No.1.
6th Lancs.Fus.	"	No.2.
5th R.Innis.Fus.	"	No.3.
6th R.Dublin Fus.	"	No.4.
198th L.T.M.B.	"	No.5.
No.3 Sig. Sec.	"	No.6.
A/331st Bde R.F.A.	"	No.7.
430th Field Co. R.E.	"	No.8.
Coy. 25th Bn. M.G.C.	"	No.9.
Sect. 100th Bn M.G.C.	"	No.10.
Troop 12th Lancers.	"	No.11.
Section Cyclists.	"	No.12.
B.I.O.	"	No.13.
Staff Captain.	"	No.14.
199th Inf. Bde.	"	No.15.
150th Inf. Bde.	"	No.16.

6 Royal Scots Fusiliers Order No 20.

Refers Map.
SHEET 57A

Copy to 8th R.S.F

1) According to latest reports our line now runs from X roads on Southern Corps boundary J.21.b.5.5. – J.16. central – J.10. central – J.5. central – D.29.d.0.0.
The enemy is occupying the EAST bank of the stream in advance of this line.
At 16.00 on 7.11.18 enemy were holding spur in J.11. central and probably LA CROISETT FARM with a few M. Guns.

2) The 19th Inf Bde with the 199th Inf Bde on the RIGHT and the 150th INF BDE on the LEFT will continue the pursuit at 07.30 today 8th inst.

3) Boundaries – Northern Brigade Boundary – D.29.d. 0.3 – E.26.c.0.3. along LES TROIS PAVES – SARS POTERIES road (inclusive to 198 Bde.) E.28.a.9.5. – E.23.c.0.1.
Southern Bdy GRID LINE J.3.c.0.0. – K.5.c.0.0.

4) Objective – General line K.4.d.9.0 – E.28.d. 5.0 – E.28.b.1.5. where a liaison post will be established with 150th Inf Bde.

On securing this line Infantry patrols will clear the ground 500 yards EAST of the objective whilst cavalry patrols will ascertain whether FELLERIES and BEAUGNIES are held by the enemy or not.

5/ 5th R. Innis. Fus. will carry out the attack as far as the AVESNES — MAUBEUGE road, between K.1.d.1.0 and road junction F.25.d.9.2 inclusive.;
6th LANCS FUS will pass through 5th R. Innis. Fus. when the latter have reached their objective.

6th ROY. DUB. FUS. will be in Brigade Reserve and will keep in close touch with 6th L. Fus. 6th ROY. DUB. FUS will follow the 6th LANCS. FUS through the 5th ROY. INNIS. FUS & in close support and pay particular attention to the flanks.

When 6th L. Fus have captured final objective 6 R. DUB. Fus will concentrate in SUPPORT if situation permits, in valley in K.3.

6/ Success signals — 5th R. INNIS Fus will fire two RED very lights in quick succession after capture of their objective and 6th L. Fus three white after capture of final objective.

INSTRUCTIONS

7. The Battalion will form up at the cross roads K.2.a.8.8. soon as possible in following order 'B' - 'D' - 'A' - 'C' - HdQrs.

Route — via Kraai J.2.d.

8. Formations — 'B' Coy Left leading Coy — 'D' Coy Right leading Coy — 'A' Left support 'C' Right support.

If any artillery fire is experienced Coys will open out into Platoon artillery formation on leaving BOMPIERRE.

A distance of 500 yards will be maintained in rear of L.F.s until reaching the valley in K.3 when Coys will halt unless otherwise engaged.

Coys will send connecting files forward to ensure touch being kept.

Centre line of advance — CRIA LANE D.2 central K.3 central.

9. Btn Hd Qrs will advance along this line. Boundary for Bn HQrs 1st point J.2.b.6.5.

2ⁿᵈ Bound J.4.a.10.00, — 3ʳᵈ Bound J.6.a.3.0.
4ᵗʰ Bound K.1.a.5.1. — 5ᵗʰ Bound K.2.b.9.1.

10. Assembly position. In rear of lines from
J.2.d.0.5 to J.2.b.0.5. Two right Coys
south of the road and two left Coys NORTH
of road.

This position may be altered by the C.O.
according to whether the position the 6ᵗʰ Life
occupy.

O.4.30

5/4/18

[signature]

...ES AND SIGNALS. Form C. 2121

Prefix	Code	m.	Words	Charge	This message is on a/c of:	Recd. at	m
Office of Origin and Service Instructions.			Sent			Date	
			At	m.	Service	From	8/11/18
			To				
			By		(Signature of "Franking Officer.")	By	

TO { 6: ~~Leins~~ ~~Fu~~
6: ~~Innis~~ ~~Fus~~
6: Dublin Fus

Sender's Number.	Day of Month.	In reply to Number.	AAA
DM126	8		

50th Division report right
and centre battalion on
at AVESNES-MAUBEUGE 2nd

From AA 198 Rd
Place
Time 12.00

The above may be forwarded as now corrected. (Z)

Censor. Signature of Addressee or person authorised to telegraph in this name

"A" Form — Army Form C. 2121 (in pads of 100).
MESSAGES AND SIGNALS.   No. of Message..........

| Prefix ..... Code ..... | Words | Charge | This message is on a/c of: | Recd. at .....m |
| Office of Origin and Service Instructions | Sent At .....m To ..... By ..... | | .....Service (Signature of "Franking Officer.") | Date TLR 8/11/18 From By |

TO: [struck through]

| Sender's Number | Day of Month | In reply to Number | AAA |
| BM 125 | 8 | — | |

Pf OP closing at J.9.2 and opening at LA TUILLERIE (J.10 d 5.5)

From 19 Inf Bde
Place .....
Time .....

The above may be forwarded as now corrected. (Z)   [signature] Capt
Censor.   Signature of Addresser or person authorised to telegraph in his name
* This line should be erased if not required.

SECRET.   Copy No...4..

198TH INFANTRY BRIGADE ORDER No.136.

                                        8th Novr., 1918.

1. SITUATION.   General Line appears to run as
    follows :-
        Copse K.20.a.5.9. - K.15.b. - K.8.Central -
    K.2.Central - K.26.c. - thence along track
    through E.26.a. - E.20.c. - E.20.Central.
        An attempt is being made to capture SEMOUSIES
    tonight.

2. The attack will be continued to-morrow
    Novr.9th, with a view to gaining objectives as
    given in 198th Infantry Brigade Order No.135.
        The Brigade will attack on a One battalion front.

            Leading battalion, 6th R.Dublin Fus., Support
    battalion, 5th R.Innis Fus, Reserve Battalion,
    6th Lancs.Fus.
        5th R.Innis.Fus. will follow in ~~close~~ support
    ~~with~~ 6th R.Dublin Fus., and will be prepared to
    protect the flanks.
        When 5th R.Innis.Fus. pass through 6th Lancs.
    Fus., the latter will concentrate in Brigade
    Reserve in K.1.

3. Boundaries as previously ordered.

4. With a view to ascertaining the enemy's defensive
    line, 6th Lancs.Fus. will push out patrols towards
    the road in K.9.a. - K.3.c. - K.2.b. - K.26.d.,
    to-night, when light permits.
        Early reports as to the disposition of enemy
    are required.

5. The following will be attached to 6th R.Dublin Fus.
    to assist them in their attack.
        1 Sec. 18 pdrs. (150 Bde.R.F.A.).
        1 Sec. 4.5" Hows. (D/150 Bde.R.F.A.)
        1 Sec. "D" Coy. 100th Bn. M.G.C.
        1 Platoon Cyclists.
        198th L.T.M.B.

        Troop 12th Lancers will be sent up when the situation
    permits.

                                        /7. Artillery

7. **Artillery.** Artillery arrangements will be notified later.

8. Objectives of left flank Brigade will be notified later. Right flank Brigade, as for to-day, i.e., due South from 198th Infantry Brigade objective.

9. Axis of Liaison, will be as for to-day. (198th 198th Infantry Brigade Order No.135).

   The next Brigade H.Q., FME LA JONQUIERE.
   Next Brigade Report Centre, farm in K.2.b.

10. Troops at present attacked 6th Lancs.Fus., less 198th L.T.M.B., and one section "D" Coy. 100th Bn. M.G.C., will come into Brigade reserve at Zero, remaining near FME LA JONQUIERE till Brigade H.Q. arrives there.

11. Brigade Signal Officer will synchronise watches.

12. Zero hour will be 0900 hours, Nov.9th, 1918.

13. **ACKNOWLEDGE.**

                                    Captain,
                                 Brigade Major,
                             198th Infantry Brigade.

DISTRIBUTION.

66th Division "G"	Copy No.1
6th Lancs.Fus.	" No.2.
5th R.Innis.Fus.	" No.3.
6th R.Dublin Fus.	" No.4.
198th L.T.M.B.	" No.5.
No.3 Sig.Sec.	" No.6.
Troop 12th Lancers.	" No.7.
"D" Coy. 100th Bn.MGC.	" No.8.
Platoon Cyclists.	" No.9.
150th Bde.R.F.A.	" No.10.
199th Inf.Bde.	" No.11.
149th Inf.Bde.	" No.12.
Staff Captain.	" No.13.
B.I.O.	" No.14.
War Diary.	" No.15, 16, 17.
File.	" No.18, 19, 20.
Spare.	4 Copies.

S E C R E T.   Copy No. 4

ADDENDUM TO 198TH INFANTRY BRIGADE ORDER No.136.

ARTILLERY PROGRAMME   4.5" Hows and 18 pdrs.

From Zero to Zero plus 20 minutes on targets, Houses -
(1st Bound).   K.3.c.1.2. - K.2.b.9.2. -
                        E.26.d.5.0. and Cross roads
                        E.26.d.
From Zero plus 20 mins. to Zero plus 65 mins, High ground
(2nd Bound).   in K.3.b. and d. - houses E.27.d.2.2.
                        and E.28.c.3.2. - Fork road
                        E.27.b.5.0.
From Zero plus 65 min to Zero plus 95 min, house, K.4.b.5.5.
From Zero plus 65 min. to Zero plus 120 min., houses
(3rd Bound).   E.29.c.5.9. - E.29.b.1.8.

   Rate of fire, 1 round per gun, every 4 mins. for 18pdrs.
   Rate of fire, 1 round per gun, every 6 mins. for 4.5"
                                                    hows.

6" Hows. to fire one bound ahead of former, commencing
         on 2nd bound, and to conform to times stated. When
         targets on 3rd bound are being engaged, 6" Hows
         will fire on houses and junction of tracks in
         E.30.c.1.4.

                                    E. [signature]
                                         Captain,
                                     for Brigade Major,
                                 198th Infantry Brigade.
8.11.18.
RV.

DISTRIBUTION.

   Copies to all recipients of Order No.136.

C.O.X.70

Artillery programme   4.5 How's & 6" How's.

From hero to 2+20 minutes on targets - houses - K.3.c.1.2 -
(1st Bound)   K.2.b.9.2. - E.26.a.5.2 and
                    X roads E.26.a.

From 2+20 to 2+65 - High ground in K.3.b. and d. - houses
(2nd Bound)   E.27.a.8.2 and E.28.c.3.2, -
                    fork road E.27.d.6.0.

From 2+65 to 2+90 - houses K.4.D.3.5.
    "   2+120 - houses E.28.c.8.9 - E.29.d.1.9.
(3rd Bound)
                        per gun
Rate of fire 1 rd/gun 4 rounds per minute per 18pdrs.
                        4.5 How's.
6" How's. To fire one bound ahead of former,
commencing on 2nd Bound, and to conform
to times stated. When targets on 3rd
Bound are being engaged 6" How's will fire
on houses and junction of tracks in E.30.
d.1.4.

4/4/18   [signature]
                        6" H.P. Batt. Heavy

6th Lancs. Fus. 198th Inf.Bde.
5th R.Innis.Fus. No.G. 32/14
6th R.Dublin Fus.
198th L.T.M.B.
Sec."A" 100th Bn. M.G.C.
"D" Coy. 100th Bn. M.G.C.
66th Division "G"

The following moves will take place to-morrow, 10th inst

    6th Lancs.Fus. to ST.HILAIRE-sur-HELPE.
    6th R.Dublin Fus. to DOMPIERRE, E.of the Railway.
    5th R.Innis.Fus. will not move.
    Brigade H.Q. to DOMPIERRE.
    "D" Coy. and 1 Sec "A" Coy. 100th Bn. M.G.C., to
      rejoin battalion at BASILEU.

Detailed Orders follow.

                                          Captain,
                                    Brigade Major,
9.11.18.   198th Infantry Brigade.
RVm

ACCOUNT OF OPERATIONS.

PART VII.

2nd November, 1918 - 11th November, 1918.

PART VII.

2nd November - 11th November, 1918.

Reference Map Sheet.
57A, 1/40,000.

On 2nd November the Brigade marched from PREMONT to HONNECHY.

On 3rd November the march was continued to LE CATEAU, which was reached at about 18.00.

On 4th November an attack was delivered on a front of about 50 miles. The attack involved troops of the First, Third and Fourth British Armies and the First French Army.

XIII Corps attacked with the 25th and 50th Divisions.

66th Division was in Corps Reserve ready to go through the 25th Division and continue the advance.

The Brigade marched to POMMEREUIL on the evening of the 4th November.

The attack was completely successful and on the morning of 5th November the Brigade Group, constituted as follows, moved to the valley in G.9.a and c.

        198th Bde. H.Q. & No. 3 Signal Section.
        6th Lancs. Fus.
        5th R. Innis. Fus.
        6th R. Dublin Fus.
        198th L.T.M.B.
        431 Field Co., R.E.

A/331 Bty., R.F.A., and a troop of 12th Lancers and 1 section, 100 M.G. Battn., joined the Brigade Group on arrival in the valley.

/As the enemy offered little

As the enemy offered little resistance to the advance of the 25th Division the 66th Division were not committed to the attack and the Brigade moved to the portion of LANDRECIES, West of the Canal on the evening of the 5th November.

Troops of 12th Lancers rejoined their Regiment early on the morning of 6th November.

On 6th November XIII Corps continued their advance with the 25th and 50th Divisions.

At 14.30 a message was received from Division that the Brigade Group would not move on the 6th.

At 14.45 further orders were received for a move that evening to BASSE NOYELLES.

The conditions for the march were very bad. Traffic on the roads was hopelessly congested and it was raining hard and became very dark soon after 17.30. In spite of this all troops of the Brigade reached their billets in BASSE NOYELLES by 22.30.

On the afternoon of the following day the Brigade Group moved to DOMPIERRE. Orders were received from Division while on the march that the Brigade was to take over the front held by 7th Brigade and continue the advance as far as the AVESNES - MAUBEGE Road, at 07.00 on the 8th if this line had not already been reached by the 7th Brigade.

Orders were accordingly issued for 5th R. Innis. Fus. to take over the line held by 21st Manchesters and for 6th Lancs. Fus. to take over the Support position on the road from J.2.c.c.h. - J.3.d.c.c.

6th R. Dublin Fus., 195th L.T.M.B., Section 100 Bn., M.G.C., and A/331 Bty., R.F.A. remained in DOMPIERRE.

The line to be taken over by 5th R. Innis. Fus. was roughly along the road through J.10.b. J.4.d. and b. O.C., 5th R. Innis. Fus. was given instructions to use his own discretion as to taking over any posts in front of this line.

The relief was successfully carried out, but was rather delayed owing to the deviation round the demolished road bridge at BOMPIERRE STATION being so deep in mud that Lewis Guns had to be off loaded from limbers and carried forward by hand.

During the night the locations of enemy M.G's. were reported by 5th R. Innis. Fus. Most of these were on our right flank opposite 199th Infantry Brigade. These locations were given to 199 Infantry Brigade.

on 4th Nov.
At 07.30 the attack began in a thickish mist, which however soon thinned, on which enemy M.G. fire became considerable, particularly from the right flank, taking our advance with oblique fire. The centre and left, however, got well forward and the threat of envelopment eased the situation on the right. (This was the general tendency during the whole advance up to the AVESNES - MAUBEGE Road.)

The AVESNES - ST. AUBIN Road was the enemy's next M.G. position, and whilst this was being dealt with he brought a few guns into action.

This position was carried quickly, enveloping tactics being used where necessary, and our troops were reported entering the wood in J.6.b. and d. at 09.40.

Brigade H.Q., which had moved at 0840 to a house at J.3.d.5.3, then moved forward to TUILERIE in J.10.d. On arrival there reports were received from both attacking and Support Battalions that the right flank was being fired into from flank and rear, from the spur in J.12.c. and J.13.a.

/One section, 100 Bn.,

One Section, 100 Bn., M.G.C., was therefore sent up by the TUILERIE - J.6.c.cen. road to occupy the high ground and houses in J.12.a, to protect the right flank.

The left flank, which had never got touch with 150 Brigade was also reported moving forward. The reason for this lack of touch was that 150 Brigade had made an encircling movement avoiding the marshy ground in D.29. and 30.

At 10.30 the right flank of the 109 Brigade was much held up, as the Division on their right were still fighting in the neighbourhood of LE BALBAQUI (J.20.)

There was a certain amount of desultory fighting on the wood in J.6.b. and d., but the enemy's next line of defence was obviously the AVESNES - MAUBEGE Road. His M.G. resistance stiffened there and it was only after considerable fighting that the line of the road was gained. The enemy had mean time ceased troubling the right flank from the spur in J. 12 and 18 but was enfilading the main road badly from BASLIEU and the high ground to the E. of it. In consequence the right Company of 5th R. Innis. Fus. spread out to the right, and sent one platoon down to the houses in K.13.a. On the way they captured a lorry and an abandoned tractor and also disturbed some pioneers who were busy about the culvert in K.16.a., but unfortunately were not able to prevent them blowing the mine there. This platoon was preparing to attack the high ground E. of BAS LIEU but as the Company was already very much extended the Coy. Commander gave orders that it was not to go further S. but to engage the enemy M.G's. there with L.G. fire and so to enable the troops on our right (who were unable to advance down the Eastern slopes of the spur in J.18, and who were digging in there) to get forward. This was successful and on their arrival the Company front was shortened by withdrawing troops to the North.

/Meantime arrangements had

Meantime arrangements had been made with 199 Infantry Brigade for their Support Battalion (Connaught Rangers) to be put through as soon as 6th Lancs. Fus. were ready to advance from the AVESNES - MAUBEGE Road. It was further arranged that Connaughts should start as soon as 6th Lancs. Fus. reported ready and that 6th Lancs. Fus. should be launched ½ hour later, as 6th Connaughts had further to go, being assembled near the TUILERIE.

At 12.55 the success signal went up from the left Co. of 5th R. Innis. Fus. who had been having some trouble with M.G. nests round the road junction TROIS PAVES (E.25.d.)

6th Lancs. Fus. then moved forward and were prepared to advance at 14.00.

Meantime, as the situation had eased somewhat on the right it was arranged that Connaughts should start at once (13.20). Moving round through K.7.c. and d. with the intention of seizing high ground in K.9 and 10 and so threatening the retreat of the enemy in AVESNES, who were still holding out, 6th Lancs. Fus. meanwhile going for their final objective which included the high ground in K.3. and 4.

Enemy resistance had, however, stiffened considerably. The 200th Jaeger Division fighting well and placing their M.G's., of which they had a great number, with considerable skill.

The short day was also a disadvantage as by 16.30 what with lack of light and mist it was impossible to locate friend or foe with any certainty.

The chief resistance was from the road in K.3.c. and 2.b., which is sunken for most of its length, and a particularly strong concentration of M.G's. in and round LA CORNELLE.

Orders were issued for the continuation of the attack by 6th R. Dublin Fus. on the morning of 9th October at 09.00.

The advance of 199 Brigade on the right was timed to begin 45 minutes earlier in order to

/ensure the capture

ensure the capture of the high ground in K.13.
and K.6. before the advance of the 8th R. Dublin
Fus. was begun.

Patrols were sent out by 6th Lancs. Fus.
at dawn, and it was quickly discovered that the
enemy had withdrawn during the night.

6th Lancs. Fus. were accordingly instructed
to continue the advance to the final objective and
to push out patrols as far as the FELLERIES –
LES CROUPIAUX – BEUGNIES road.

A troop of 12th Lancers was attached to 6th
Lancs. Fus. This troop patrolled well forward
of the infantry, and encountered no enemy
opposition.

6th Lancs. Fus. reached the final objective at
10.00.

6th R. Dublin Fus. remained in support on the
AVESNES – MAUBEGE Road and 5th R. Innis. Fus. in
Reserve on the AVESNES – ST. AUBAN Road, in J.6.

At 17.00 the South African Brigade forming
part of the Fourth Army Advanced Guard passed
through the line held by 6th Lancs. Fus. and billetted
in BEUGNIES.

Early on the morning of 9th November the 190
Infantry Brigade took over the Brigade front, the
18th K. L'pools. taking over the line of resistance
held by 6th Lancs. Fus.

By 14.00 on 9th November the Brigade was
disposed as follows :–

  188th Brigade H.Q.   DOMPIERRE.
  6th Lancs. Fus.   ST. HILAIRE-SUR-HELPE
  5th R. Innis.Fus.
    & 168th L.T.M.B.   MAUBEGE – AVESNES Road in J.6.
  6th R. Dublin Fus.   DOMPIERRE (E. of the Railway).

The Brigade disposed as above until 11.00
on the 11th November, when the armistice brought
hostilities to an end.

TOTAL CAPTURES, 1st Nov. - 11th Nov., 1918.

PRISONERS.

Off.	O.R.
1	6

OTHER MATERIAL.

M.G's.	A.T. Rifle.	Motor Lorry.	Steam Engine.	G.S. Wagon.
7	1	1	1	1

TOTAL CASUALTIES, 1st Nov. - 11th Nov. 1918.

	KILLED		WOUNDED	
	Off.	O.R.	Off.	O.R.
6th Lancs. Fus.	1	5	-	31
5th R. Innis. Fus.	-	6	-	27
6th R. Dublin F.	-	-	-	3

SECRET.   appx "9"   Copy No.

198TH INFANTRY BRIGADE ORDER No. 135.

11th Novr. 1918

1. The 198th Infantry Brigade will move to-morrow, 12th instant, as follows :-

    5th R.Innis.Fus. to SARS POTERIES, move to be complete by 10.00

    6th Lancs.Fus. to BEUGNIES via BAS-LIEU, move to be complete by 11.30.

    6th R.Dublin Fus. to BAS-LIEU. Not to enter BAS-LIEU before 10.30.
    Move to be complete by 11.00.

    198th L.T.M.B., to SARS POTERIES, move to be complete by 12.00.
    Not to pass FME JONQUIERE before 10.30.

    198th Bde.H.Q. and Signals, to BEUGNIES. To pass the Church DOMPIERRE at 08.30.

2. Usual distances will be observed.

3. Brigade H.Q. will close at DOMPIERRE at 08.30 and open at BEUGNIES on arrival.

4. Transport will march in rear of their own units.

5. ACKNOWLEDGE.

                                    Captain,
                                Brigade Major,
                            198th Infantry Brigade.

Issued through Signals at 20.30.

DISTRIBUTION.

    BETHELS Force,   Copy No.1.
    66th Division "Q"   "   No.2.
    6th Lancs.Fus.   "   No.3.
    5th R.Innis.Fus.   "   No.4.
    6th R.Dublin Fus.   "   No.5.
    198th L.T.M.B.   "   No.6.
    No.3 Sig.Sec.   "   No.7.
    150th Bde.R.F.A.   "   No.8.
    Staff Captain.   "   No.9.
    B.I.O   "   No.10.
    B.T.O.   "   No.11.
    War Diary.   "   No.12, 13, 14.
    File.   "   No.15, 16, 17.

Appx 10   108th Inf.Bde.
           No.G. 32/16

- 8th R.Dublin Fus.
  8th R.Innis.Fus.) for information.
  Bethels Force.   )

8th R.Dublin Fus. will move by march route to BARS POTERIES to-morrow, 13th instant. Move to be complete by 12.00 noon.

Transport will accompany the battalion.

Billeting parties will meet the Staff Captain, at Brigade Headquarters at 10.00.

ACKNOWLEDGE.

                                    Captain,
                                  Brigade Major,
                              108th Infantry Brigade.
12.11.18.
RV

~~6th~~
~~5th Innis Fus.~~
6th R.I.D. Fus
~~198 LTMB~~.

SC 1

Reference ~~68 D.B~~ Order No.

I. 6th R.D.F will be responsible for making their own billetting arrangements in BAS-LIEU. (Information for 100 ~~issued~~ MGC.)

II. 5th Innis Fus will be responsible for ~~billet~~ making their own billetting arrangements in SARS-POTERIES ~~wish~~ in addition allot accommodation to 198 LTMB in that town.

III. CC 198 LTMB will get into touch with 5th Innis Fus, as stated above for accommodation in SARS POTERIES

IV. Billetting party from 6 L F will meet Staff Capt at Road Junction E 24. C. 6 2. at 09.45 tomorrow

V Acknowledge

11/11/18

P. Hughes Capt
Staff Capt
198 Z B

6. R Dub. Fus.

198 Inf Bde
no. G32/17

ORDER OF BATTLE FOURTH ARMY ADVANCED GUARD
And LOCATIONS on 12th NOVEMBER 1918.

COMPOSITION.	LOCATION.
66th Divisional Headquarters.	SOLRE LE CHATEAU. (200 yds west of Church).
66th Divl Signal Company.	- do -
Divisional Units:-	
198th Brigade H.Q. & 1 Battn.	BEUGNIES.
1 Battalion.	SARS POTERIES.
1 Battalion.	BAS LIEU.
S.A. Brigade Group H.Q.	½ inch N. of X in HESTRUD.
199th Brigade Group H.Q.	SIVRY.
100th Bn. M.G.C. (less 2 Coys).	BEUGNIES. FONTAINE
2 Coys 100th Bn. M.G.C.	1 each with 199th and S.A. Bdes.
C.R.A. 66th Division.	SOLRE LE CHATEAU.
A/331 Bde R.F.A. (4 18-prs).	with 199th Brigade.
B/331 Bde R.F.A. (6 18-prs).	with S.A. Brigade.
D/331 Bde R.F.A. (4.5" Hows).	1 Sect. with 199th Brigade, 1 Sect. with S.A. Brigade.
Mobile Ammunition Column.	
C.R.E.	SOLRE LE CHATEAU.
430th Field Coy. R.E.	with S.A. Brigade (L'ECREVISSE).
431st Field Coy. R.E.	SOLRE LE CHATEAU.
432nd Field Coy. R.E.	- do -
9th Bn. Glouc.R.(Pioneers).	SOLRE LE CHATEAU.
1 Coy 9th Bn.Glouc.R.(Pioneers).	~~SARS POTERIES.~~
1st S.A. Fld Amb. with 4 light and 3 heavy Ambs of 2/2nd & 2/3rd Fld.Ambs.	SOLRE LE CHATEAU.
17th Armoured Car Battalion.	LIESSIES.
XIII Corps Cyclist Bn.	SOLRE LE CHATEAU.
IX Corps Cyclist Battalion.	
35th Squadron R.A.F.	GRANDFAYT.
80th Squadron R.A.F.	- do -
1 Section A.A.	
Divisional Artillery.	DOMPIERRE Area.

5th Cavalry Brigade:-   AVESNES & ST. HILAIRE.
   12th Lancers.   ECCLES.
   R.S. Greys.   AVESNES & ST. HILAIRE.
   20th Hussars.   - do -
   E Battery R.H.A.   - do -
   5th C. Fld. Amb.   - do -
   7th M.V. Section.   - do -
   A and B Echelon.   - do -
   2nd Fld. Troop R.E.   - do -

J. Marriott Capt.
for Major General.
Commanding, Fourth Army Adv. Guard.

12th November 1918.

SECRET.   appx- 11   Copy No...5.

198TH INFANTRY BRIGADE ORDER No.139.

15th November, 1918.

Ref.Map. NAMUR, Sheet 1/100,000.

1. Moves will take place to-morrow, 16th November, 1918, in accordance with the attached March Table.

2. Transport will march in rear of their own Units.

3. Brigade H.Q., will remain at BEAURIEUX.

4. Troops will not halt on the main road.

5. ACKNOWLEDGE.

                                    Captain,
                                Brigade Major,
                            198th Infantry Brigade.

Issued through Signals at 19.40.

DISTRIBUTION.

66th Division "G"	Copy No.1.
66th Division "Q"	" No.2.
9th Lancs.Fus.	" No.3.
5th R.Innis.Fus.	" No.4.
5th R.Dublin Fus.	" No.5.
198th L.T.M.B.	" No.6.
No.3 Sig.Sec.	" No.7.
431st Field Co. R.E.	" No.8.
2/End Field Amb.	" No.10.
5?? Coy, A.S.C.	" No.11.
Staff Captain.	" No.12.
War Diary	" No.13, 14, 15.
File.	" No.16, 17, 18.

MARCH TABLE to accompany 198th Inf.Bde.

Order No.139.

Serial No.	Unit.	From.	To.	Time of passing Stg.Pt.	Remarks.
1.	6th Lancs.Fus.	SARS-POTERIES HARNAUT.	L'EPINE	09.15	(a) To make their own billeting arrangements. (b) Not to march through SOIRE LE CHATEAU.
2.	6th R.Pub.Fus.	do.	SOIRE LE CHATEAU.	09.30	Advance party to meet Staff Captain at Area Commdts.office, SOIRE LE CHATEAU at 08.15.
3.	198th L.T.M.B.	do.	BEAURIEUX.	09.45	Advance party to meet representative of Staff Captain at Bde.H.Q. at 09.00.
4.	2/2nd(E.L.) Fld.Amb.	do.	SOIRE LE CHATEAU.	09.50.	Advance party to meet Staff Captain at Area Commdts.office, SOIRE LE CHATEAU at 08.15.

15.11.18.
RV.

Appendix

198th Inf. Bde.
No. G.

6th Lancs. Fus.
6th R. Dublin Fus.
66th Division "G" (For information).

Ref. Map. Sheet 1/100,000, NAMUR.

1. 6th Lancs Fus. and 6th R. Dublin Fus. will move by march route to RANCE to-morrow, 17th November, 1918.

    6th Lan. Fus. will pass starting point at 10.30.
    6th R. Dub. Fus. will pass starting point at 10.45.

    Starting Point:- Road junction 200 yds N. of first E. in SOLRE LE CHATEAU.

    Route:- BEAURIEUX - SIVRY.

2. Transport will march in rear of battalions.

3. In the event of the direct road from SIVRY to RANCE being sufficiently good, units will move by that road; if not, they will march via SIVRY Station.
    An Officer from Brigade Headquarters will meet the column on the western outskirts of SIVRY, and inform units which of these two roads will be taken.

4. ACKNOWLEDGE.

                              Captain,
                              Brigade Major,
16.11.18.   198th Infantry Brigade.
RV.

"A" Form.
MESSAGES AND SIGNALS.

Army Form C. 2121.

TO: 6° Lanc Fus
6° Dublin Fus

Sender's Number: G. 180
Day of Month: 16
AAA

You will ~~probably~~ move to TRANCE to-morrow 17° instant aaa To be clear of SOLRE LE CHATEAU by 12.00 aaa detailed orders follow aaa Inspection by G.O.C. will take place in the afternoon aaa Fatigue dress aaa 6° Lanc Fus 15.30 6° Dublin Fus 16.00 aaa Ground for inspection to be Selected by units.

From: 198 Bde
Time: 22.25

Signature: W Eden Capt

Secret.

Advanced Guard Commander's Order No 1.   Copy No :- 5

(xxth Division.)

1. The march to the RHINE will be resumed on the morning of 20th Nov. 1918.

2. The 20th Hussars will cover the Divisional front.

3. The Advanced Guard will consist of :-
    6th Royal Dublin Fusiliers (less 2 Coys).
    A/291 Bty R.F.A.
    1 Coy (Pioneers) 5th Gloucester Regt.
    1 Sect. 1st Australian Tng Coy.
    1 Sect. 491st Field Coy R.E.

4. O.C. Advanced Guard :- Lt Col. C.H.Lange, D.S.O.,M.C.

5. The line to be held from the afternoon of 19th inst until further orders will be VOERENDE — St. ANNA.

6. Order of March :-
    Vanguard — 'B' Coy (6th R.D.F.) less 2 platoons, with 1 Sect. moving as Point under Lieut Parish.
(a)   1 Sect of 491st Field Coy R.E.
    Commander — Major Woodhouse.

    Mainguard — 2 platoons 'B' Coy.
    'C' Coy.
(b)   1 Coy 5th Glouc. Regt.
    1 Sect. (less 1 squad) 491st Field Coy R.E.
    1 Sect. 1st Aust. Tng Coy.
    Remainder transport of above.
    A/291 Bty R.F.A.

7.(a) The respective Units of Mainguard will join the Advanced Guard at points as already arranged.
  (b) An Officer from each Unit will move at the head of the Main Guard with the O.C. Ad. Guard.

8. Route :- Froidchapelle — Cerfontaine — Beauville — Fig... — on Silenrieux — Philippeville road.
    Starting Point :- 6th R.D.F. — Hence station.
    Time :- 07.30 hours.

9. The Main Guard will march 500 yards in rear of Vanguard.

10. Flank Guards will be ordered out if the situation necessitates.

11. Should any opposition be met with it will be dealt with boldly without delay.

12. The usual clock hour halts will be observed.
    A halt will be made from 11.30 to 12..... hours.

13. The line gained will be plaquetted as arranged with O.C. Units concerned. (para 3)

14. Reports will be forwarded to O.C. A.G. Guard who will move at the head of Main Guard.

                                        Lt Colonel,
                            O.C. Advanced Guard.

Copy to :- O.C. Vanguard.
         - A/33 Coy R.E..
         - Coy of 4th Middx. Regt.
         - 1st East Lnc Coy.
         - 91st Field Coy R.E.
         - O.C. "B" Coy.
         -     "C"
         - Tpts

6th Bn. Lancs. Fusrs.
5th Bn. R.Innis.Fus.
8th Bn. R.Dublin Fus.   Copy to
108th. L.T.M.B.   66th Division, "A".

108TH INFANTRY BRIGADE
14 NOV 1918
No. 19a.7144

ADMINISTRATIVE ARRANGEMENTS IN REFERENCE TO THE MARCH TO THE RHINE.
-o-o-o-o-o-o-

1. 66th Division, "Q" are arranging to collect all surplus kits from all dumps except PREVENT and deliver to battalions, where they will be re-sorted and re-despatched again the same day to a surplus kit dump, probably at VAUX-ANDIGNY.

2. Four G.S. wagons will be attached to each battalion to carry one blanket and one greatcoat per man. A second blanket will be carried in the pack.

3. In view of the bad state of the roads, transport must not be overloaded. All unnecessary kit must be dumped, *including*
   (a) All mobilization stores intended for trench warfare.
   (b) Battalion reserve of gas stores.

4. Any stores that are dumped must be dumped at VAUX-ANDIGNY. There is no possibility of dumping after the march commences.

5. One spare pair of H.D., four spare pairs of L.D. and four spare riders will move with each Brigade group to replace casualties.

6. Supplies will be delivered by echelon of lorries under Army arrangements.
   Men proceeding on leave or courses will be sent back by returning supply lorries.
   Supplies of clean clothing will be supplied by lorry if possible.
   No lorries will be on the road by day. Refilling will therefore generally be at night. Railhead is VAUX-ANDIGNY.

7. Divisional Reinforcement Camp will be at VAUX-ANDIGNY.
   Men unable to march will concentrate at SOLRE-LE-CHATEAU to-morrow by 18.00 hours.
   Names of any men with bad characters or under suspended sentences whom battalion commanders consider it advisable to leave behind, will be reported to Brigade Headquarters by 18.00 hours to-morrow.

8. In addition to the emergency ration, one day's hard ration will be carried on the man. The emergency ration and this hard ration will be completed immediately with large hard biscuits in place of any of the small round pattern that may be in possession.

9. Battalions will report by noon to-morrow whether they are in possession of frost cogs, Winter, taps and wrenches; also whether the cogs fit the shoes.

10. Strict attention will be paid to discipline and turnout.
    When billetted in villages, great care will be taken to respect the property of civilian inhabitants; against fires, the barking of trees by horses and other such details.
    The Regimental Police will be stiffened up and adequate picquets always posted.

/11.

11. Arrangements are being made for trench shelters to be carried, as billets will by no means always be obtainable.

12. The Trench Mortar Battery will carry six trench mortars but no ammunition. A G.S. wagon will be allotted to them in place of the limber they have at present.

13. Units will report forthwith the names of any officers or other ranks who speak German.

14. 30 officers per battalion will be taken, viz; 6 on Battalion Headquarters, 4 Company Commanders, 16 Platoon Commanders and 4 spare. The remainder will be sent to the Reception Camp.

15. Battalions will report by 6-0 p.m. to-morrow whether they are complete in boots, clothing, cleaning gear. Other deficiencies in tools etc. must be reported forthwith.
Units are reminded that they must carry their full complement of S.A.A. and bombs.

16. Acknowledge.

Captain,
Staff Captain,
198th Infantry Brigade.

14.11.18.
HBC

66th Division.
7948/1/Q.

Camp Commdt.	197th		D.A.P.M.	Copies to:-
C.R.A.	199th	50.	A.D.M.S.	9th Clos.N.	IX Corps Q
C.R.E.		S.A.Inf.Bd.	D.A.D.V.S.	254 D.E.Coy	XIII Corps Q.
					O.//.Div. Recep.
					th Camp.
					'G'

Officers to be leftbehind
All Officers and Other Ranks unfit to march, together with/
, will be sent to the 66th Divl. Reception Camp at VAUX ANDIGNY.

The above personnel will concentrate at SARS LES POTERIES (the Church) by 15.00 hours, 15th instant, Units providing necessary transport for kits, blankets, etc.

An Officer will be in charge of the personnel of each Brigade Group, and the Senior Officer will be in charge of the whole.

1 Officer from each Formation will report to Staff Officer, 66th Division, at the Church, SARS LES POTERIES, at 11.00 hours, 15th instant, to arrange billets.

The Officer, or N.C.O. in charge of personnel of each Unit will be in possession of a nominal roll of all Officers and Other Ranks proceeding. Duplicate copies of these rolls will be forwarded to these Headquarters.

The above personnel will bring rations for consumption 16th instant.
(Rations for consumption 17th inst. will be delivered at SARS LESPOTERIES.
They will proceed on the 16th instant, at 11.00 hours, by empty supply lorries, from SARS LES POTERIES to 66th Divl. Reception Camp at IX Corps Reception Camp, VAUX ANDIGNY.

Major.
D.A.A.G.
66th Division.

14.11.18.

SECRET.

66th Division.
7948/Q.

ADMINISTRATIVE INSTRUCTIONS NO. 2

in connection with 66th Div. Preliminary Order No.123

dated 15.11.18.

1. **ESCAPED PRISONERS OF WAR**

   Lieut. F.J.ROURKE, 5th Bn Connaught Rangers, who is established at Divl. Headquarters, is detailed to deal with escaped Prisoners of War. He will receive the same, feed them, and despatch them in a formed body to VAUX ANDIGNY by returning empty supply lorries.
   All escaped Prisoners of War in the Divisional Area will be directed to Divl. Hd.Qrs.
   Lieut. ROURKE will inform "Q" office daily the numbers and nationalities of escaped Prisoners of War received by him up to 18.00

2. **TRANSPORT.**

   Units in possession of unauthorised transport will render a return of the same forthwith through the usual channels, so that authority may be obtained for them to retain the same if they so desire.
   Captured German G.S.Wagons will on no account be allowed to be taken on the march.
   No unauthorised transport other than that for which application has been made for authority to retain will be allowed on the line of march.

3. **WATER.**

   One Water Lorry will be attached to the Brigade Headquarters of the leading Brigade Group, and will proceed under the orders of the former.
   This lorry will be handed over by the Brigade concerned to the Brigade which takes its place as leading Brigade. This lorry will be for the use of the leading two Brigade Groups.
   One Water Lorry will be similarly attached to Div. Hd.Qrs. for the use of Div. Hd.Qrs. Group and the Rear Infantry Brigade Group.
   Application for the use of these Water Lorries will be made to the Formation in whose charge they are.
   Div. Train will supply 8 gallons Petrol daily for each of these Water Lorries.
   In the event of the water supply being insufficient, or unfit to drink, application will be made to theop headquarters for a Sterilizer, of which there is one allotted to 1st Division, for use of that Division and 66th Division.

4. **VETERINARY.**

   The Mobile Veterinary Section will march in rear of Div. H.Q., In cases where Units cannot, owing to exceptional circumstances, evacuate animals to the M.V.S. or where the M.V.S. cannot collect from Units, animals may be left in farms, with Horse Recovery Form No. I, and 3 day's forage. The Form should state the number of days Forage left with the animal, and D.A.D.V.S. will be notified by the Unit of the exact location of the Farm in question.

18.11.18.

Lieut.-Colonel.
A.A.& Q.M.G.
66th Division.

(Distribution overleaf).

Distribution.

War Diary.	A.D.M.S.
" "	IX Bn.Glouc.R. (Pioneers).
File.	IX Corps.
198th Infantry Bde.	IX Corps Cyclist Bn.
199th do.	1st Division.
S.African Inf.Bde.	169th French Division.
C.R.A.	2nd Cavalry Division.
C.R.E.	32nd Division.
Signals.	A.D.S.
G.	D.A.P.M.
Div.Train.	D.A.D.V.S.
100th Bn. M.G.C.	O.C., 66th Div.Reception Camp
Camp Commdt.	66th M.T.Coy.
D.A.D.O.S.	

S E C R E T.   Copy No. 5

198TH INFANTRY BRIGADE PRELIMINARY ORDER No.140.

16th November, 1918.

Ref.Map. 1/100,000. NAMUR Sheet.

MARCH TO THE RHINE.

1. In accordance with terms of the Armistice, occupied portions of FRANCE, BELGIUM, and LUXEMBURG, are to be evacuated by enemy by November 26th.
   A further withdrawal to East of the RHINE will take place at a later date.

2. The advance of the Allied Forces will commence on November 17th.

3. 66th Division will lead the advance on the right of the British Army.
   169th French Division will be on its right, and 1st (British) Division on its left.
   66th Division will be preceded by the 2nd Cavalry Division, which will cover the front of the Fourth Army.
   32nd Division will follow 66th Division 1 day's march in rear.

4. Divisional Boundary to the MEUSE will be as follows:-

   (a) Northern Boundary:-
       L'ECREVISSE (Excl) - FRASIES (excl) - SIVRY Station (incl) - RENLIES - SILENRIEUX - FONTAINE - FLORENNES - JUSAINE (all excl) - ROSEE (incl) - ROSEE- DINANT Road (excl.)

   (b) Southern Boundary:-
       EPPE SAUVAGE (incl) - through BE of FOREST LE RANGE - Railway crossing ⅜ inch south of J of CERFONTAINE - SAMART (excl.) - VILLERS-LE-GAMBON (incl.) - SURICE (incl.) - Road junction ⅜ inch W. of H of BEER.

5. (a) By 18.00 November 16th, 198th Inf.Bde.will be disposed as in Appendix "A".
   (b) On November, 17th, 2nd Cavalry Division will pass

-2-

5. (a) By 18,00 November 18th, 198th Infantry Brigade will be disposed as shown in Appendix "A".
(b) On November 17th, 2nd Cavalry Division will pass through our present outpost line. The Cavalry will be followed by billeting parties to be detailed by 66th Division "Q" and by working parties to be detailed by the leading Brigade Group; reconnaissance will be carried out to ascertain whether state of roads will permit a full days march on the 18th.

6. On November 18th. the Division will advance in Brigade Groups with 198th Brigade Group leading, along the road, RANCE - FROIDCHAPELLE - CERFONTAINE - PHILIPPEVILLE - ROSEE.
Should the road be sufficiently good it is intended that the march on 18th. should be to the line of L'EAU D'HEURE.

7. Military precautions will be observed during the march as follows :-

   (i) Leading Infantry Brigade Group will detail an escort and covering party of 2 Coys to accompany the billeting and working parties which will be moving a day in advance of the main body of the Division.
Working parties will consist of :-
1 Field Company R.E.
1 Section Tunnelling Company R.E.
Proportion of Pioneer Battalion.
and additional working parties will be held in readiness at the head of the Brigade Group in case they should be required.

   (ii) Leading Brigade Group will march with an Advance guard including 1 Battery R.F.A.

   (iii) In billets the leading Brigade will picquet the roads leading from front and flanks to their billets.

   (iv) Troops will be distributed in sufficient depth to facilitate supply, but arrangements will be

/made to ensure

made to ensure that a sufficient force can be
available at 48 hours notice to overcome the
resistance of the enemy should he attempt to
oppose our advance.

8. (a) Subject to the above, the comfort of the troops
will be the principal object in the conduct of the
march.
Bands will be, and colours may be, taken on the march.
The strictest march discipline will be maintained
by all units on the march.
(b) DRESS:-
Full Marching Order; 1 blanket in lieu
of greatcoats; helmet worn in lieu of cap; 70 rounds
S.A.A. carried by each man in lieu of 120 rounds;
1 day's hard ration to be carried by each man in
addition to emergency ration and unexpended portion
of days ration.

9. COMMUNICATIONS.
During the march communications will be maintained
entirely by wireless, visual, D.R.s, and orderlies.

10. ACKNOWLEDGE.

Captain,
Brigade Major,
198th Infantry Brigade.

Issued at 20.00

DISTRIBUTION.

66th Division "S"	Copy No.1.
66th Division "Q"	" No.2.
6th Lancs.Fus.	" No.3.
5th R.Innis.Fus.	" No.4.
6th R.Dublin Fus.	" No.5.
198th L.T.M.B.	" No.6.
No.3 Sig.Sec.	" No.7.
431st Field Co. R.E.	" No.8.
2/2nd Field Amb.	" No.9.
543 Coy. A.S.C.	" No.10.
Staff Captain.	" No.11.
B.I.O.	" No.12.
War Diary.	" No.13, 14, 15.
File.	" No.16, 17, 18.
Spare.	" No.19, 20, 21.

APPENDIX "A".

198th Infantry Brigade H.Q. & No.3 Sig.Sec.	BEAURIEUX.
8th Bn. Lancashire Fus.	L'EPINE HARNAUT.
5th R.Innis.Fus.	CLAIRFAYTS.
8th R.Dublin Fus.	SOLRE LE CHATEAU.
198th L.T.M.B.	BEAURIEUX.
431st Field Co. R.E.	SOLRE LE CHATEAU.
No.3 Coy. Divl.Train A.S.C.	do.
2/2nd(E.L.) Field Ambulance.	do.

16.11.18.
RV.

SECRET.   Copy No. 5

MARCH TO THE RHINE.

INSTRUCTION NO. 1 ISSUED WITH REFERENCE TO
108TH INFANTRY BRIGADE PRELIM'RY ORDER No. 140.

17th November, 1918.

1. On the march each Brigade will lead in turn, being responsible for protection for a day and the following night, until the relieving Brigade passes through its outposts.

The Battalions of 108th Infantry Brigade will therefore lead in turn for three successive marches, as follows :-

        1st three marches.   6th R. Dublin Fus.
        2nd   "   "   6th Lancs. Fus.
        3rd   "   "   5th R. Innis. Fus.
                               etc.

This will give each Battalion the protective duties in turn.

2. Leading Battalion will be known as "A" Battalion, second Battalion as "B" Battalion, and third Battalion as "C" Battalion.

3. Order of march for Brigade Group will be :-

(a) When Leading Brigade.

    Two Companies "A" Battn. under Second-in-Command.
    (escort to working parties, probably one day
    ahead).

    "A" Battn. less two Companies.) Advanced Guard
    1 Battery R.F.A.   )

                                         / Main Body.

Main Body.

198th Brigade H.Q. & Signal Section.
B. Battalion.
Surplus Transport, "A" Battalion.
"C" Battalion less 1 Company.
198th L.T.M.B.
431 Field Co., R.E. (less troops on advanced working parties).
2/2nd E. Lancs. Field Ambulance.
543 Coy., A.S.C.
1 Coy., "C" Battalion. (rear guard).

(b) When NOT leading Brigade.

198th Inf. Bde. H.Q. & Signal Section.
"A" Battalion.
"B" Battalion.
"C" Battalion, less 1 Coy.
198th L.T.M.B.
431 Field Co., R.E.
2/2nd (E.Lan.) Field Ambulance.
543 Coy., A.S.C.
1 Coy., "C" Battalion. (rear guard).

4. "B" Battalion will be prepared to find working parties on the road if required.

5. The duties of the rearguard are to collect stragglers, assist transport if necessary, and clear any obstructions, such as abandoned vehicles, off the road. This does not absolve units from clearing the road of any of their own vehicles which may break down, and leaving a guard if necessary; Nor from the responsibility of taking along their own stragglers.

6. The following distances will be observed on the march:-

In rear of Infantry Company.	10 yards.
" " " Battery or other similar formation.	25 "
" " " Bde. R.A. or Infantry Bn.	50 "
Between units and their transport.	20 "

/7.

7. Any Germans encountered will be made prisoners and sent in to Brigade Headquarters at the end of the day's march.

8. Transport will march in rear of own units except as given in para. 3 (a) of this Instruction.

The order of march of Transport is given in the "Pink File".

9. Dress.

    (a) Steel helmets will be worn on the head.

    (b) Leather jerkins, one blanket, mugs, mess tins, ration bags and caps will be carried inside the pack. Ground sheet under flap of pack.

    (c) S.B.R. on top of the pack, with sling across chest and pulled taut under left arm.

    (d) Attention is drawn to the fitting of equipment.

    (e) Officers will conform to the dress of the men.

10. March Discipline.

    (a) The column will march in 3's.

    (b) No smoking except at halts.

    (c) No hanging on to the back of vehicles.

    (d) All transport details who are marching, except necessary brakesmen, cooks and water men, will march in a formed body in rear of the transport of their unit.

    (e) THERE WILL BE NO TEN MINUTES HALT ON THE WAY TO THE STARTING POINT. After passing the starting point the ten minutes halt will be rigidly observed.

11. Water.

No water will be drunk except from water carts. M.O's. of units are responsible for testing water from wells etc. in their Battalion areas. Field

/Ambulance.

Ambulance will give all assistance in this and in marking sources of water supply with the amount of chlorination necessary.

12. The Report Centre on the march will be Brigade H.Q. (See para. 3 (a) and (b).

A Report Centre will be notified in March Orders. Units will send an officer to this point immediately on arrival in billets. They will be shown the location of Brigade H.Q. and report the position of their unit H.Q., numbers of men fallen out and arrival of their units in billets. Watches will be synchronised and any necessary orders and instructions given.

13. Units are responsible for the cleanliness of G.S. Wagons attached to them

14. Battalion Messes will be formed.

Officers' Messes will be on this system unless local conditions make it quite impossible. Should this occur they will be reformed at the earliest opportunity.

15. ACKNOWLEDGE.

Captain,
Brigade Major,
108th Infantry Brigade.

Issued through Signals at 0700

DISTRIBUTION.

Issued to recipients of 108th Inf. Bde. Preliminary Order No. 140.

6th Lancs. Fus.
5th R. Innis. Fus.
6th R. Dublin Fus.
198th L.T.M.B.
No. 5 Sig. Sec.
151st Fld. Co. R.E.
545 Coy. A.S.C.
2/2nd Fld. Amb.
Staff Captain.
B.TO..

198th Inf. Bde.
No. G. 2876

DAILY NOTES.

1. Ref. 198th Inf. Bde Instructions No.1. dated 17.11.18, para. 9.
Leather Jerkins will be carried rolled on top of the pack, and secured under the retaining straps, and not inside the pack. S.B.R. will be carried on top of jerkin.

2. No flags or banners, except the Regimental Flag, will be carried on the march.

3. Mounted men, drivers, and men on wagons, may wear greatcoats, or jerkins, or both, at the discretion of Commanding Officers.

4. Ref. 198th Inf. Bde. Instruction No.1 dated 17.11.18., para. 6. A gap of 30yds will be maintained between every 3 vehicles.

5. With reference to G.R.O. No.55, the wearing of flowers and other unsoldierly trinkets in the cap, other than the French National Colours, will immediately cease.
(G.RO..60.)
No colours, or other unsoldierly trinkets, will be worn on any other part of the dress.

Captain,
Brigade Major,
198th Infantry Brigade.

18.11.18.
RV.

No. 1907/7/A.

Administrative Instructions.
-o-o-o-o-

66th Division letters 7946/Q and 7946/8/Q are amplified as follows:-

1. **SUPPLIES.**

    Normally the guides left by units to meet their Supply wagons will be posted at the point at which billetting parties meet the incoming units. The guides should move with the advance party, learn the location of the Quartermaster's Stores in the new area and meet the Train on arrival.

2. **ORDNANCE.**

    The representative attached to the Train Company to take over Ordnance Stores at the Refilling Point should be a capable N.C.O.

    x *If we have always 2 men there one can be used for this purpose*

3. **MEDICAL.**

    The Field Ambulance attached to the Brigade group in rear will establish a Main Dressing Station at the end of each day's march.

    Sick will be collected from units in the early morning prior to the Brigade marching off.

4. The suggested pooling of all G.S. wagons by battalions and allotting 1 per company, 1 to Battalion Headquarters and one to Quartermaster's Stores will enable companies in advance to move complete.

5. Steel helmets will be clean but not oiled. They will be kept dull as long as a state of war exists.

6. Billetting parties should, if possible, all be mounted on horse or bicycle. The billetting officer must always be mounted.

P. Hyslop
Captain,
Staff Captain,
198th Infantry Brigade.

17.11.18.
HBC

Copies to; all recipients of 198th Infantry Brigade Order No.140.

SECRET.
66th Division.
7948/Q.

ADMINISTRATIVE INSTRUCTIONS NO.1.

in connection with 66th Div. Preliminary Order No. 123 dated 15.11.18.

---

1. AMMUNITION.

Horsed Echelons will move full, with the exception that grenades will not be carried.

2. SUPPLIES.

In addition to the Iron Ration, one day's preserved ration will be carried by units.
On the line of march each echelon will move full.
Supply Section, 66th Div. M.T.Coy will leave lorry head in order of march of Formations.
Units will ensure that guides are left to meet their supply wagons, these guides will be posted at the approaches to billets.

3. ORDNANCE.

Ordnance Stores will as far as possible be delivered to Refilling Points. Units will attach to their affiliated Train Coy a representative to take over Ordnance Stores at Refilling Point, and deliver the same by Supply Wagon to the Unit.

4. TRANSPORT.

Extra Transport for the conveyance of blankets and great coats will be provided. In addition, it is hoped to allot 1 Motor Lorry to each Brigade Group for conveyance of stores etc.
Horse Transport will be under-loaded as roads will be met with of difficult gradients. Replacement of broken down vehicles will not be possible. The replacing of animals will be extremely difficult.
All units will be in possession of horse shoes tapped for frost cogs, and will satisfy themselves that the thread of the cogs received fit the sockets. The D.A.D.O.S. will carry a reserve of both of these.

5. PROVOST ARRANGEMENTS.

(a) Police will be strengthened in Formations and Units, great care will be taken in selecting men for this duty.
(b) Group Commanders will be responsible for the adequate picqueting of their areas, and for taking the necessary precautions against fire.
(c) Necessary steps will be taken by all concerned to prevent damage to property. The tying of animals to trees is prohibited.
(d) Group Commanders will be responsible for the collection of stragglers of their respective Groups.

6. BILLETING.

The Division will be billeted in four Groups: Three Infantry Brigade Groups, and one Div. Hd.Qr.Group.
Group Areas will be allotted in Divisional Orders, Group Commanders will then send on Billeting Parties mounted on bicycles ahead of the Division to make detailed arrangements for billeting and meeting units on arrival.

P.T.O.

(2)

6. **BILLETING** (Contd.)

C.R.A. in conjunction with an Officer to be detailed by Camp Commandant will be responsible for billeting Div. Hd.Qr. Group.

The following Units of Div. Hd.Qr. Group will send Billeting Parties in accordance with instructions to be issued to them by C.R.A.

    Camp Commandant.
    100th Bn. M.G.C.
    Div. Train for Hd.Qrs. and No. 1 Coy.
    Mob. Vet. Section.

7. **TRAFFIC.**

(a) No Mechanical Transport other than Motor Cars and Motor Cycles will be allowed to proceed along the line of march until the day's march has been completed by troops.
(b) Lorries and wagons will not be loaded or unloaded on any main traffic route.
(c) Broken down vehicles will be moved clear of the road by the first troops to discover them.

8. **LEAVE.**

All ranks due to proceed on leave up to and including 25th November, and desirous of so proceeding, will be despatched to Divisional Reception Camp, VAUX ANDIGNY, and will not proceed on the march.

9. **MEDICAL.**

Sick will be collected by Field Ambulances from their respective Brigade Groups. Those of Div. Hd.Qr. Group will be collected under arrangements to be made by A.D.M.S.
Cases will be evacuated to C.C.S. through the Field Ambulance with the Rear Brigade Group.

10. **SANITATION.**

(a) Latrines will invariably be dug immediately troops reach billets or camp, and also during prolonged halts.
All Latrines must be filled in before troops move off, and the site marked.
(b) Water for drinking purposes will only be drawn from water carts.
Group Commanders will make the necessary arrangements to ensure that water is tested before it is passed fit for drinking, and that the amount of chloride of lime necessary for sterilisation is clearly indicated.
(c) Camphor Powder for the feet should be freely used during the march. Supplies can be obtained by units from the Field Ambulance collecting their sick.

    Lieut.-Colonel.
    A. & Q.M.G.
    66th Division.

16.11.18.

(Distribution overleaf).

Distribution.

War Diary.	A.D.M.S.
" "	
File	9th Bn. Gloucester Regt.(Pioneers)
198th Infantry Bde.	
199th do.	IX Corps.
S.African do.	IX Corps Cyclist Bn.
C.R.A.	1st Division.
C.R.E.	169th French Division.
Signals.	2nd Cavalry Division.
G	32nd Division.
Div. Train.	A.D.C.
100th Bn. M.G.C.	D.A.P.M.
Camp Commandant.	D.A.D.V.S.
D.A.D.O.S.	O.C., 66th Div. Reception Camp.
	66th M.T.Coy.

6th.Lancs.Fus.
5th.R.Innis.Fus.
6th.R.Dublin Fus.
198th.L.T.M.B.

198TH
INFANTRY BRIGADE.
17 NOV. 1918
No. 1907/57A

Forwarded for information and necessary action.

Staff Captain,
198th. Infantry Brigade.

17.11.18.

66th Divn.
7948/8/Q.

G.	9th Gloucester R.
Camp Commandant.	Train.
C.R.A.	A.D.M.S.
C.R.E.	D.A.D.V.S.
Signal Co.	D.AD.O.S.
198 Infantry Bde.	D.A.P.M.
199 do.	66th Div. M.T.Co.
S.A. Bde.	Div. Baths Officer.
100th Bn. M.G.C.	Div. Canteen Officer.
	N.C.O. i/c F.P.O.

-----

1. The following G.S. wagons will be allotted for the march to the RHINE.

        Div. H.Q. .. 2
        R.E. H.Q. .. 1
        Each Inf.Bn. 4   40   (excludes baggage wagons)
        100th Bn. M.G.C. 2
        Each Field Co. 1 3
        Each Field Amboo.1 3

                Total 51

These wagons will report to respective formation Headquarters on evening of 17th.
Instructions as to wagons for 2 battalions of 198th Brigade are being issued separately.
The above transport is to be used primarily for the carriage of blankets and greatcoats.

2. Lorries for move are allotted as under, and will report to formations on evening of 17th.

    1. Div. H.Q. .. 6
    2. Signal Co. .. 1
    3. D.A.D.O.S. .. 4
    4. Post .. 2
    5. Each Inf. Bde.
        Group 3... 9
    6. Div.Baths Officer 2
    7. " Canteen Offr. 1
    8. R.A. H.Q. .. 1
    9. R.E. H.Q. & Pnr.Bn. 1

Serial Nos. 1, 7, 8 & 9 will march with Divisional Headquarters Group.
Serial Nos. 2, 3, 5 & 6 will march with 66th Divnl. M.T.Coy.
The above lorries are primarily to be used for the carriage of trench shelters, but are available for other stores as space permits.

The normal daily procedure will be as follows. Lorries will park under Brigade Group arrangements during the night and will start to rejoin Groups until all troops have completed their day's march.

↙ no lorries

                                contd........

2.

3. Infantry Brigades will indent on 66th Div. Train for the necessary patrol. This will be sent up on supply wagons of the Train, as required.

4. Under no circumstances will any transport be loaded with more than 80% of the normal load.
 N.B. 1 lorry carries 150 Trench Shelters loose.
       or 200   "   "   in bales.

5. A supply of trench shelters will be distributed. It is not known how many can be made available, but it is hoped to send a supply to formations on the lorries referred to, on 17th.

R.E. Oller
Major,
D.A.Q.L.G.
66th Division.

16.11.18.

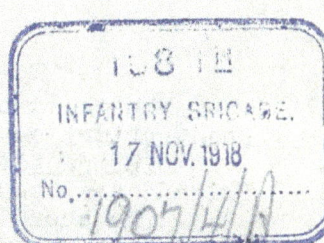
198TH
INFANTRY BRIGADE.
17 NOV. 1918
No. 1907/4/A

6th.Lancs.Fus.
5th.R.Innis.Fus.
6th.R.Dublin Fus.
198th.L.T.M.B.

Forwarded for information and necessary action.

Captain.
Staff Captain.
198th. Infantry Brigade.

17.11.1918.

66th Division.
7948/8/Q.

To all recipients of 66th Div. No. 7948/8/Q
of 16.11.18.

This office No. 7948/8/Q para. 2 is amended.

Serial Nos. will accompany Formations as under :-

    Nos. 1, 2, 8 & 9 ..... D.H.Q., Group.
    "   3, 4, 6 & 7 ..... Divl. M.T.Coy.
    No. 5 ..... Respective Infantry
                                 Brigade Groups.

R. E. Otty
Major.
D.A.Q.M.G.
66th Division.

17.11.18.

SECRET.   Copy No. 5

108TH INFANTRY BRIGADE ORDER No.149.

17th November, 1918.

Ref.Map. NAMUR 8, 1/100,000.

---

1. The 108th Infantry Brigade Group, (less
   6th Lancs.Fus. and 6th R.Dublin Fus.), will
   move by march route to RANCE, to-morrow, 18th
   instant, in accordance with the attached
   March Table.

2. Billeting parties will meet the Staff Captain
   at Road Junction TRIEU BOUCHAUX, at 07.15.
   Incoming Units will be met at this point.

3. Brigade Headquarters will close at BEAURIEUX
   at 08.45 and open at RANCE on arrival.
   A Brigade report centre will be maintained
   at the head of the column on the march.

4. ACKNOWLEDGE.

                                    Captain,
                                    Brigade Major,
                                    108th Infantry Brigade.

Issued at 20.00

DISTRIBUTION.

66th Division "G"	Copy No.1.
66th Division "Q"	" No.2.
6th Lancs.Fus.	" No.3.
5th R.Innis.Fus.	" No.4.
6th R.Dublin Fus.	" No.5.
108th T.M.B.	" No.6.
No.3 Sig.Sec.	" No.7.
151st Fld.Co. R.E.	" No.8.
2/2nd Field Amb.	" No.10.
543 Coy. A.S.C.	" No.11.
Staff Captain.	" No.12.
B.I.O.	" No.13.
B.T.O.	" No.14.
War Diary.	" No.15, 16, 17.
File.	" No.18, 19, 20.
Spare.	" No.21, 22, 23.

MARCH TABLE to accompany 198th Inf.Bde Order No.141.

Serial No.	Unit.	From.	To.	Starting point.	Time of passing Stg.Pt.	Route	Remarks.
1.	198th Inf.Bde H.Q. & Signals.	BEAURIEUX.	RANCE.	Cross roads on frontier 200 yds S. of M in MOULLARD.	07.10.	SIVRY - TRIEU BOUCHAUX	TRIEU BOUCHAUX - RANCE Station road to be clear by 10.30.
2.	198th L.T.M.B.	do.	TRIEU-BOUCHAUX.	do.	06.15.	do.	
3.	5th R.Innis.Fus.	CLAIRFAYTS.	RANCE.	CLAIRFAYTS Church.	07.00	do.	
4.	2/2nd Fld.Amb.	SOLRE-LE-CHATEAU.	TRIEU BOUCHAUX.	do.	07.15	do.	
5.	431 Fld.Co.RE.	do.	do.	do.	07.25	do.	
6.	543 Cpy.A.S.C.	do.	do.	do.	07.35	do.	

17.11.18.
RV.

198th. Infantry Brigade.

A.81.   22.11.18.

War Office wires that applications are being received from Units for colours to be sent out aaa   Issue instructions forbidding independent applications pending Army Council decision on this matter aaa

66th. Division "A".

6th. Lancs Fus.
5th. R. Innis. Fus.
6th. R. Dublin Fus.
198th. L.T.M.B.

198th. Inf. Bde.
No. 1923A

The above copy of wire is forwarded for information.

Captain,
Staff Captain,
198th. Infantry Brigade.

22.11.18.

File

6th   (s) Bn Royal Dublin Fusiliers.

Movement Order No.29.

Ref Map. NAMUR 1:100,000

(1) 6th R.D.F. will move to...... Exact place later ...... at...0845....
in following order. H.Q. B. C. A

(2) Route:- ANTHEE - HASTIERE LAVAUX

(3) Billeting party meet Staff Captain at..0.8.00..........
at...S.W. Rd. Slope.. ON HASTIERE-ATHEE. Road

(4) D Coy will act as rear guard to Bn and pass
starting point (X roads ½ N of M in MORVILLE) at
1005 am

J Monde
Captain.
Adjutant 6th (s) Bn Roy.Dub.Fus.

23/11 1918.

6th (S) Bn Royal Dublin Fusiliers.

Movement Order. No.29.

Ref Map. NAMUR 1:100,000

(1) 6th R.D.F. will move to..................at....................
in following order.........

(2) Route:-

(3) Billeting party meet Staff Captain at......................
at....................

23/11/18.
J. Emonds
Captain.
Adjutant 6th (S) Bn Roy.Dub.Fus.

SECRET   Copy Nº 5

198TH INFANTRY BRIGADE ORDER Nº 143

1918.
22nd November,

March To The Rhine

REF. MAP.

Namur, 1/100,000.

1. The 198th Infantry Brigade Group will move on the 23rd November, in accordance with the attached March Table.

2. Starting Point: Cross roads at 14th Kilo.Stone, ¼" N. of V of VODECEE.

   Report centre on arrival :- Cross roads 200 yds N. of ROSEE Church.
   Meeting point for billet guides :-   do.
   Meeting point for Supply wagons.   do.

3. Brigade Headquarters will close at PHILIPPEVILLE, at 07.30 and open at ROSEE on arrival.

4. Billeting parties will meet the Staff Captain, at Cross rds. 200 yds North of ROSEE Church, at 08.00.

5. ACKNOWLEDGE

Holden
Captain,
Brigade, Major,
198th Infantry Brigade.

Issued at 13.30

DISTRIBUTION. (overleaf).

MARCH TABLE TO ACCOMPANY 198TH INFANTRY BRIGADE ORDER N° 143.

Serial N°	UNIT.	FROM.	PASS. STARTING POINT AT.	TO.	ROUTE	REMARKS
1.	Bn R.Innis.Fus. (less 2 Coys).	PHILIPPEVILLE.		MORVILLE.		Advanced Guard
2.	A/351 Bde R.F.A.	HEMPTINNE.		MORVILLE.	ROSEE.	Under orders of Lieut.
3.	1 Sec.,431st Fld. Co. R.E.	PHILIPPEVILLE.		MORVILLE.		Col. W. J. Paterson, D.S.O.
4.	198th Inf. Bde.H.Q. & No.3 Sig. Sec.	PHILIPPEVILLE.	08.36.	ROSEE.		
5.	2 Cos.,5 R.Innis.Fus.	PHILIPPEVILLE.	08.39.	MORVILLE.	ROSEE.	
6.	6th Lancs. Fus.	JAMAGNE.	08.46.	ROSEE.		
7.	6th R.Dublin Fus. (less 1 Coy.)	HEMPTINNE.	09.03.	ROSEE.		
8.	198th L.T.M.B.	PHILIPPEVILLE.	09.11.	ROSEE.		
9.	100 M.G. Bn.	JAMIOLLE.	09.12.	ROSEE.		
10.	431 Field Co., R.E. (less 1 section).	PHILIPPEVILLE.	09.27.	ROSEE.		
11.	2/3rd Fld. Ambce.	PHILIPPEVILLE.	09.32.	ROSEE.		
12.	543 Coy., A.S.C.	PHILIPPEVILLE.	09.37.	ROSEE.		
13.	1 Coy., 6th R. Dublin Fus.	HEMPTINNE.	09.42.	ROSEE.		Rearguard

6th Lancs. Fus
5th R. Innis. Fus.
6th R. Dublin Fus.
106th L.T.M.B.
No. 3 Sig. Sec.
121 Field Co. R.E.
3/2nd Field Ambce.
543 Coy., A.S.C.
B.T.O.

  Reference 106th Infantry Brigade Order No. 144.

  Starting Point is as follows :-

    Cross Roads, ½ mile N. of M in MORVILLE.

            Captain,
           Brigade Major,
         106th Infantry Brigade.

25.11.18.

SECRET   Copy No. 5

198TH INFANTRY BRIGADE ORDER No 144
1918.

23rd November,

March To The Rhine

REF. MAP.

NAMUR, 1/100,000.

(Miscellaneous Documents for Nov. 1918)

1. The 198th Infantry Brigade Group (less 100th Bn. M.G.C.) will move on the 24th November, in accordance with the attached March Table.

2. Starting Point: Cross Roads ½ mile N. of M in MORVILLE.
   Report centre on arrival :- HASTIERE LAVAUX, Church.
   Meeting point for billet guides :- }
   Meeting point for Supply wagons. } To be notified later.

3. Brigade Headquarters will close at ROSEE at 07.30. and open at HASTIERE LAVAUX on arrival.

4. Billeting parties will meet the Staff Captain, at 5th kilo stone on the HASTIERE - ANTHEE Road, at 05.00.

5. ACKNOWLEDGE

                                                         Captain,
                                                      Brigade, Major,
                                                 198th Infantry Brigade.

Issued at 19.00

DISTRIBUTION. (overleaf).

MARCH TABLE TO ACCOMPANY 198TH INFANTRY BRIGADE ORDER N° 144.

Serial N°	UNIT.	FROM.	PASS. STARTING POINT AT.	TO.	ROUTE	REMARKS
1.	6th Lancs.Fus. (less 2 Coys.).	MORVILLE.				Advanced Guard under orders of Lieut.Col. R.F. Gream, D.S.O.
2.	198th Inf.Bde.H.Q. & No.3 Sig.Sec.	ROSEE.	09.15.	AUSEVIERRE — LERNE — HASTIERE LAVAUX.	ANTHEE — HASTIERE LAVAUX.	
3.	2 Coys.6th Lancs.Fus.	MORVILLE.	09.18.			
4.	5th R.Irish.Fus.	MORVILLE.	09.24.			Exact destinations of units will be notified later.
5.	6th R.Dublin Fus. (less 1 Coy).	ROSEE.	09.32.			
6.	198th L.T.M.B.	ROSEE.	09.35.			
7.	431st Fld.Co. R.E.	ROSEE.	09.40.			
8.	2/2nd Fld.Amb.	ROSEE.	09.45.			
9.	542 Coy.A.S.C.	ROSEE.	10.00.			
10.	1 Coy. 6th R.Dublin Fus.	ROSEE.	10.05.			Rear Guard.

NOTE: O.C. 431st Fld.Co. R.E. will detail 3 cyclists to accompany the advanced guard.

www.ingramcontent.com/pod-product-compliance
Lightning Source LLC
Chambersburg PA
CBHW081422300426
44108CB00016BA/2281